I0245424

Other books in print by

Nik C. Colyer

Channeling Biker Bob 1 Heart of a Warrior
Channeling Biker Bob 2 Lover's Embrace
Channeling Biker Bob 3 Magician's Spell
Channeling Biker Bob 4 Wisdom of the King
Maranther's Deception Lost in the desert
Kicking Ass and Taking Names
Poetry through the eyes of a tough guy

All books available through
Singing Reed Press
P.O. Box 1395
Nevada City, CA 95959
530 265-3566
www.NikColyer.com

Acclaim From Readers:

"It's a great book. . .great insight and incredible knack to put it in story form. . ."

-Sandie Sage (White Springs, Montana)

"Hard to put down. Loved that I felt so much for the characters."

-Joell Sweeny (North San Juan, California)

"Fabulous work!

-Kate Henry (San Diego, California)

"Not a lot of books have left me wanting more. Your book has done that for me. . . .(it) has inspired me.. ."

-Jay Titus (Denver, Colorado)

" I've suggested this book to everyone I know. . ."

-Julian Fonders (Jacksonville, Florida)

"I was enthralled! I finished the book in two days flat. "

-Linda Grotke (Nevada City, California)

"Riveting, captivating."

-Sanchez Prusso (San Anselmo, California)

"Bravo! I couldn't put down. The ride was wonderful."

-Darlene Hawkins (Myrtle Point, Oregon)

"I not only enjoyed the book, but even better it made me think. . .You have something important to say and we need to hear it."

-Marsha DeFilippo (Bangor, Maine)

Colyer has a way of telling a story that keeps you on the edge. This one is no different. I couldn't put it down.

- Bill Sandersson (Dallas, Texas)

Keep ‘em coming. I love your writing.

- Sinclair Jones (San Francisco, California)

Trillian Rising

Colyer, Nik C.
Trillian Rising / by Nik C. Colyer. — 1st ed.
p. cm.
LCCN pending
ISBN 978-0-9708163-8-2

1. Fiction. 2. End of the world- fction. I. Title.

1. pandemic-virus-world die off-fiction. 2.adventure-vacation-jungle-journey-fiction. 3. utopian community-mystical-clarivoinat-community dynamics-new order-fiction. 4. life after-surviving-illness-fiction 5. romance-love-fiction

Printed in the United States of America
10 9 8 7 6 5 4 3 2 1

This book is dedicated to
the coming times

I do hope our species can survive
the changes being thrust upon us.

To my Dad
who, through his tenatious insistance to
be individulistic, taught me how to
be my own man.

Trillian Rising

Nik C. Colyer

Singing Reed Press
Nevada City, CA

Chapter 1

Awakening

I awake on my couch with a start. Sweat pours from my face and I have a dry taste in my mouth. I reach for the bottle on the floor next to me, untwist the cap, then take a long drink of warm liquid. I guess by the temperature of the water that she's been gone for hours.

I glance at my watch. It's 5:47. On a note pad left for me by Cynthia —or was her name Claudia— I scribble the exact time of day as if my life depends on it, and I guess it does.

I stand, wobbly at first because, hell, I haven't been on my feet for more than a week. I haven't been coherent for five days. Will this nightmare ever end?

I walk to the kitchen, look at my answering machine while I round the breakfast nook. Thirty-seven messages.

People are desperate, just as I will be in a few hours if one of those thirty-seven isn't a match.

I open the fridge and see that Cynthia/Claudia left me some fried chicken and a cold beer. Both are almost impossible to get during these days of shortages.

I grab a chicken leg, the bottle of beer and sit at the table in my kitchen. I push the button of my answering machine. "Beep. . . This is Frank. My awake time is 12:37pm July seventeenth, 2016. My number is. . ." I delete the message. His time isn't right.

"Beep. . . This is Caroline." She has a deep-throated, sexy voice, but I'm not interested in sexy voices these days. "My time is 2:24am July twelfth. Call me if you're a match."

The chicken has a slight smoked flavor and I devour three pieces before I've deleted all the messages without finding a single match remotely close to mine. Damn, I hate the first hours of being awake. I feel so frantic. The timing is never right because so few people are left.

I now begin the never-ending nightmare of phone calls, hoping someone out there will match my time who lives close enough that they can attend to me during my incapacitation.

I pick up the telephone. Thank God the phones still work. I open the phone book randomly to the "S" pages and key in my first set of numbers. "Beep. . . Hi, this is Tammy Steel and my time is seventeen thirty hours, July fourteenth. Leave a message if you're a match and I'll call you back. Please tell me your phone number slow and clear." She lets out a short, teenage giggle, not one of playfulness, but a nervous, frantic titter.

I hate military time. Let's see. Seventeen hundred, twelve hundred is noon, so seventeen would be 5:30 in the afternoon. Can I be that lucky? I mean right off the bat I find someone.

The second beep has come and gone before I realize I'm supposed to leave a message. I call back. "Hello," I say in a jerky manner, "My name is Jason Oakley and my time is 5:47." I look out of my west window and see vestiges of the sun through the trees. "It's morning," I shout. "I live on Bloomfield Road here in Nevada City." I'm so excited, I almost forget to tell her I just woke up. I look at my watch and its little calendar reads, July 17. I hang up and hope against hope that she's the one. Because I can't be sure, I have to keep calling until I find a positive match.

I lose count at twenty-two calls, when the phone rings. I snatch the receiver. "Hello?"

A timid voice breaks three seconds of silence. "Mr. Oakley?"

"Yes, this is Jason Oakley. What's your time?"

After another moment of silence, she speaks in her high-pitched female voice. "This is Tammy Steel."

"Tammy, do we have a match?"

"Yes, I can care for you."

I let out a deep lungful of stale air and take in a fresh breath of relief. "I've been awake for an hour, and things were already looking pretty shaky."

"It's okay, Mr. Oakley, I can take care of you, and because you live on Bloomfield Road I can almost walk. I'm on Nubian Way."

"No need Tammy, I still have gas coupons from last month. I'll come get you when my time comes."

"That would be nice, Mr. Oakley. Thank you."

I'm about to say goodbye when she speaks with a soft, unsure voice. "Umm, you don't by chance know anyone who might match me?"

"What?" I yell. "You don't have a match yet? You're about ready to go into your cycle and you don't have a match?" My entire moment of relief returns to panic. If she doesn't have a caregiver, she could die while I go into my second phase of this nightmare, then I could expire myself of over-exposure, especially in this heat. "Why don't you have a caregiver at this late date?"

She says with her annoyingly nervous titter, "He died during the last cycle. I guess his caregiver wasn't real accurate with her timing. Geez, Mr. Oakley, I hate all of this."

I calm. "I hate it too Tammy, but until the scientists figure out a cure for this, depending on one another and making these calls is our only choice."

I think I'm being supportive, but she starts to cry. I sit silent on the phone until she can speak. "I'm only an hour away from my first triad and I have no one to help."

"Is there no one in your family who can fill in?"

"They all died last year during the early days when no one understood."

"You live alone out here?"

"Yes," she says through sobs and sniffles.

She is my only possibility for a caregiver so far, and we're committed, at least for the next cycle. Although it's the last thing I want to do, I say, "Look Tammy, you still have another five days before you go into the catatonic. If you can't find anyone by the time you go in, I'll continue your calls until we find someone for you."

"Really?"

"We're in this together, at least for the next ten days until I go to sleep. You watch my back and I'll watch yours. You keep trying to find someone and call me if you can't. I'll be close to the phone. Call me either way, okay?"

"Thank you Mr. Oakley. My last caregiver wouldn't take the time. Oh, he was here all right, but he ate all of my food and left the house a mess. I had to cook my own first meal. That was bad enough, but he found the storage food in the basement."

"You have storage food?"

"Not much left now, but a little."

She pauses for a long time, then with a deep breath and a voice of resolve, says, "I'll share all my food with you if you make me pregnant."

"Pregnant? That's a pretty big request."

"I know who you are. I've seen you in town before Trillian struck. You're the writer, right?"

"Yes, but do I know you?"

She sniffles. "No, I was just a college student. I used to see you in Flower Garden Bakery."

"College student? Aren't I a little old for you?"

"Not too bad, I was twenty-five before I went back to school." Another long pause. She breaks down again. "I was studying to become a teacher." After a thirty-second battle to regain control, she says, "I was almost finished and ready to go on to a university for my M.A. I got straight A's, for all the good any of that does now."

"Listen Tammy, I think it's best that you try and find a caregiver for this next cycle. When you come to care for me, we can talk about this getting pregnant thing, but I have to warn you, I'm kind of a loner and relationships have never been a successful enterprise for me."

She sniffles. "Okay, but can I ask you to keep an open mind? Remember, if you make me pregnant then you will have a full time caregiver, at least until the baby is born and during lactation. Some women can stretch nursing out for years."

"Tammy."

"Yes."

"Make your calls and call me back before you go into the cycle. If I don't hear from you in a few hours, I'll call you. Does that sound okay?"

She has a somber tone. "Okay, Mr. Oakley."

I don't know why, but I say, "I haven't totally rejected your offer. I would be relieved to not have to scramble for a new caregiver every cycle, but we have to talk about the possibilities."

Her chipper tone returns. "Okay, Mr. Oakley, we'll talk."

"Tammy."

"Yes?"

"Call me Jason."

She says my whole name in a reverent tone. I hate that tone, like I'm some kind of God or something. I just wrote some books. What's the big deal, especially considering what we have to face these days?

She says goodby and the line goes dead.

I check my watch and it's 8:45. If I have my caregiver settled, then I'm left with four-and-a-half glorious days to myself. Well, not exactly to myself. I have laundry, groceries, but I'm free of Trillian for one hundred and eight hours. I want to see the birds. I want to go to the river and lay on the rocks naked. I want to watch a few sunsets and for four-and-a-half days, except for being a caregiver for Mason Anderson two days from now, I'm free.

I would love to walk to town, but because my physical

state is weakened, and I live five miles out, I can't. I take a shower, shave, and dress in town clothes, then get into my car and take the twenty-minute cruise along curvy Bloomfield Road. Close to Cooper Road, I pull over for a young man hitchhiking.

When I unlock the rider's door, he climbs in with a smile. We both know he's going to town, so the question is dispensed for the moment. His first words, in an exuberant burst of energy are, "Man, don't it feel good to be alive?"

I smile, but don't answer.

He turns to me, "How much time you got?"

"Almost all of it. I just woke up."

"Very all right. I got two days left and I'm making the best of it. I'm looking for some babe and I'm gettin' laid."

"You sound sure of yourself."

He snickers. "One up side of Trillian is women want to get pregnant and they don't care who knocks them up. It's guy heaven."

"What about becoming a dad? Don't you have any problems with the responsibilities of fatherhood?"

"Shit, man, where have you been? They don't want a father, they just want a donor, and for the next two days, I am here to help."

We ride in contemplative silence for the final two miles along Bloomfield, then down the hill on Coyote Street. The entire Nevada City valley opens into view. Nothing has changed. The forest blankets all of the people who are lying sick in their beds with the second flu stage of Trillian. I hope the third-stage people have a caregiver to force water and food into them during their last five days of the cycle. The catatonic stage is where all of the people died before anyone knew what to do.

When are the scientists going to come up with some answers? They've figured out cures for other diseases. What's taking them so long?

At the bottom of the hill, we cross the highway and slip into the backside of what used to be our thriving little tourist town. I turn right off Coyote and drive behind the county courthouse, in front of New Moon restaurant, by Ike's Café, all closed now. I come to the final stop sign on Broad Street.

"I'll get out here." The kid opens the door and gets out of the car.

I nod. "Good luck."

Before he closes the door, he bends. "These days luck has nothing to do with it. Where I'm about to go is a certainty."

"What happens when all the women get pregnant?"

He rolls his eyes. "Hey man, don't fuck up my good mood."

I smile while he closes the door. Before I drive down the hill, I watch him strut diagonally across the street toward Bonanza Market.

I make my left and notice two more businesses have closed. The windows aren't boarded up, but they have been painted with something on the inside so no one can see. Two more closed businesses doesn't leave much open. There's Cirino's, probably because they have a bar; farther down the street on the left is the Asian restaurant; and the National Hotel is open, though they always look closed with that dark, Victorian interior.

I make a right onto the freeway and, except for the kid, I saw no one walking along the sidewalks.

On the freeway, I quickly get up to speed and merge

onto the highway, but there are no cars. When I come to the business part of my community, the Brunswick Basin looks the same; stores, gas stations, burger joints, signs, and motels. At the bottom of the hill I exit the freeway and sit idling, waiting for the light to turn green. Once it turns, I drive over the freeway, where I see my first moving car going the opposite direction. An older man drives, with a young girl in the passenger seat. He honks and waves. I wave back. On the other side of the overpass, I pull into the huge, empty parking lot of the grocery store. I drive to the front door and park in the first space. Twenty other parked cars are spread out in the parking lot, though few look like they run.

I get out and silence pervades the atmosphere. There is no freeway noise, no air traffic overhead, no sound of children screaming or couples arguing. I hear only the sound of my steps. I walk to the front doors. They automatically open, and I step into the store.

One lone cashier trims her nails. She's more than a few months pregnant. She looks at me as I step past the long string of empty cash registers.

"Hi," she says with a bored voice, then turns back to her nails.

With a simple nod, I walk past the woman, grab a cart, and go to the far left of the store where the fruits and vegetables are kept. I've had a craving for an apple since I awoke. I don't expect much, but when I push the cart around the corner where towering islands of potatoes, carrots, pears, and glossy waxed apples used to be, only empty tables remain. I spot a few bags of last year's potatoes. They're soft to the touch, filled with stringy eyes and pockmarked with bug bites. I search for the bag that looks the best and drop it into the bottom of my cart. I pick some local apples, but it's too early in the summer. They look green. The carrots, the only remaining vegetable, are limp and unappealing, but I grab a bunch and put them in the cart. Along the back wall I find beer and cold drinks, though only a local brew is featured and the never-ending supply of Coca-Cola. I grab a six pack of each and make my way to the end of the aisles, looking down each one as I pass. Any row that once had food is now stripped clean. Shelves with toilet paper and laundry soaps remind me of the old days before Trillian, when stores carried everything.

I go down the third aisle, and a woman stands eyeing the one other thing I came for, the only thing abundant in this part of the country. Bags and bags of long-grain and short-grain rice are stacked fifteen high the entire length of the aisle.

I pull up short of the woman, grab a fifty-pound bag, and toss it in next to my other meager grocery supplies.

Chapter 2

Serenity

"Can you help?" the woman asks, which startles me. I didn't expect her to speak.

I step over to her. "Which one?"

She points. "The long grain. They put them in such huge bags, I can't lift them."

I roll the bag to my knees, grab under it, and hoist it up to her cart.

"You're the writer, aren't you?"

I smile. "Yeah, I guess I am."

"I was just reading one of your books before I came into town. You paint a wonderful picture of before. . ." Her voice drops and she gets a depressed look on her pale face. We all have pale faces from too much time lying on our couches or in bed.

"Thanks."

"Are you working on anything new?"

I frown. "I spend my time catching up with life, I'm not sure I know how to write anymore."

"I know what you mean." She stands in awkward silence. I'm almost ready to return to my cart when she says, "It's lonely too."

My lifestyle has not allowed me to feel the loneliness of being a writer. I've always lived inside my stories and came out only when distractions were forced upon me. Lately I have felt lonely. When the young woman made me the pregnancy offer, I was tempted to take her up on it mostly to alleviate my growing feelings of isolation.

I say, "Yeah, lonely. . ." I shrug, not able to finish the sentence.

She searches my face with her big brown eyes and, for the first time, I see her as more than another shopper getting the only real commodity this store has to offer. I look at her cherub face, her small-toothed smile, the little turn at the corner of her mouth. For a moment the entire store disappears, my fucked-up life vanishes, and that damn Trillian doesn't exist. All I see is her peach blouse, her soft-looking hands with metallic green nail polish, her overly accentuated lips with dark red lipstick, a little smeared on one of her front teeth.

She reaches a hand out. "I'm Serenity."

I fumble my right hand out, and she grips me tight with a full handshake, not one of those wimpy woman shakes with just the tips of fingers.

"Jason," I say with a nervous titter. "Jason Oakley."

"I know who you are," she says.

I stand, still shaking her small hand, unaware of my

surroundings. I barely notice when a logger type walks up and grabs two bags of rice at once.

"I. . . uh. . . well." God, I'm stammering.

She finally cuts in. "Can I buy you a cup of coffee next door at the bakery? Thank God they're still open."

"Sure."

She lets go of my hand. The brilliance of the moment fades back into the drab rice aisle and my lost life, the remains of which Trillian has equally divided into three distinct sections: five days of flu-like sickness, as many of deep sleep, and five glorious days of life.

Why did I have to go to Brazil? Guilt lies heavily on my soul, but no one else knows anything except Sam, and he died in the first wave. How long has it been, eighteen months?

"I'll meet you out front," she says, which brings me back from the ancient burial site in the rain forest.

"Okay."

She pushes her cart to the end of the aisle, then makes a right toward the vegetable section. I grab a second bag of rice and cruise the remaining aisles in a daze of nightmare memories.

Chapter 3

Amazon

Sam had a bottle of champagne he'd saved for that occasion. Although it was warm, the celebration was the intent, not the taste of the bubbly.

"We found it," he said, hanging off the bow of the flat-bottom boat with its noisy Donkey steam engine making a pop-pop sound while we floated through the murky waters of the Amazon.

I came for the adventure and to possibly find a story to end the writer's block that had plagued me for six months. I was sure an Amazon adventure would spark some kind of creative inspiration.

When Sam popped the top, the plastic stopper shot over the bow, high into the air, and arched all the way to shore thirty yards away. The champagne burst forth with an exuberant overflow, so warm and shaken up, it almost emptied itself. Sam poured his portion into a roughly thrown pottery mug and mine into a small, stainless steel cup I kept on my backpack. What was left of the bottle half filled each of our cups.

He gave me his famous boyish grin, looked around, and whispered, "To the find of a lifetime."

I clicked my cup against his but didn't respond. I didn't want to go back to the ongoing argument we'd had since he stumbled upon the site.

I don't know how many times I'd said it. "We can't take things from burial sites."

"It's gold, Jason. How many chances will we get to find so much gold? Hell, the person is dead. What use does he have of this thing, anyhow?"

"Sam, it was sacred ground."

The argument had gone on for two days while Sam searched the surroundings looking for other burial sites. If there had been any, the forest was much too dense to find them.

The one site we found had been opened by a split in the earth. The gap was wide enough to drive a small car into. The gold medallion the size of a CD disk, with a heavy gold link chain, lay fully exposed, face up, glinting at us.

Our guide had unpacked for lunch. Before anyone but me saw anything, Sam unwound the links from the bones of that long-ago rotted soul, slipped the medallion over his head, and slid it inside his shirt. He kept his shirt buttoned high to hide the glint of the metal.

"That'll be eighty-seven fifty-three." A voice demands my attention and draws me out of the memory of the first days after finding the medallion.

I reach in my pocket, pull out four twenties, and hand them to the cashier. She rambles through her drawer, then gives me change.

Although no one is in line behind me, I'm forced to bag my own groceries. The woman continues filing her nails. I push my cart to the car and put my groceries away. The brown-eyed woman watches me.

I close my door and lock the car out of habit, then walk in her general direction.

She smiles. "I hoped you wouldn't stand me up. You looked so distracted, I was sure you'd forgotten."

I had forgotten, but I say nothing. We walk the length of the sidewalk, across a short section of the parking lot, then up to the front door of the bakery.

Inside, the aroma takes me back to a much simpler time before Trillian, before the food shortages, when I didn't stop at the bakery for fear of my expanding waistline.

The smell of coffee and croissants fills my senses. We order. She leads me outside to a small table in the sun and sits. "The sun feels nice, don't you think?"

"Yes, but my eyes aren't used to it." I slide my chair around the table so that my back is toward the glare.

I take a sip of coffee.

"I loved your last book. Have you written anything lately?"

There is innocence to her question. Heaven knows I've asked the same questions too many times of other authors. She's simply filling in during our nervous first few moments. It's the logical question. Only a few years ago, I reveled in the answer. I always had at least three manuscripts I was working on at any one same time, so the answer was easy. Since Trillian, except to look for possible matches, I haven't sat in front of the keyboard to write once. The two books I was working on still sit, one half-finished, the other completed but not edited.

"I've finished the seventh, and number eight is over the hump."

She cuts the roll with her fork. "It's good that someone has the time to work. I haven't been able to do anything except survive since Trillian began."

I want to tell her the truth. I want to look deep inside her big brown eyes and spill my guts. I want to tell her I haven't been able to work either, and that I've been lonely lately, but I say nothing.

I take another sip of coffee to keep from looking at her.

A moment of silence goes by before she speaks. I've already blown my one chance. She's talking in a nervous chatter to fill the empty space I left unspoken. I hear the fidgety delivery of her voice. She's not talking to me any longer, but at me. It's my fault for not answering honestly. How can I tell her of my two-week hike out of the jungle? How can I explain the arguments Sam and I had about the pendant?

I wanted him to leave the damn thing in the jungle, and he, with the glint of gold fever in his eyes, continued to wear it around his neck. That hike was the longest two days of my life. I knew something was wrong, but I didn't fully understand until we reached the banks of the Amazon and waited another two days for the boat to pick us up. By the time the boat rounded the bend and pulled to the dock, Sam, our three couriers, and I were in the first days of a full-blown flu. I'd thrown up three times that morning alone. We all sat with pale faces on the edge of the dock puking our guts out. We didn't have enough energy to leave the dock to get water.

The natives had already given us the sign of the hex and staying clear of the dock. The boatman got close enough to see us, then steered his thirty-foot flatboat out to the center of the river. Its little one-cylinder engine thumped and puffed away from us. I yelled an offer of three hundred bucks extra, but he didn't slow or turn. I raised the ante to a thousand, cash in hand. He turned the boat and reluctantly accepted the cash, barricading us at the nose of the boat with boxes of hardwood statues made by a tribe upriver.

We were forced to string a makeshift tarp over us to keep the sun from baking us into prunes. It was a five-day ride back to civilization, and somewhere along the route, I blacked out. I awoke, and the boat was adrift and banging along the northern shore, slowly spinning while it floated in the current. I was almost dead from thirst. I climbed over the boxes and found the helmsman shriveled in a corner. Three vultures were picking at his flesh. I scared the birds away, found the water, and drank almost a gallon. I took some to Sam and woke him.

Once Sam was rehydrated, I stoked the fire under the boiler and built up a head of steam. In an hour we were on our way.

"What the hell happened?" Sam asked between long draws of water and chews from a loaf of a local hard bread.

"If it was a flu, then it was a whopper." I steered the boat downstream. "I think it's got something to do with

that gold necklace you found."

"Jason, will you give it a rest?"

"Then what killed our helmsman?"

"Any number of things. He looks like he had a heart attack to me. I mean look at the guy. He carried an extra two hundred pounds and smoked like a chimney. He looks forty-five or fifty, and that's the age when his kind of debauchery catches up. It was just our luck to be with him at the end."

I rotated the tiller to the left to miss a downed tree in the river. I looked at Sam. "I don't know how you expect to get that thing out of the country anyhow."

He gave me a sly smile. "I've got a plan."

"I guess there's no way I can talk you into selling the damn thing here."

"Jason, you're paranoid."

It was the dead end of the conversation. We'd been at that particular junction God knows how many times. Sam had his heart set on bringing that frightening disk of gold back to the States, and from what I knew of Sam, tight security or not, he'd pull it off.

A single word pulls me from cruising the Amazon on that noisy skiff, with the dead helmsman and my stubborn friend. The word jerks me into the present, sitting across the table from an attractive woman with the sun reflecting off her long, dark hair. The word is "pregnant." It's a popular word these days.

When the word invades my daydream, I focus on her lovely forty-year-old face and the gleam in her eyes. I concentrate on words forming on her rose-petal lips. "I might be too old to get pregnant."

"What?" I ask.

She blinks one time. It's a long, slow, contemplative blink. "Getting pregnant, I'm too old to get pregnant."

I want to join her in the discussion, though it's been one-sided for I don't know how long. Apparently, she hadn't noticed my blank stare. "I don't think you're too old to get pregnant, it's just that a baby this late sometimes brings complications."

"Maybe you're right." Her face drops into thought for a few seconds. She scowls with concentration. "Maybe I could get pregnant for a few months, then if the baby has problems, I could abort and get pregnant again."

"Abort?"

"Oh, I see," she glares at me. "You're one of those Right to Lifers, are you?"

"No, no, far from it, but it's a little crass. Could your body hold up to that kind of stress?"

A silence falls over our little metal table. She puts her hands up to her face and breaks into a long, quiet sob. After a moment, she says, "I can't do this any longer. I can't go in and out of this illness, never knowing if the caregivers are going to be responsible enough to keep me alive or if they'll miscalculate their timing."

I put my hand on her shoulder, but say nothing.

In five minutes she pulls herself together, grabs the paper napkin and dabs at her eyes. Even puffy, her eyes are arresting.

She looks at me for a long time, searching, then says, "I need to be pregnant. I need to get clear of this sickness, and if my baby turns out to be fine, I want a baby from a man who is creative and intelligent.

"The young boys around town are more than willing,

and I'll find one of them if necessary, but it's a crapshoot with them. They could be a genius or a mass murderer. One can never tell, because they're much too young. You've proven yourself."

I take a sip of my coffee and pick at the croissant. I look at her questioning eyes. "I don't make good father or husband material. I've always been a loner and never too successful when it comes to relationships."

"Jesus, Jason, I'm not asking you to be a father or marry me. I just want a good solid man to sire my child. I want to rid myself of this sickness for a few years. Maybe by then the scientists will have figured something out."

"I'm sorry, I can't—"

A flash of anger crosses her face. Her next words are not from a plaintive woman, but from some demanding monster. Her voice drops an octave and three decibels. "You chicken-shit bastard."

She stands, grabs her coffee, turns on one heel, her hair whips to follow the arc of her spin, then stomps off toward the parking lot.

"Wait!" I yell.

She stops before she steps off the curb. She turns, and glares at me.

"Come back for a second."

She puts her free hand on one hip. Her dress pulls slightly up, showing a hint of a lace slip. "What?"

I open a fist I hadn't realized I'd closed and rotate my palm up. I point at her chair. "Please come back for a moment. Sit down."

She takes a sip of her coffee and walks the three paces back, then settles herself onto the metal chair. She puts her coffee cup down and gives me a cautious gaze.

"I've felt the same way, lately. I'm so tired of having

to search out whatever teenager is available to care for me while I'm in the third stage. Some are responsible. Others eat my food and leave the place a disaster. Who knows how they cared for me?"

Her big, brown eyes soften and return to the windows of her soul. She has eyes I could jump into and get lost forever. She smiles again. "So, you're considering?"

I take a sip of my coffee. "I've been considering for months, I just hadn't met anyone who looked like she might hold up her end of the bargain."

She leans forward and puts her soft hand over my balled-up fist. She rubs my white knuckles, and I remind myself to relax. My hand goes flat. She slides one finger between mine and says, "What's the bargain?"

I look up from her hand. "I don't know yet, but I do know I want someone to take care of me while I'm in my third stage."

She smiles. "I can do that."

"We both agree this is not a traditional relationship, so I want no emotional ties."

Her mouth turns down, but she agrees with a nod, then says, "It's best if I live at your house or you at mine. Either way works for me."

My mind is racing, but I can't come up with anything coherent. "Maybe we can use both houses."

She looks embarrassed. "I live in a crappy apartment overlooking the freeway. These days it's not as noisy, but there isn't much of a view."

I smile. "Because my uncle died during the first wave, I'm living in his house in the woods. It's not a mansion, but it is large enough for two people and a child."

She asks, "Can we go to your house?"

I nod toward the freeway. "I've got more shopping.

Can I meet you in an hour?"

"Yes," she says. "My last stop is the Nevada City post office. We could meet there in an hour."

"Okay." Being a man, I think the conversation is over. Although I'm nervous, we made a clear agreement, set up a time to meet, and as far as I'm concerned, that's the end of it. I take a last sip of coffee, set my cup on the table, and stand. "Okay, then, I'll see you in an hour."

She grabs my wrist, then guides me back to the seat. "I need a bit more time. This is a little quick for me."

I settle back into my seat and look at her. "What do you mean?"

"Let's talk a bit more."

"About what?"

She scrunches her face slightly revealing cute crow's-feet that crinkle at the edge of her eyes. "Oh, anything at all would be fine. I just need to sit here for a few more minutes and get to know you."

"I thought—"

"Just a little longer, Jason. I know we have things to do and precious little time to do them, but let's give it a little more time."

"Okay, but I don't know what to say."

We sit for a moment in silence until she speaks. "How about you tell me one important thing in your life."

"You first."

"Okay, that's fair. Let's see, I was married, but two years ago when Trillian hit, my husband died. He was my best friend, and I miss him terribly."

Oh God, she's telling much more than I'm willing to reveal. "I've been a writer most of my life and didn't have time for marriage. I've been in a few relationships, but

I'm not well suited to living with a woman."

"Does our arrangement make you nervous?"

"Yes, but I can't get any work done the way things are. I've been thinking about this for a long time, I just haven't met anyone the right age and temperament."

"Temperament?"

"You know, someone reasonably stable. Not some airy-fairy nutcase like most of the single women in this town."

"That's not fair. I know a number of stable women."

I sit through a moment of thick silence, then say, "You look stable and that's enough for me."

She smiles.

We make another dozen awkward exchanges, then agree to meet at the post office. I stand, put my hand out and shake, then walk to my car.

The rest of my town experience is a blur; the bank, drug store, hardware store, video store and finally back to the post office.

She stands by the front door. I park. She walks to my door and opens it. "I'll follow you in my car."

"I'd like to go to the river before this cycle is over. Maybe we could drop your car close to my house and ride together to Edward's Crossing."

A smile crosses her face and she nods. "I'll follow."

I drive along Coyote Street, cross the highway and up the steep hill to Bloomfield. The closer I get to my house, the more nervous I get and the more I realize I'm taking the first steps on the long, dark road of being in a relationship with a woman. Stable as this one might be, she's still a woman and so different from me, which forecasts problems, none of which I can ever overcome.

We reach the summit of our climb and I pull in next

to a string of mailboxes. She drives beside me and rolls her window down.

"Park here," I say. "We can go to the house after."

"What about the groceries? They'll wilt in this heat."

She's right, but here is the first in what is sure to be a long series of corrections she'll have me consider. I hate being corrected by a woman. It's the main reason why I've lived alone the last four years since Joanne, who was the epitome of a correcting female.

Serenity's words of correction are between us for a moment. At any other time in history, I'd have simply driven away, but this isn't any other time. Trillian has all of us by the throat, and it isn't going to let up.

I smile. "You're right; we'll drive to the house, put groceries away, then go to the river."

She closes her window and follows me. I make the first right down my little country one-lane road, weaving through the forest for a half mile until I turn into my driveway. I pull up to the house and notice a cardboard box sitting on my porch.

I turn off my engine, grab my bag of limp carrots and the bug-riddled potatoes, and get out. She opens her door with her bag of groceries and walks over to me. "I'll put my things in your refrigerator while we're at the river. We'll decide later whether to keep them here or not."

"What do you mean decide?" Oh shit, she feels my ambivalence.

"Maybe this isn't going to work out. I can already see you're not used to having a woman around. Maybe staying here isn't the best idea."

Like an idiot, I stand and look at her. How can she understand this even before I do? How do women pick up on subtle things so easily?

"Look, Serenity, I'm just not used to having anyone around, especially lately, but this is a unique situation. I'm a confirmed bachelor in normal times, but these are not normal times. We have special circumstances here, and though every fiber of my being wants to continue to be alone, I know it's not good for me, and it's also dangerous to my health.

"Things may not work out, but we might get lucky. God knows, we could use a little luck right now, and I'm willing to give anything a try."

She gives me a furtive smile. The little lines on her forehead crinkle. She shifts her groceries to her left arm, slides her right hand around my elbow, then walks with me up the stairs I rebuilt last summer.

I open the door and lead her into my messy house to the kitchen table where we set our groceries. She fumbles through her bag and removes the perishables.

In these days of shortages, the refrigerator that used to be packed tightly with everything in varying stages of decomposition is almost empty. A stick of butter, three bottles of locally brewed beer, a box of baking powder, and assorted half-empty bottles of catsup, mustard, and all the things that can keep for long periods and aren't used much.

I slide my carrots and potatoes onto a shelf and she slips her things below mine. She closes the refrigerator door. I look at her. "Let's go to the river."

Chapter 4

The River

There's her smile again. "Okay, but I have no bathing suit, and I never got used to being naked in public."

A flush of embarrassment floods my face. "I'm sorry; I never wear clothes. You could wear your panties and bra. It's almost the same thing."

Without the self-consciousness I'm feeling, she says, "That works for now. When I go home, I'll get my suit."

We walk down my front steps and get into the car. On Bloomfield, I make a right and continue into the canyon. At the bottom of the hill, before we cross the steel bridge, I park. We wind our way along the side of the river on a narrow footpath I've taken endless times.

A quarter mile upstream we see a wide pool of clear,

emerald water and wind our way over boulders and between water-torn willow and deer brush until we come to the river. I pull my shirt over my head, remove my shoes and pants at the same time, and climb onto a familiar white granite boulder the size of a house. I know the water is deep under this boulder, so I take a leap into the air, arch my back, point my toes, and toss my arms over my head. I cut the cool water like a pro, come up for air and look at Serenity. She has removed her shoes, lined them next to one another and is working on folding her socks carefully, one into the other.

"Come on in, the water's wonderful."

"Turn around."

She's shy, and I understand. I turn toward the canyon walls on the opposite side of the river. I'm standing, patiently waiting, when I feel her hand on my shoulder. She says, "this water is wonderful. I forget how amazing this river is."

We swim and lie on the rocks until late afternoon without one other person walking by. It's not unusual these days, but there were times when people had to claim their space on the sand with towels and share the beach with a hundred screaming kids and barking dogs. The day is silent and hot, with the cool water to refresh us. Although we try a few times, Serenity and I have little to talk about. After a time, we give up and simply lie on the beach next to one another, baking in the afternoon sun, listening to the gurgle of water over rocks that have been here a million years.

It's the same gurgle I heard when Sam and I awoke from our first nightmare sleep in that noisy boat, with the helmsman dead from exposure and dehydrated so much we couldn't recognize him.

We continued downstream for a half day before we came to a small village. Neither Sam nor I spoke the local language, and we had a hell of a time finding someone to talk to. Finally, one old man was able to tell us we'd drifted forty miles beyond our rendezvous. Sam bent to pick up his bag. The gold pendant slipped from inside his shirt. The old man paled, crossed himself, said a few words of warning, and scampered away, yelling some unintelligible gibberish to the villagers. In minutes, we stood alone in the middle; every man, woman and child had vanished.

Sam and I walked back and sat at the edge of the dock, tossing pebbles into the murky water. He turned to me. "The last thing I want to do is take the boat back upriver with that body getting riper every minute."

"What did you have in mind?"

"We could rent canoes from the villagers."

I tossed another rock. "I don't think they rent canoes, plus, have you ever tried to paddle upstream?"

Sam stood and pulled his loose shorts up. "Guess we're stuck with the cadaver another day."

"If we're going back, then the quicker we get started, the sooner we rid ourselves of that body."

I stood, stepped into the boat, and tossed a few sticks into the little firebox. The remaining coals lit the sticks. In five minutes, I added more wood, and ten minutes later the first hiss of the engine rotated the drive shaft. Sam loosened the tie ropes and pushed us away from the dock. The noisy engine hissed and spit its way to the center of the river. While I stoked the fire late into the night, Sam sat at the till and kept us in the middle of the river. The full moon helped us navigate in the dark.

About midnight, Sam pointed. "I see lights."

I stood and looked over the helm of the boat. Electric lights of a civilized community reflected through the trees. I grinned big. "I've never seen anything so inviting. I'm never leaving civilization again."

"Jason, how many times have I heard you say that?"

"This time, I'm serious. The last forty miles have cured me. I'm close to home from now on."

I didn't know how true my statement would be. I had no idea that most transport systems would shut down.

Now that gas is precious as gold, the days of imported beer and cheeses, or even fruit from the next state, are gone, maybe forever.

I come out of my dream state when Serenity touches my shoulder. With a sigh of relief, I pull myself away from the Amazon Basin and look into Serenity's dreamy chocolate eyes.

"It's time to go back, Jason."

"What time is it?"

"Six thirty. I'm hungry, and it's going to take a bit of time to make something. Let's go to your house, and I'll fix dinner."

I stand, gather my towel, take a long drink of water from my bottle, and slide my sandals on my feet.

The walk back reminds me of the miles Sam and I walked in the jungle, him with that damn gold pendant jangling around his neck. It's ironic that after all of his conniving, paying off officials, greasing the palms of each little person who stopped and inspected us, I would be the one who would end up inheriting the damn thing.

When we get in the car she speaks for the first time

since we started walking back. "You seem distracted."

I try to smile. "There's a lot going on in my head."

"Working on your next book?"

"Working on what's left of my life. I guess I'm not the best company."

"It's okay, we all have a lot to think about. My entire family died from the sickness. I'm the only one left to carry on the Lockheart name."

"Lockheart is your last name?"

She gives me a sad smile and nods.

"I'm sorry."

"Did you lose anyone special?" she asks.

I start the engine and back the car out of the parking space, then drive up the long hill. "I was pretty much always alone. I never knew my family of origin. I was orphaned when I was six months old. My folks died in a freak tornado in the Sacramento Valley. The twister took them and half of the houses in our neighborhood. I was in the other half."

She puts her hand on mine.

I shrug. "Too long ago to remember."

"Anyone else since?"

"My uncle and my ex-wife. Four years ago she packed her stuff while I was in town one day and disappeared. Sam, too, but I don't know if he counts."

I break my gaze from the road to see her staring. "Was Sam a friend?"

I nod, shift into second gear, and round a sharp turn. "My friend from high school. We got together once a year to travel. The last place we went was the Amazon. He died during the early stages of Trillian sometime after I got back. I think he was in a Mexican jail at the time."

"I'm sorry," she says, but I'm not listening that well. All

I'm aware of is the road and the damn hastily wrapped box that showed up at my doorstep with the shaky penmanship addressed with pencil in Sam's disjointed script. There was no letter inside, not even a note, just that damned gold pendant he was so determined to get back to the States.

"Jason?"

I come out of my stupor. "Yes?"

"Just checking to see if you're still around."

"I was back in the Amazon for a second."

"Did a lot happened there?"

I round the last hairpin and drive up a straight part of the narrow two lane road. I glance at her. "More than you could ever imagine."

She continues to try to keep me in conversation for the rest of the two miles back to the house. I want to talk to her and share my secret with her, but I can't. It's way too big to put on anyone else.

When we pull up to the house and park, I turn the key off and look at her. "You must be pretty disappointed, me being a space case and all."

Her smile warms the inside of the car. "Not really. I just figured that's how writers are."

"How's that?"

"Introspective."

"Maybe someone like Toltec or Steinbeck, but I'm just a crappy run-of-the-mill fiction writer. I don't have much to say, just a nice way of saying it."

"Jason, that's not true. I've read your last two novels, and you had a lot to say."

"Most of what I write is schlock."

She opens her door and reaches to the back seat for the towels. Before she gets out she looks at me. "I don't think it's schlock. I like what you have to say though, and I like the way you say it."

We get out and I speak over the car's roof. "Thanks."

We walk into the house.

I open the fridge and grab a beer. I show her the chilly bottle. She smiles. I grab a second one, close the fridge, and open hers. I sit at the kitchen table and slide her the open one, then pop the top of mine. We both take long swigs before we say another word.

I put my bottle down. "Thanks for keeping me here with your conversation. I guess I'm not in my body much these days."

She looks around. "Maybe we'll get the rice started so it'll be ready when everything else is. Where is it?"

I point at the revolving cupboard at her knees.

She turns, leans down, and pushes the door with her right hand. I see the muscles strain in arms that have worked hard. Her slim arm bulges as she pushes the door inward, grabs a gallon jar and hoists it up to the counter. She snatches a pot from the wall and puts it on the stove, then turns the flame on. "You wouldn't possibly have some olive oil, would you?"

"Not for more than a year, but I have some fat from a butchered hog my neighbor gave me last month. Will that do?"

"Sure." She leans down to adjust the flame.

I stand, open the fridge door, dig out the two-pound coffee tin and hand it to her. Without taking it, she dips a teaspoon in the lard and drops it into the sizzling pot.

By the time I've returned the tin to the fridge and close the door, she's measured out one cup of rice and drops it dry into the melted lard.

I raise an eyebrow, and she smiles. "My maid taught

me. That was years ago, when life was much different."

She stirs the rice while the pot screams from the spitting lard. Just as I think things can't get much hotter, she dumps in two cups of water. "Stirring in hot oil first gives the rice a nutty flavor."

"No kidding?"

She puts a hand on her hip and turns to me. "I've followed your career for years. You've always been interesting and I'm curious about what makes you tick."

As anger flushes my face, I try to keep my ire under wraps. "So, I'm some kind of experiment for you?"

She sets her bottle down. "I'm probably going to be a character in one of your books someday."

I smile. "Okay, I'll give you that, but everyone seems curious about what makes me tick. I hate that."

"Sorry, buddy, curiosity comes with the territory. You're famous, and everyone wonders what the other side of the fence looks like."

"I'm famous?"

"Before Trillian, Baker's Corner was a big deal. Your name was everywhere. I'd say you're famous."

"You're not going to believe this, but most of my fame was hype from my publicity people. Their job was to market me, and they did a good job. I'm not as famous as they say."

She shakes her head. "Don't you get it? No one cares if your fame is hype or not. To them you're famous."

I shrink into my seat. "I never wanted to be."

"Too late."

"I guess you're right." I take another long drink from my bottle. Because it's homemade beer, I'm careful not to let the sediment rise to the top.

She takes some limp vegetables from the fridge, pulls

out some venison I got from my neighbor last week, and slices things into a hot pan. "I'm not so interested because you're famous, but because I wonder how you're able to write your stories. Where do they come from?"

I take another sip of beer while I watch her ample hips rotate with the cutting of each slice of carrot. She has welcoming hips, unlike the skinny model types who starve themselves.

She turns to me and almost catches me gawking. I quickly look up into her chocolate eyes. She flips the knife and uses the blade as a scoop for the carrots. "So, where do they come from?"

"The stories themselves come from somewhere even I don't know. When I sit and write, and lately it's been seldom, something takes over. I find myself following the rabbit in Alice in Wonderland. The rabbit leads me to places even I wouldn't have guessed."

"No kidding? It's that easy?"

"Not exactly. The way I put the words down is the skill I have acquired from twenty years of novel writing."

We talk about nothing in particular for the next thirty minutes before she starts cooking the vegetables. The rice smells delicious.

Her back is to me while she dumps a load of sliced celery into the pan, takes a wooden spoon from the drawer, and stirs everything. "Do you have any soy sauce?"

"Gone six months ago. I did manage to sock away a load of salt and I still have a little pepper. Other than local herbs, it's all I have."

She turns to me again, and I admire the twist of her slender waist. "That'll do. Where's the salt?"

I step to the spice rack, snag the salt container and

hand it to her. My belly touches her elbow. It's enough to feel a spark that startles me. I'm not expecting the contact to be more than a simple nudge, like on a crowded bus or train. I jump back and awkwardly hand her the salt. "Sorry, didn't mean to . . ."

Our second or two of silence feels like an hour. I hold out the salt. She turns her whole body and backs to the counter. Her eyes flash. Thinking I frightened her, I step back another foot to give her room. In the same stretched out move, quick as a cat, she closes the gap between us, lifts to her toes, and plants a fast peck on my lips. I feel her soft lips. I taste the faint lipstick and smell a hint of some forgotten perfume, long ago applied and still lingering. Maybe it's her natural odor. I'd like to think she carries a hint of lilac.

While I sit back in the chair, she stirs the vegetables, then cuts thin slices of venison from the small steak. Deer meat is tough and stringy, but it does just fine cooked thin and mixed into something to hide the gamey flavor.

After a long silence, she says, "I've wondered what your lips felt like since I met you in the rice aisle."

I'm silent. What do you say to something like that?

"Did you like it?" she asks.

"Yes, I guess I did, but you startled me."

"Startled me too. I wasn't planning on kissing you, if that's what you think."

"I know you were being spontaneous, but you caught me off guard."

She smiles, turns, and drops the slices of meat into the pan with the vegetables, then flashes an odd expression.

I give her an awkward smile. "Maybe if you were to try again, I'd be more prepared."

She sets down her spatula, takes the three steps to

where I'm sitting, leans down, and touches her soft lips to mine. Her slippery tongue pushes farther into my mouth. She slides in, not in an intruding manner, but more to invite playfulness, enticing my tongue to participate. In an automatic response, my tongue joins hers, though it hasn't acted in this way since long before my wife left four years ago.

I feel an immediate reaction down there, a tingling stiffness. It's another sensation I haven't felt in a long time.

Her kiss lasts thirty seconds, though I try not to keep time. She disconnects from my lips and pulls back. She steps to the sizzling pan and stirs the meat. "You seem a little nervous."

I feel flush. "Maybe I am."

"Why?"

"I'm not used to kissing so early. Not since I was a teenager have I been so reckless."

She stirs dinner, plucks a slice of carrot from the pan and blows on it. "I started ovulating this morning. I thought this might be the perfect time, because when you wake up from your next round of flu, who knows when our cycles might match up again?"

"I see."

"Plus, I like kissing you. Did you like it?"

I say, "I liked it, but things are moving so quick."

"It's the times, Jason. These days we have to make snap decisions and no preamble. I hate this new way, but there is little either of us can do about it."

I'm silent for a moment.

She plucks two plates from the cupboard, plunges the spoon into the rice, dollops a large portion onto both plates, then divides the vegetable venison stir-fry over the rice. She sets a plate in front of me, sits, and closes her eyes for a moment. During that moment, I get a chance to study her face, the wrinkles around her eyes, the small dimple high on one cheek, the shape of her round little nose, her small mouth with surprisingly sensual lips.

She opens her eyes and picks up the fork. "I never used to thank anyone for my meals, but lately things have been so skimpy, I've taken to appreciating each one."

"Are you Christian?"

While she chews her first bite, she gives me a smile. "I don't know who I'm thanking, not some patriarchal Christian God, but I know it's someone."

I take my third bite. She's still chewing her first. I'll probably finish my entire meal before she gets her first bite swallowed, so I slow down. When no one is around, I shovel food. A burrito on the run is fine by me.

I attempt to match her mastication techniques but fail miserably. She's not paying attention.

When we're finished and the kitchen is clean, I break out my last bottle of cognac, stashed from a case I got two years ago.

With half-full snifters in hand, we retire to the living room and I sit across from her.

She shakes her head with a slight movement, gets up from the couch, and sits on the love seat next to me. "I don't know what's made you so cautious, Jason, but I don't think we have time for coyness." She sets the glass on the coffee table and takes my free hand.

I've positioned the brandy next to my lips, not taking a sip, but there to protect me from any surprise kissing attacks. I take a small sip, then smile. "Coyness?"

She reaches for my glass, sets it on the table, then looks into my eyes. "We can do this without romantic overtures if you feel more comfortable."

"Overtures?"

She lets go of my hand and leans back. "You know, no kissing or petting, just get down to business, but we won't have half as much fun."

I flush. "I want a little romance, don't you?"

She smiles and nods.

I take another swallow, not a sip this time, but a good healthy slug, almost finishing the glass. I set the snifter down and look at her. Although my insides have turned to jelly and my hands are shaking, I take her hand. "I'm not used to moving so fast, that's all. It's been a long time since I've been with a woman."

That said, I'm a bit less shaky. I pull her closer and allow my old horny teenager to take over. It's not the gangly, unsure, harsh, I've-got-to-have-it-now teenager, but simply allowing myself to embrace the moment.

She leans close. At the last second I close my eyes. Her lips touch mine. A long forgotten tingle begins in my chest, then quickly shoots to my loins. My cock stands at immediate attention. I slip my free arm around her waist and pull her closer.

Her one hand fumbles my shirt out of my pants and I feel her cool fingers sliding through the fur of my chest. Her lips are soft and yielding. With a surprise move, she releases her lock on my lips. In one quick movement, she pulls my shirt over my head without unbuttoning it. She tosses it across the room. In another second, I feel her warm breast against my skin. She rubs her nipples across my chest.

I'm relieved not to take the assertive role in this little drama. I sit back and experience the moment, rather than what I've always done, which is to try to figure out what she wants next, what to do that might please her. I don't even have to think, and it's exciting.

Her lips are on my neck, my shoulder, my chest before I realize she has undone my slacks. She slides them down a few inches, freeing up my hardness. She kisses my bellybutton, and I know what is about to happen. I've never had this before. The surprise makes me shudder, though not from nervousness this time.

Before long we are having one another on the couch, the floor, the coffee table, spilling the brandy, then finally crawling across the floor toward the bedroom. She helps me to find my moment by reaching her climax, pulling me deep into her and rotating her hips, coaxing the baby-making sperm out of me in one of the most pleasurable ways I've ever experienced.

We make the last movements, the last twitches of pleasure and I go soft and slip free of her. She rolls onto her back and pulls her knees to her chest.

Although I don't want to waste a moment of my short time left during this cycle, the last thing I see is her in the knee-up fetal position before I drop into a slumber even the third cycle couldn't produce.

I awake to a gray dawn with the birds calling to one another in a celebration of another day. I feel dread. It's one of realization that I have three days left before I drop back onto the couch with the flu again. Three days left, and I've done so little.

Serenity lies next to me with her back exposed to the morning coolness. I slip from bed, slide the covers up to her chin and tiptoe out of the room, closing the door quietly behind me.

Three hours later, after I have a remarkable session with computer keys flying and words slinging onto the screen, the story unfolding like never before, Serenity opens the door. She walks to the bathroom and glances in my general direction.

I look up just long enough to see her hair tangled, her face without makeup, and for a second, because I don't want to stop writing, I realize that she looks good without all of the foo-foo stuff.

Holy shit, I've got a girl I'm supposed to check on. I look at the phone and the answering machine is blinking with forty-seven messages. I search for Tammy's number on my phone pad and dial it. On the third ring, a male voice answers. "Tammy Flanders house."

"Is Tammy around?"

"She's in second stage in the back room," the voice says. "I'd get her, but she's not doing too well."

"It's okay. You her caregiver?"

"Yes, I'm Bill Sanders. I'll be caring for her through the third stage."

"Oh, good. Tell her I called, will you?"

I want to relieve her of the responsibility of taking care of me, but if Serenity's pregnancy doesn't take, then I'll need Tammy in seven days.

"Sure," the voice says then abruptly hangs up.

I replace the receiver and look at Serenity.

She puts her hand on one of her luscious hips and twists her body slightly to glare at me. "Well?"

During the three seconds of silence between her question of finality and the moment I'm expected to say something, my mind leaps back to that damn boat and the ride out of the jungle.

Chapter 5

Flu

When we got back upstream to our original meeting place and moored the boat, a silence lay over the little village. No one was on the dock to greet us, not even the children who plagued the docks fishing around the boats.

"Where is everyone?" I asked aloud.

Being a good Catholic, Sam crossed himself, kissed his fingertips and stepped off the boat onto the dock. "Hello," he yelled with his hands cupped to his mouth.

No answer.

He gave another longer, louder yell with the same results, then turned to me. "I think we better find out."

I stood, climbed out of the boat onto the firm wood of the dock. Both Sam and I walked the hundred feet to shore and climbed the root-infested bank to the first building.

"Hello," he said, in a quieter tone. We looked in the hut. A child of five sat blank faced next to her dead mother or grandmother, I couldn't tell. We walked in. The child didn't look at us. On the straw mats next to the far wall lay two figures, one the blue color of death on her lips, the other looked like he could die any minute. Although he hadn't moved a muscle, the guy's lips were parched, so I poured a dribble of water on them from a roughly formed clay cup that sat on the table. His lips move slightly while he lapped the liquid.

Sam whispered, "he's dying of thirst."

I poured another small amount into his mouth and he responded. In five minutes, I'd given him two cups from the pitcher. His color looked better.

Sam asked the girl what happened, but she couldn't answer.

I motioned Sam to follow. Outside I said, "looks like we have some work to do."

Sam grimaced. "What do you mean?"

"If everyone is dehydrated, we've got a lot of water to pour."

Sam stepped thirty paces to the next building and looked in. "Looks like they all are either dead or in some kind of catatonic state."

"Either way, they need water." I pointed at a row of mud huts to my right. "I'll take these and you continue with that row. When we get to the end, we'll both take the last row."

Sam was never a man for much talking. He turned and walked into the hut. I stepped across the compound and poked my head into the first cottage. A woman lay peacefully next to a young man; He was breathing, she was not. I found a gourd of water and slowly poured some into his mouth. He spat and sputtered in his sleep state, but drank the water. When he was satiated, I went to the next hut and found both people barely alive. I gave them water and moved to the next building where two adults and one child were dead. In the next, out of six people, only a child of eight was alive and coherent. He helped me give some water to everyone we found alive in the next seven buildings.

We finished the string of huts before Sam and I—

"We don't have time," she says, pulling me back from my nightmare. "What are you thinking?"

"I wouldn't be able to tell you in the one day I have left."

"If I'm pregnant, we have many days. Before we go any farther, maybe we better make another attempt to get me knocked up."

Although it's the driest approach to lovemaking I've ever heard, still my old wanger stands at full attention. I pull her into my arms. My stiffness pushes hard against her belly.

She rubs her body into mine. "I didn't know you were so ready."

I smile and lean down to kiss her. Our lips meet. I pull her one little baby-step at a time toward the stairs, then up to the bedroom. I open the door and get her close, then push her onto the bed and grab her bare feet. I kiss her ankle and she sucks in a breath. With each kiss up her lovely torso, her breathing becomes more pronounced.

We couple three more times before the next morning.

That evening, while I'm splitting firewood, she dances out the front door and over to me holding a pregnancy test packet. I look at her and grin. "I guess we're pregnant?"

She smiles. "Come inside. I've made soup."

"Do you like to cook?"

We step through the kitchen door and into the warm room filled with the scent of fresh bread.

I take a deep breath. "This is the best this room has smelled since I was a teenager."

She's humming. "You sit at the table and I'll serve."

I find a chair and plop myself in at the end of my family-size table, the one thing I was left with from my marriage.

She ladles hot liquid out of a pot and fills a bowl, pulls off the nose-cone shaped end of the loaf and drops it on a plate, sets the bowl next to the bread and walks them over.

I look up at her. "I could get used to this."

She smiles. "Tonight is special and I'm cooking my best tonight."

"Special?"

She sets the bowl in front of me and puts both hands on her hips. It's obvious she's waiting.

I point at the plate with the steam rising. "Maybe I'll let the soup cool."

She scowls and takes a cute little hop. Maybe it's only a leap of a quarter inch, but it signifies the mandate of the entire female population. Now!

I grab a piece of bread, tear it in half and make a quick stab at the bowl, soaking the bread to cool the scalding liquid.

When it touches my tongue, I'm expecting to fry off a layer of skin, but surprise, it's not hot. I take a healthy bite, then grab for the spoon. "This is good."

She gives me a devilish grin.

I don't shovel my food, but I'm not taking my time either. The soup is amazing. The bread is incredible.

I taste each vegetable and maybe the barley hides the gamy taste of the venison.

"How did you learn to cook like this?"

She crosses her arms in front of her, turns slightly to the left and for the first time I notice the little scar above her right eye. She smiles. "I never learned, cooking just happened."

She rips a hunk of bread from the loaf, steps to the stove and dips directly into the pot. With the bread ready to go into her mouth she asks, "So, you going to call your sitter and cancel?"

I nod and grab the phone.

When my call is finished and I've left a message, Serenity and I sit across from one another sipping the soup. We eat the entire loaf of bread.

"Tomorrow you go into Trillian?"

"Yup, and it's a day I don't look forward to."

She puts a spoonful of soup to her lips. "I'll take good care of you."

"Oh, that's not it. The problem is, it's such a waste of time. Why can't the scientists figure this out?"

She takes the spoonful of soup, chews the chunky parts, then sets the spoon down. "Haven't you heard?"

"Heard what?"

Chapter 6

Medallion

"They're looking for the original strain of virus. When they find it, or at least one close, then they can study it. I guess the mutated forms aren't so useful."

I stop eating my soup. "Oh really, and just where do they want this original virus?"

"No one said. I guess somewhere in the body would be useful."

"I mean, where do they want the virus delivered?"

She looks up with a smirk. "How would I know?"

"Where did you hear about this?" I get out the phone book from the hutch against the back wall.

"The newspaper, I read about it. Let's see." She holds up one hand and counts fingers. "Three days ago I met you, and I was awake for a day before that, so it must have been the Saturday paper, because they don't print on Sunday."

I find the number of the paper and call. "Hello, you had an article about Trillian in Saturday's paper, can you give me some information on who to contact?"

I take a pen from the table and scribble a number, then thank the young woman and hang up.

I dial the number and wait interminably for the auto operator to give me an endless list of options. Finally out of frustration, I hit the "O" for operator and the line passes over to an actual person.

"Is this the Viral Health Institute?" I ask after she rushes through a welcome.

"Who can I connect you with?"

"Are you looking for a pure strain of Trillian?"

In a bored voice, like she'd been fielding millions of these calls for weeks, she says, "Yes sir, we need the virus to further the research. Most people call with the second generation version; we've already studied that. We need the first strain."

"What if I said I have the first strain?"

She gets an irritated tone, "You and about a hundred other callers today. Sir, just how did you come by this virus?"

"In the Amazon jungle."

She laughs aloud, holds her hand over the receiver, and in the background she yells, "this one found it in the Amazon." I hear laughter from the background.

"Sir, if you found—"

"Who am I talking to?" I yell. "Let me talk to your supervisor, now!"

That said, the young woman hangs up on me.

I look at the receiver, then at Serenity. She says, "I'd

have hung up too. You're not going to get anywhere yelling." She picks up the phone and re-dials the number. In her soft voice, she asks for the address and to talk to the person in charge. I look over her shoulder while she writes: "332 Park View Lane, Palo Alto."

When the operator hangs up on Serenity, I see a hint of anger in her face. "That bitch hung up on me."

"Are you ready to scream now?"

We called three more times and got rerouted, got the wrong people and finally hung up on again.

After dropping the phone on its receiver, Serenity asks, "why are you so interested in that particular lab in the first place?"

"I'm sure I have the original strain on a pendant Sam found while we were in the Amazon. Everything leads to the necklace. This catastrophe began when we brought the thing out of the jungle."

In the brief seconds between my last word and her next question, my mind dives back into the darkenss of the Amazon jungle.

Chapter 7

Jungle

We helped the people in the village, then hiked ten miles to the top of the mountain and called bush pilot to fly us out. We had to hike twenty more miles to an airstrip carved out of a section of the forest on the side of a hill. The plane had enough room to land, turn around, and take off.

The pilot flew in with an oversize Cessna, grabbed our bags, got us on the plane, and was out of there in five minutes. Once we were in the air, he asked, "You two get wind of some kind of sickness going on down there? I heard it was something nasty. No use in sticking around to catch any bugs, if you know what I mean."

"You have the pendant?"

Her question brings me back to my kitchen.

"Sam found the damned thing and he was determined to bring it back."

She raises one eyebrow. "Where is Sam now?"

"Died in a Mexican jail. I should have gone back for him."

She puts her soft hand on the bare skin of my arm. "It's okay, Jason. We all have a bunch of should's."

"I guess, but he was my friend, for God's sakes."

She squeezes my arm.

I say, "I think we better get this virus to the lab in Palo Alto."

"You're not going anywhere now. Starting tomorrow morning, you have Trillian to deal with and for the next ten days, it's my job to take care of you."

I look at her. "You know how good that sounds?"

She turns and opens the cupboard. "Want a cup of tea? It's a good herbal that will help during the first few hours of the stomach upset. It's coming any minute, you know."

I look at the clock on the wall. "Coupla more hours." "Between now and then, I have something I would like to try again. It has something to do with a soft fluffy part and another thing that's getting harder by the second."

She blushes. "I'm already pregnant."

Her words shatter all the pleasant dreams of copious amounts of sex with her. I smile. "We'll practice for the next pregnancy."

She turns her head slightly, and her little scar lights up like a Christmas tree bulb. In a sudden movement across the table, she leans forward, grabs my jacket, and pulls me to her, slapping a sloppy lip-lock on me. "In the bedroom," she says helping me to my feet. She leads me upstairs and through the door. "It's much more comfortable on the bed."

In the morning, nausea has arrived, and by noon I'm flat on my back in the full throes of the first stage.

Serenity cares for me like a full-time nurse. She sees to every detail. I hurl my lunch an hour after I eat. She dutifully cleans the mess and me. On the morning of the second day, during a coherent moment, I say to her, "When I get finished with this set, I want to take the pendant to the lab in Palo Alto. Wanna come along?"

"I'd like that. It's been ages since I've been to the city."

"San Francisco won't be the same city."

It's the last conversation I remember, though she says I went on talking for another day and a half. Things get strange inside this sickness.

When I awake in my bed, the sheets are fresh. I touch the back of my hand to my forehead. My temperature is cool, which means it's over, at least for the next five days. I get up, dress in clean clothes, and go to the kitchen, where Serenity sits sipping a cup of something hot.

"Do we have coffee?"

"Herbal tea. It'll be better for your system anyhow."

I rummage through the cupboards until I find the remnants of last month's pound of Sumatra. I pour out a spoonful. She sips her brew while I make a cup. After it's steeped a minute, I sit at the table.

She asks, "you still want to go to Palo Alto?"

"We should get started. I have enough gas coupons to get us there and back, though there'll be no more for the rest of the month. We'll have to slip in a food shopping trip at the same time before we leave."

She stands. "I'll be ready in an hour."

I take her hand. "It's good to feel good again."

She smiles. "And not to worry."

On my way out the door, I turn. "I'm jealous."

I dig up the pendant from where I buried it in the basement, wrap the gold in a piece of leather, and hide the whole package in the trunk. I check the oil and tighten the fan belt that's been squealing the last few months. Up until now, the squeal hasn't bothered me, but now that a woman is riding with me, I want the car to sound as good as it can.

The right rear tire is showing wear, but it's still in good enough shape to make a journey to San Francisco. I hope this isn't a mistake.

The car is packed. Serenity sits in the passenger seat, and I turn the ignition key until the engine starts. I drop the shift lever into gear and we move forward with a slight lurch. "We're off," I yell and look at her. She smiles.

The ride into town is always the slowest part of any journey.

"How come the road is so lumpy?" she asks.

"It's a mess because now everyone works part time. It's about all anyone can do with Trillian around."

She turns to me. "As a writer, how do you go part time?"

"Little gremlins come in at night and write for me."

She smiles.

Finally off of the windy little road and out on the highway, I go a mile, then onto Highway 49 and crank up the engine until we're traveling sixty-five. Nevada City disappears in the rearview mirror. We pass through

Grass Valley and along the wooded corridor toward Auburn, thirty miles to the south.

At the Bear River Bridge separating Nevada County from Placer County, we run into a roadblock. Not many cars are on the road, so we pull behind four cars. When we get to the officer, he asks for our ID and grills us about why we're leaving the county.

"We're going to Sacramento to see her mother," I point at Serenity. The answer pleases the cop. He hands our cards back. "It's easy getting out of this county. Getting back in will be a whole other deal."

"We live here. Surely we'll get back in."

"Depends on the cop. I'm here between six a.m. and two in the afternoon on the days I'm not sick. You could get Deluth. His wife died last month, and he's not letting anyone in."

"What days are you sick?"

"I got two days left before I'm down again."

"We'll make it."

"Either that or try coming back in through Colfax." He waves us on.

As my car picks up speed again, I look at Serenity. "Are we going to hit every little tyrannical cop?"

She gives me an odd glance. "And then some." She looks back through the windshield.

Lush foothills go by, with valley oaks, and long open meadows of drying grass.

In ten minutes we leave the lush grasslands and come to the first stoplight. It's the beginning of the never-ending city all the way to San Francisco. God, I hate driving into this mess. The strip malls, gas stations, burger joints, automobile dealerships; the list is endless.

For ten miles we drive past stores, hospitals, banks,

restaurants, and office supply businesses to Interstate 80, which leads off of my cherished mountain to Loomis, Rocklin, Roseville, Rancho Cordova, then eventually to Sacramento. I point slightly to the left of the car far off on the horizon.

She looks and glances back at me. "What?"

"Mount Diablo. In the old days, you would never see it because of smog. Another good thing about this sickness is the air is cleaner."

She looks again while I point west. "You see way off in the distance to the left of the tallest building in Sacramento."

She smiles. "Oh, yes."

"That mountain can be seen from hundreds of miles in every direction."

"It looks big."

"Not so much, maybe a few thousand feet. Diablo's uniqueness is it stands alone."

When we get to the flatlands, the ride is tunnel like, with the freeway walls built up on both sides and not much to look at.

She turns to me. "I never got much chance to get down here the whole ten years I've lived in Nevada City. I don't know, I never got around to it."

"What's the point anyhow? It's pretty ugly."

"It's exciting."

I look at her for a moment, then back at the road. "I guess I came down here too often. I used to drive to Sacramento almost every week to fly out for some kind of book signing or talk my agent set me up with. Traveling was a pain."

"Hey, Jason, we're going into the city, and I haven't been there in years. It'll be an adventure."

I don't want to sneer, but one slips out.

We drive in silence for a half-hour until we go under Interstate five in Sacramento. She points to the sky, "A plane is landing. I haven't seen an airplane for ages."

I look up and a small commuter jet is in a landing pattern flying north toward the airport.

Moments later we drive over the Sacramento River, then pass through the town of Davis. It's like some long freeway nightmare, but she's enjoying herself, so I continue along the almost abandoned freeway, looking in directions she points, trying to capture her exuberance.

In an hour, we climb through the Coast mountains. Compared to the majestic Sierras these hills are hardly bumps above the flats of the Sacramento Valley.

The freeway cuts through a dozen valleys until we come to the rusting metal bridge of the Carquinez Straits. We go over the bridge and to the top of the next hill. The entire northern end of the San Francisco Bay comes into view.

I've seen the bay too many times, but she goes into a childlike gasp, directs my attention toward the Golden Gate Bridge, then pans her finger the entire length of the panoramic view. "Would you look at that. It's like some crystal formation."

"Too much concrete."

The car drops off the hill and once again the view gets swallowed up with overpasses and road signs. We travel through the ugliest part of the entire journey, Richmond and adjoining towns.

Passing Berkeley and Oakland there are more cars on the road, though we still have an entire lane to ourselves.

Serenity points at San Francisco across the bay. "Are

we going over the Bay Bridge?"

"Wasn't planning on it. There's a faster route along the East Bay to San Mateo."

"Come on, Jason, let's have an adventure."

I swing across four lanes without coming within five hundred yards of another car, and get into the far right lane for San Francisco. "Hey, a little jaunt into the city might change my mood a bit."

I follow the freeway into a long sloping right bank, which leads us to the entrance of the bridge.

One toll booth is open and a long string of temporary cones funnel traffic to the far left. I pull up to the booth. Only one car is in front of me. I give the operator the money and look back before I take off. Two cars are behind me and it's three in the afternoon.

Serenity points. "Things have changed. I remember having to wait fifteen minutes to get to the booths."

The rise of the bridge takes us high over the water with a spectacular view of the entire Bay Area. We go through the bridge tunnel and come out the far end. San Francisco, in all of its angular glory, stands tall. Serenity says, "I'd forgotten how beautiful the city is."

I look at her. "For a man-made thing, I guess, but I much prefer the beauty of a high mountain lake or rocky craig of some cliff in the Sierras, or Andes, or Swiss Alps."

She looks at me while we cross the final span of the bridge and merge into the San Francisco freeway system. "You sure have an attitude about anything man-made."

I glance at her while we come into a sloping turn. "I don't have an attitude."

As I look back at the road, she turns to me. "I don't know what else to call it."

"Most things man-made have been under built by uninspired designers. You have to admit that many modern buildings could just as well be dumped into the bay for landfill."

"But they house people, and my guess is they do a pretty good job of it too."

"Oh, sure, but ugliness abounds in this country and when you add in the millions of strip malls and crappy box warehouse stores, the whole thing is like some kind of joke on the people who are forced to look at them."

"Okay, Jason, I agree with you. Most strip malls are the blight of this country, but because most of them are thrown up as cheaply as possible, they will disintegrate in fifty years."

"The problem is I have to look at them during those fifty years."

We come to a split in the freeway. I slide into the far left lane that leads us toward San Jose. Serenity speaks in an almost frantic tone. "Go right, Jason."

With little traffic, I swing the wheel at the last second, cross three lanes and guide the car into the right fork. "Why this way?"

She turns. "I want to see the city. This may be the last time in my life. We have plenty of time. I was hoping to go down to the surface streets and cruise around a bit."

I give a reluctant nod.

"Come on, Jason, it'll be fun. We'll see what things look like and be on our way in an hour."

"Okay, just an hour though. We have to get to the lab and back home in time."

The freeway goes to the right and I prepare to exit on the first off ramp, but a large flatbed truck sits blocking the exit. A guy with Army fatigues rises from his sitting position on the first step of the truck, bringing his rifle with him. He extends his hand directing us farther along the freeway.

I'm not going to argue, so I swerve back onto the freeway and continue driving above the trashy buildings of the warehouse district.

Two more off ramps are blocked in the same manner, but the fourth, Van Ness, is open. I slow and drop off the overhead freeway down onto city streets. Another large delivery truck with big-lettered words, "Bill's Beef Steaks," blocks the ramp. I halt next to a young man with short blond hair and a grimace. He has his rifle up, not aimed directly at us, but in our general direction.

I stop, open my window and smile.

He demands, "State your business."

I look at Serenity, then back at him. "Gas," she says quickly.

I add to the charade. "We're headed for Palo Alto. There used to be a station two blocks from here. Is it still there?"

The kid relaxes a little, lowers his rifle, turns toward the way we're going and points. "Two blocks and make a right. It's on the far corner." He leans down so he can see both of us. "Only one way out of the city though. After you get gas, you must come back to the freeway here. He pulls a slip of paper, makes a mark in one of the printed boxes and hands it to me. "You've got twenty minutes to get to the checkout station, otherwise you got trouble."

I toss the paper on my dash. "Just gas, then we're out of here."

The kid rises and waves us on.

We drive around the truck and the first thing I notice

is three cars traveling the length of Van Ness. One is coming toward us and two stagger a mile ahead.

I whisper, “there’s no one here.”

Serenity rolls her window down. “I expected more people in San Francisco. This place is deserted.”

“We don’t need gas, but we have twenty minutes. Where do you want to go?”

“To the Financial District.” She has an excitement in her voice. “We’ll get there and back in fifteen.”

“Financial District it is.” I turn right and drop down the long hill of Post Street.

She pokes her head out the window. “I lived in that apartment twenty years ago.”

I don’t look, but keep driving.

The ever-constant grind of traffic in San Francisco proper no longer exists. Sure, we see a few people here and there. Cars and delivery trucks weave in and out of the concrete monoliths, but the crush of humanity no longer fills the streets of San Francisco.

In five minutes we drive under the towering pyramid, then farther to Embarcadero at the edge of the water. We might have passed fifty people walking along the sidewalks and it’s three o’clock on a Tuesday.

I drive a large circle through a parking lot that would normally be packed.

In a cautious voice, she says, “I hope your necklace has the original virus.”

As I pull back onto Embarcadero and drive south through the myriad of unnecessary streetlights, I look in her direction. “I don’t have much hope. I never wanted the damn thing in the first place. Sam had the fever and there was nothing I could do to persuade him.”

“Fever?”

"Gold Fever."

"The thing is made of gold?"

"Almost two pounds."

Although I'm still driving, stopping at every red light, maneuvering my way toward the Bay Bridge again, then south toward San Jose, my mind leaps back to the first time Sam and I were barred from entering a village.

We'd traipsed through overgrown, narrow jungle paths working our way toward the larger townships down river, always moving in the direction of Rio. We'd hiked for miles. Tired and hungry, we came upon a mountain village. It had been four days since the boat. A child leapt from a tree and ran screaming to the center of the village. Before we'd come within a hundred yards of the first hut, the entire male population, spears in hand, arrows strung into their makeshift bows, stood in a line aiming at us.

Sam understood the language. "They say we carry the mark of death."

"The mark of death?"

He asked them a question, then turned to me with wide eyes.

"They know we have the necklace."

I rolled my eyes. "You should have left that blasted thing in the damn jungle."

The villagers jabbed their spears toward us and pulled back their bows. Fast, threatening words were spoken. Although I didn't understand, the intent was clear.

Both Sam and I were forced to backtrack for a mile to go around the village.

The next morning, still deep in the jungle, out of food, I awoke feeling a sense of nausea and dizziness.

We had to hike to the next township, but the word

was out and we were turned away. Sam and I found ourselves dropping to our knees next to a small stream. I puked my guts out and he tried to attend to me, though he was getting sick too.

For days we laid next to the stream, then blanked out. When I woke again I felt fine. I looked about at the crystalline quality of the morning and saw an old man sitting across the small fire from us. He offered me water and a strip of meat, then spoke in a fast jungleese I didn't understand.

When I looked at my watch I was amazed to realize five days had passed. Sam awoke and I looked around for the old man, but he'd disappeared. I leaned down to get a drink of water from the creek and saw my reflection and that squiggly vertical line with three crosshatches. I cupped a handful of water and tried to wash it. Although the crust of the application washed off, the underlying brown stain stayed. I looked at Sam. "Your forehead is tattooed."

"Yours too."

He rubbed the crust away, but not the stain. "The old man must have tattooed us while we were asleep."

I said, "I'm not sure we were asleep."

"What do you mean?"

"No one sleeps for five days."

He rubbed his forehead, as if rubbing would make it disappear. Finally, without looking up, he asked, "where are we?"

"Somewhere lost in the Amazon."

"That's great."

A low rumble, starting far off toward the rising sun, thundered toward us at breakneck speed. The intensity of the sound quickly rose until both Sam and I were forced to put our hands over our ears. The fronds and leaves of trees trembled.

I searched for the source as I got to my feet, ready to bolt deeper into the forest. The noise was unbearable. A flash of silver brilliance blotted the sky. The trees were cast into shade for a split second. The thunder washed over us. A jumbo jet, less than a hundred feet off the ground, rumbled over our heads. The sky returned to its former radiance. The sound dropped from a scream to a howl. The huge jet washed the trees and us with a hurricane intensity. Both Sam and I were almost blown over.

I expected it to hit the trees any second. I waited with gritted teeth for the first crunch of metal, the fireball to follow and a race to escape the burning trees.

As the sound lowered to a bearable level and both of us took our hands away from our ears, I grabbed Sam's arm. "We've got to get out of here."

Sam grinned. "The plane isn't crashing, it's landing."

Not two seconds later, I heard the skidding sound of rubber against pavement, then the roar of the reverse thrusters. The engines cranked up to another howl.

Thirty seconds later, the engines stopped roaring and the jungle was silent once again.

"Let's go." Sam moved toward the distant sound of the idling engines.

He rushed headlong through the fronds and jungle brush, not paying much mind to any trail or even trying to duck under branches. I followed at a safe distance.

After a hundred yards of weaving my way through dense jungle trying to follow him, I pulled a last frond aside and ran into an eight-foot Cyclone fence with a double strand of razor wire strung along its top. Sam had his fingers laced through the mesh of the fence. The jumbo jet turned at the end of the mile-long runway, then taxied toward the terminal.

Sam looked at me. "Last I remember, we were a few hundred miles from any airport. How did we get here?"

I looked through the fence at a flat, treeless patch of land of maybe three square miles. A tractor pulling a mower was doing crisscross patterns on the three-inch undergrowth. The driver was dark skinned and smoking a large cigar.

"Maybe the old man who tattooed us had something to do with it. A whole team of natives couldn't have carried us a hundred miles in five days."

We stared as the mower reached us, then turned to trek back across the tarmac heading for the far fence.

"Whatever," Sam said after the noise of the mower receded. "We're here and that's all that counts. Let's find a way to the terminal and get on a plane. I'm ready to go home."

"Me too."

We moved along the fence for a hundred yards until we came to a place where animals had dug under. When we stood on freshly cut grass, Sam pointed. "We'll follow the parameter. Airport authorities frown on pedestrians crossing airports." He pointed at the building on the far end of the tarmac. "It's not far."

I followed him around the outer edge of the airport property. While we walked, two more planes landed and one took off. We finally stepped on asphalt and walked along a paved road. I was relieved to be out of the jungle. How long had we been in there, a month or six weeks? Whichever, it was too long. I made a secret promise never to set foot in the jungle again.

After a quarter mile, we climbed three concrete steps to the terminal building and went through the big double glass doors. San Francisco International it wasn't, but we found a ticket desk and a few passengers sitting in the forty-seat waiting area. Best of all, there was a burger joint and I was starved.

After we ate and drank, in our torn and filthy clothes, Sam and I walked up to the bored looking, middle-aged woman standing with one elbow on the counter to prop her head. When we approached her desk, her attitude shifted. Her arm dropped to her side. She straightened as we leaned against the counter. I noticed she was looking at our foreheads. I remembered the tattoo and hoped it would wash away after a shower.

"Good afternoon." She spoke fast Spanish, extending her r's with a roll of her tongue. I never could get the rolling tongue part, but I answered with the few Spanish words I knew.

She asked a question, but I didn't understand and looked to my ever-constant interpreter for clarification. Sam smiled and spoke perfect Spanish, "Do you have a flight to the United States soon, preferably the West Coast?"

I caught the words United States.

She looked at her computer screen, clicked a few keys, waited for an interminable thirty seconds, then snapped off a string of sentences. Sam turned to me. "Nothing for three days, then they fly to Denver. Nothing to the West Coast for a week."

Sam spoke in quick Spanish, then turned to me and winked. "She's checking on a connecting flight here in Brazil."

She let out another string of incoherent Spanish and

Sam brightened. He reached into his side pocket and blanched. "Holy shit, my wallet's missing."

"Maybe it's in your pack."

"I never keep it anywhere except in this pocket of my cargo pants. It's the only safe place."

He looked and found nothing.

"What about your passport?" I pulled mine from the hidden pouch hanging around my neck.

He reached under his shirt and yanked his passport. "But, my money and credit cards were in my wallet."

"It's okay Sam, we'll use mine." I unslung my small backpack, unzipped the side pocket and found nothing. I checked the rest of my outer pockets, then dropped the pack to the floor and dug through dirty clothes. I found nothing.

I looked at him. "We're screwed."

I stood slowly and looked at the woman. Her brown eyes had a patient softness. Her demeanor was relaxed. Sam and I continued to check pockets and packs while she dropped back to one elbow on the Formica counter, resting her cheek on her knuckles.

"What'll we do now?" Sam asked.

We thanked the woman, walked away, and sat in the waiting area.

"I'll bet those bastards on the boat robbed us," Sam said. "I didn't trust them from the get-go."

"Either way, we're without money and no way to get anywhere without walking, and I'm finished walking."

Sam checked and rechecked his pockets, backpack and every other place he could think of. I leaned back in the cheap plastic chair, laced my fingers together and put them behind my head.

I sat for five minutes while Sam rifled through his

gear for the third time, then I noticed a small, single-engine plane taxi out to the gigantic runway and leap into the air.

I put my hand on Sam's shoulder. "I think I've got an idea. You still have the necklace?"

He felt for the center of his chest. "Sure, but I'm not trading this thing for flights out of here. No way man. It ain't going to happen. It's gold."

I smiled. "How about trading a few beads from the top of the necklace."

He sneered. "Don't be ridiculous. If that woman even had the authority to make a deal for some gold trinket, do you think she would trust that what we had was the real article?"

"Not her," I pointed out the window at the single engine plane as it banked to the right and flew in an easterly direction. "Someone in a small plane could take us to a bigger city where we could wire for money."

Chapter 8

San Francisco

"What are you thinking?" Serenity asks while I drive onto Montgomery Street.

"Oh nothing, just some memory."

I sense an expectation for me to say something else. It's what women want —no, more like demand— spoken out loud or not.

The light crossing Market Street changes yellow and I slow to a stop in the first position with one other car next to me. When the light turns red, two cars and one taxi move across the intersection and disappear down Market going toward the bay. For a long minute, not one other car crosses the intersection.

Serenity gazes out the window and looks up at the concrete walls filled with glass and steel.

"I was thinking about the fiasco that Sam and I went through trying to get back into the States with his chunk of gold."

"Chunk of gold?"

"You know, the pendant that cost so many lives."

When the light changes, I step on the gas and race through the intersection. It's halfway across that I feel something. It's slight, not worth noticing, but my car has been so dependable the last five years I've forgotten anything could ever go wrong. The engine gives one distinct chug, then continues through the intersection almost to Franklin Street before the second hesitation surprises me. I look at my gauges and everything is fine, oil pressure, battery, fuel level, but something happened twice now. Downtown San Francisco is no place to have car problems.

Serenity doesn't notice anything until we're halfway through the Franklin Street intersection. The car gives a marked buck, spits once and coasts to a halt.

She looks at me. "What's happening?"

I pump the gas twice and crank the starter for ten seconds, but it doesn't start. "I don't know."

I fiddle with every switch and knob I can think of.

She says, "This is no place to get stuck."

I nervously crank the starter. "But here we are and there isn't much I can do about it. This car's been so dependable."

When I turn the key off and rest my head on the headrest, I take a deep breath and let out a quiet whistle. It's something I do when I'm extra tense.

"Geez, Jason, what the heck do we do now?"

Normally there would be a half dozen derelicts and shopping cart-pushing homeless people surrounding the car in half-inebriated curiosity, but there is no one.

I look around and say, "Of course, Trillian took the street people out first thing. There would have been no one to care for them during the first few cycles."

Serenity locks her door. "That might be true, but it doesn't mean we're out of the woods here. This is still a rough neighborhood and we have to be careful, especially since the police aren't around."

"I get that, but I don't see what we can do other than walk to try and find some help."

She draws in a deep breath, lets it out and looks with her big browns. "I guess we walk to a gas station."

I reach for the key. "One more try."

I crank the engine, but it's obvious the car is not going to even pretend to start. After a final ten seconds of cranking, I release the key, then look at the gauges one last time. "We're out of gas."

She says, "what?"

"The gauge must have been stuck, because now it says empty."

"No kidding."

I point at the dash.

She leans over to look and smiles. "Would you look at that? There's a gas station up the street, just before you get on the freeway."

"You want to wait here?" I ask.

"Not on your life. I'm coming with you."

I open my door and put one foot onto the pavement. "Okay , let's get some gas and get the hell out of here."

Her door opens. In a half minute we march along the filthy sidewalk. I look in all directions for trouble.

In a long block, the street makes a slight turn toward the left and a yellow Shell sign stands towering high over the station. Serenity speaks in an out-of-breath broken sentence: "Slow down, Jason. We don't have to kill ourselves getting a gallon of gas."

I drop my pace, and she snakes her left hand through my right arm. "That's better."

After five more minutes of walking, we cross the intersection and step onto the property of the station. Other than the brilliance of the yellow sign and a single bare light bulb burning in the office, the place looks deserted. We open the door. An unshaven elf of a man looks over his newspaper without changing expression. He isn't going to speak, so I say, "We ran out of gas up the block. You got a can?"

His eyes focus on the paper. "Twenty bucks for the can, plus the gas."

"Can't I just leave a deposit and bring the can back?"

His eyes continue to scan the article. "Twenty bucks, and the can is yours."

I'm not in the mood to argue, so I dig into my pocket, pull out a twenty-dollar bill, and drop it on the counter.

"Plus the gas," he says.

"Okay, when I get the gas, I'll pay for it."

"In advance," he snorts.

I toss a five on top of the twenty.

He folds the paper, sets it on the counter, and leans down. When he comes up, he has an empty one-gallon clear plastic water jug in his hand.

"This is my gas can?" I ask.

He makes no sound, just scoops up the money the second he releases the jug and puts the twenty in his pocket. The five stays on the counter.

I snort. "You're not supposed to put gas in these."

He reopens his paper, drops his gaze about halfway down the page, and ignores me.

After another sentence of protest, I walk out of the filthy office. Serenity follows.

When gas is in the bottle and I've gotten my change, Serenity and I retrace our steps across the street, along the sidewalk, and around the only bend that keeps us from seeing the car.

The car sits at a strange angle, raked high in the back. Something's not looking right.

I rush my stroll to a fast walk. When we get closer, I see both back wheels are missing and the car sits on a short section of wooden railroad tie. I let out a long string of cuss words, give a session of kicks to the back quarter panel of my car and a few open-handed slams to the trunk.

She asks, "how could they strip the car so quickly?"

Still leaning on the trunk with both hands, I look at her. "Who knows how? All I know is if we leave the car, it'll be stripped far enough to be junked by tonight. If we don't leave, we may also be stripped by nightfall. We have to get out of here."

I search the rooftops and filthy windows of the empty buildings. Although I know someone is watching, I see nothing. She says, "This is where my cell phone would come in handy."

I smile. "I had one, but it no longer works."

"I know."

We rifle the car for anything usable and leave the rest to the thieves hiding in the buildings. In the trunk, I grab the paper bag with the pendant.

With our possessions, we start for the gas station and maybe a phone to call a car rental company, but Serenity slips her hand over my elbow and turns me toward her. "Let's go back to Market Street and get a cab. There's always an empty cab on Market."

I follow her the four blocks through the industrial area into the business section, and finally onto Market, with its camera shops, department stores, cheap liquor stores and porn shops.

We step to the corner of Market and Montgomery. Serenity holds up one hand to hail a cab. One spins a U-turn in the middle of the block and pulls in front of us. Serenity opens the door. I follow her into the stale back seat with a dark-skinned man who speaks such broken English it takes both of us together to understand what he says.

"Take us to a car rental place," she says.

The cab still sits at the curb while the man with solid black eyes tells us car rental places don't exist in San Francisco.

"Then take us to the commute train that goes south along the peninsula," I say.

The cabby turns back toward the steering wheel, adjusts his turban, pulls the meter lever down, and we are off with a squeal of tires. I slam against Serenity a number of times while he races through downtown. Although I'm sure he's going to lose control, he drives to a side street and parks next to the curb of the train station.

I pay him, and we walk up the steps.

"It's so odd," Serenity says.

"What's that?"

"This station is empty. When I worked here, there

wasn't any time of day that there weren't thousands of people milling around waiting for a train."

"Finding the medallion changed all of that."

"All the more reason why the scientists need it."

"I guess."

We step into the station, buy tickets, and walk to the platform to wait for our train, which is due in thirty minutes.

After five minutes of silence, I fade off.

Sam and I had just found out that our wallets were missing and the only thing in our possession was the death necklace. We went to the bathroom and dislodged three beads from each side of the necklace and walked to the private part of the airport. We wandered through the maze of small aircrafts.

The wait was endless while the day heated up. One jet after another landed, unloaded, reloaded, then took off.

Sam finally dragged me into the shade of the little private airport office. "We may be here for awhile, so we might as well be comfortable." He got two Cokes from the vending machine.

I took the bottle and gave him a look. "Isn't this the last of our money?"

He took a sip. "We'll be out of here sooner or later, and what else could we spend our last two dollars on anyhow?"

At dusk I looked at him, "If we don't get a plane soon, I'm finding a place to camp for the night."

He pointed at the building clouds in the western sky. "We'd better camp under this overhang. Things look a little threatening up there."

As usual, Sam was accurate with his prediction. By

dark, the clouds rolled in and let loose with a burst of rain that pounded hard on the tin roof. Lightning kept us awake all night.

In the morning, the day was calm, and though neither of us had slept much, I felt refreshed and ready.

By 9:30, Sam had talked to three pilots and gotten three rejections. A fourth approached us, a friendly Texan who spoke in a southern drawl. He was a big man with a stub of a cigar hanging from his thick lips.

Neither Sam nor I noticed him until I heard the sound of cowboy boots clunking up the little concrete path to the office. "You boys look like you could use a ride."

I was lying on top of the park bench. Sam sat facing the building. We both looked at him.

The big, bug-eyed sunglasses gave his large frame a Hollywood star kind of look.

I said, "We're trying to get to a city. "Our money was stolen."

The big guy pointed with a huge callused forefinger. "What's with the tattoos on your foreheads?"

I touched my tattoo.

He smiled and put out both arms with his palms up and fingers splayed, like he was ready to encompass the entire world. "You're in luck. I can get you to Rio, but I'll need some help loading my cargo."

Sam leapt to his feet. "No problem."

"Name's F.M. Patterson." He put out a big hand and shook mine with one solid shake, then let go.

I stretched my fingers. "Jason Oakley."

Sam introduced himself.

F.M. Patterson pointed. "My plane's there next to the van. How 'bout we get started? I got a schedule."

We followed him to the far end of the parking lot to a large two-engine prop job that needed a five-step ladder to board. We set up a fire brigade to load a hundred white plastic packages suspiciously the same size and weight of a kilo of cocaine. I didn't want to ask, but Sam broached the subject about halfway through the sweaty process of loading. Sam was always kind of naive about the world of drugs. His total experience was gleaned from the news and movies.

He asked, "So, what are we loading?"

Although I thought he was going to get angry and dump us right there, he bellowed with laughter. In his loud, boom of a voice, like there was no one around for miles, he said, "Hell, boys, it's just coke."

Sam gave him a curious stare. "Coke?"

"Well, I'll be damned, you boys don't even know, do you? Some of the best Brazilian cocaine money can buy."

I cringed, but we needed a ride, and that guy, with his two hundred kilos of coke, was our only way out of there.

He tossed me another plastic brick, and I walked it up the stairs, then handed it to Sam.

"You boys okay with my shipment?"

I came down the stairs and took another two packets. "I don't much give a shit what you do for a living. We've been stuck in this country for too long, and I just want to go home. If you're our ride out of here, then so be it."

I finished walking the next two packs up the stairs and came back for more.

In twenty minutes his cargo was loaded, and we were picking up speed on the runway. The plane leapt into the air. I looked down at the small town around the airport, then the hundreds of miles of dense jungle surrounding the settlement. God, I hated that jungle.

Chapter 9

Cowboy

Serenity brings me out of my memory. "How long were you stuck in Brazil?"

I blink as if I were asleep, then turn to her. "Maybe three weeks after Sam found the necklace, but it felt like three months."

The train takes its time rolling into the station and we wait five minutes for it to unload its measly cargo of passengers. While we wait, Serenity looks at me and asks, "What happened when you were in the air?"

"That's an entire story in itself. How about we save the next part until we're on the train?"

A tall, lanky man in his mid forties sits in the seat across from us. He takes off his felt cowboy hat, and introduces himself. "Hi, my name is Adam McFarland. They call me Cowboy."

I'm in no mood to entertain some urban cowboy,

and rather than acknowledge his introduction, I'm ready to move to a different part of the car. Jesus, he has the whole train to himself, what the hell is he doing sitting across from us? I grab my armful of worldly possessions, when Serenity speaks. "I'm Serenity, and this is Jason. We're on our way to Palo Alto. Where are you going?"

"Palo Alto," he says, like it's no coincidence.

I snort under my breath and relax my grip on my things, then face the blue-eyed wonder with his black cowboy hat. He looks ridiculous with alligator boots and tailored black slacks and sports jacket to match. Kind of a Johnny Cash look gone awry.

"What are you doing in Palo Alto?" Serenity asks. It's obvious she likes his company.

"Oh, not much. I've got two days left, and I'm going to visit my mother. She awoke this morning."

Serenity strikes a big smile like she understands and approves. "Good for you."

He runs manicured fingers through a shock of long blond hair. "Haven't seen her in three months. It's been too long."

At the far end of the train car, the doors open and a thick-chested Neanderthal-looking man steps in. He walks along the aisle and finds a seat five away from where the three of us are sitting. Cowboy glances over his shoulder at the man, then returns his attention to us while Serenity goes into a long story about where we live and how difficult it's been since Trillian came on the scene.

Although he tries not to show it, from the moment Neanderthal sat down, Cowboy is preparing. First, he unbuttons his black sports coat. Although it's a casual move, he slips his right hand around his left waist inside his jacket. That move in itself would not have drawn my attention, but though he clears his throat at the same second, I hear a definite snap of something being unbuttoned. He and Serenity chatter about the weather, Trillian, and a myriad of other subjects, but he never removes his right hand from his jacket.

My warning flags are flapping in a gale-force wind. Is he going to rob us? I pat the bag twice to assure myself the necklace is still hidden in it.

Both Cowboy and Neanderthal study my move. Are they in this together?

Something's happening, and Serenity is completely oblivious. Short of pulling out a massive loaded revolver I don't have, my guess is they're going to get what they've come for. I'll be powerless to stop them.

The train rumbles on, stopping here and there. Two passengers get on and sit at the far end. Serenity and Cowboy chatter about nothing in particular. I'm on the edge of my seat ready for something probably involving Sam's necklace. I'm trying to figure out how they know. Neither Serenity nor I told anyone we were taking this trip, and certainly neither of us told anyone why or what we're carrying.

Serenity turns to me and fires a question. "What do you think, Jason?"

"I'm sorry," I say. "I wasn't listening."

"What do you think about the Giants winning the pennant this year?"

I shrug. "I don't follow sports."

She and Cowboy look at me like I'm some kind of alien from Mars. Even the big guy behind them glares at me with disapproval.

Serenity frowns. "You don't follow sports? Why not? It's the most exciting thing happening, especially these days after Trillian."

Once again, I'm expected to defend my refusal to participate in a stupid organized game that most of America considers religion. Oh well, I'm used to being the oddball.

I say nothing. Their look of surprise transforms to a grimace of disgust, then, they both turn back to one another and leap into the chatter about individual players, the teams, and historical games. It's all a blur to me. I'm more interested in what Neanderthal is up to and how he and Cowboy will pull this off. It won't be hard. The other two passengers get off in Redwood City, just two stops from Palo Alto. Will they take us between stops and get off whenever they want? There's nothing I can do about it.

I'm ready to give up the necklace without a peep. I never wanted the damn thing in the first place.

The train gives a slight lurch and drops speed. The tinny little speakers make an unintelligible squawk, "Palo Alto," though it sounds more like, "mallo mallo."

Serenity still has no clue. I slide sideways on my seat and make the motion to stand. I look at Cowboy and Neanderthal. Both are focused in my direction. I stand. The tension can be cut with a knife. Serenity chatters about her sister in Omaha.

I motion for Serenity to get up. Without missing a beat, she grabs her things and stands. She puts her hand out to shake. Cowboy takes it. Neanderthal moves to the edge of his seat. He stands. God, he's big. His head is less than an an inch from the ceiling.

His eyes never stray from me. He takes a step toward

the exit. I look. Cowboy is getting to his feet. Okay, here it comes. I just don't want to get hurt. Neanderthal is three paces away. Cowboy stands. His hand is still under his coat. Serenity finishes her good-bye.

Neanderthal rushes me. Cowboy spins to face him, not me. I put my arms up to protect myself. Neanderthal doubles his fist and takes a long sweeping arc directly toward my face. I drop to the floor. The sound of a cannon goes off in my ears.

"Take another step and you're dead meat," Cowboy says in his Texas drawl. His friendly "ah shucks" inflection is gone, replaced by a police SWAT team demand. I land on the floor by the time the words are spoken. I hardly hear them. The ringing in my ears is loud. Another sound rocks my senses. Serenity lets out an ear-shattering scream.

I look up. The big guy's momentum carries him over the top of me. One shoe crushes my little finger. The doors open, and he sprints out onto the platform.

Cowboy stands pointing his short-barreled gun. The business end continues to follow Neanderthal sprinting away and out of sight around the tan stucco of the train station.

Cowboy holsters his weapon and puts out a hand to help me up. "You okay, Mr. Oakley?" he asks.

I grab his smooth hand and he pulls me to my feet. "I guess, but I thought you were. . ."

He smiles. "I'm here to make sure you're safe."

I brush at my pants and tuck in my shirt. "How did you know?"

"The cabby told us where he dropped you, and we followed logic from there."

"How did the other guy know?"

"Actually, Mr. Oakley, in the world of crime, you're pretty famous."

I grab my gear. We step out of the train and onto the platform. Cowboy looks around, then ushers us along.

"Will he return?" I ask.

"Probably not, but there are more where he came from. They all want your necklace."

"I guess there's a lot of gold."

"Not only for the gold, but for the virus."

All of us walk around the building and into a waiting limousine.

"What do you mean?"

"Whoever has the virus rules what's left of the world. I want to make sure you get it into the right hands."

"How did you know I had it?"

Cowboy smiles. "We found Sam Culpepper buried in Mexico a year and a half ago."

"Who is us?" I ask.

"Federal Government, of course. We backtracked his trail to Brazil, and you were in the boat with him. The problem was, you disappeared."

We get into the car. Cowboy follows us in, then sits across from us.

"I didn't disappear, I moved to my uncle's house. He died in the first few weeks."

"We waited for you to use a credit card or make a call from your cell phone."

"No reception where I live."

He turns to Serenity. "How do you fit into this?"

Her face brightens. "I'm the one who talked him into turning the necklace in."

The car pulls out of the parking area and heads to El Camino Real. We drive for five minutes along El

Camino, then climb into the hills.

I ask, "where is the lab?"

Cowboy gives me an odd stare. "A little farther, up in La Honda."

After a number of lefts and rights, the car turns into a large estate with two-hundred-year-old trees, a solid ten-foot-high brick wall and a steel gate styled from the 1920's.

Our driver clicks a button under his dash and drives up the long driveway until we come out of the trees. The building looms over a massive lawn with two long flower gardens fanned out to meet the house, if one could call the enormous building a house.

"Beautiful," Serenity says. "I never knew buildings like this existed in Palo Alto."

Cowboy smiles. "This isn't Palo Alto. La Honda is an entirely different world."

"I see that." She reaches for the window button and clicks it, but her window doesn't budge.

"We're almost there, Ma'am."

She smiles. "Call me Serenity."

The limo pulls to the entrance, a long, half-round tier of brick and blue tile to match the trim of the Georgian-style mansion. The front has eight or ten thirty-foot-high white marble fluted columns. Tall picture windows look over the entire southern portion of the Bay Area.

The driver parks, gets out of the car, and opens the door for us.

I'm the first out, with Serenity close behind. Cowboy says, "Let's go inside and meet our benefactor."

I look from the spectacular view of puffball clouds fading off into the distance toward Mount Diablo, then at Cowboy. His face is scrunched into a grimace, not the easygoing face when he boarded the train with us.

"Benefactor?" I ask. "I thought we were going to the lab."

His face makes a twitch. "We'll get there eventually, but for now we've taken a slight detour."

It's the instant shift of expression, then back to his happy-go-lucky face that causes my next move.

I leap across the stairs, land and retrace the freshly paved driveway back toward the steel gate.

Serenity yells for me.

Cowboy demands that I stop, then a bullet zings by my head; it's too close to be a warning shot. A second bullet tears a hole in a small cedar next to me. I duck into the thick forest.

I'm inside the dense woods. I plow my way through fifty or sixty feet to the ten-foot-high brick wall. I grab a renegade oak leaning against the brick and climb it to the top of the wall. Behind me, I hear a car race along the driveway. I leap onto the concrete sidewalk.

I sprint across the street and into a small creek. I'm on my knees in a trickle of muddy water. The limousine takes a casual cruise past me.

I slog my way along the wildness of the creek bed. The tangle gets thicker with vines and broken branches. I keep crashing through the underbrush.

I climb out of the six-foot trench up onto a closely cropped lawn, then sprint along the creek for another hundred yards to the edge of the property and an eight-foot-high cyclone fence with razor wire.

I'm over the mesh fence, faced with another street and another set of fences. I make it through the last property without trouble. I run to the front gate and scale the eight-foot-tall spiked railing, then sprint the fifty yards to the front door of a low-roofed ranch house. I charge the entry and slam my fist on the solid wood front door three times before an elderly gentleman with a black tux opens the door an inch. The thick safety chain stops it.

"May I help you?" he has a slight quaver in his voice, not of fear but old age.

I point toward the street and speak out of breath. "I was kidnapped. I need the police."

"Sorry," he says, and the door is almost latched shut when I leap the three steps to the door and shoulder it with all of my momentum.

The chain snaps. The door flies open. I skitter across the slippery slate floor, fall on one side, and crash into an umbrella stand.

The old man glares with indignation. He pulls out his cell phone and a small black pistol. With the barrel of the gun aimed at my forehead, he dials a number.

I stay on the floor. He says in a calm, matter-of-fact tone, "This is Colonel Williams' house at two-two-four Meadowlark Circle. We have an intruder. Would you please send an officer right away?"

I've been in neighborhoods where the police respond quickly, and I've also been in areas where the police never respond. This neighborhood takes the cake. In less than a minute, a burly knock vibrates the door. The old man, pistol still pointing at me, backs up, and while still focused on me, grabs the door handle with his free hand and opens it. A large officer with a military haircut, gun in hand, steps into the foyer and says, "It's okay, Merian, you can put your gun away. We've got him now."

Behind him a smaller, much meaner-looking officer steps in, his gun not only drawn, but dangerously aimed at my face.

The big cop holsters his gun and pulls his handcuffs from his belt. "On your stomach. "Hands behind your back."

I lay on my face and position my hands together, wondering what's next.

He has me trussed, then rotates me back and helps me into a sitting position. His nervous little buddy still has his pistol leveled at my head, but he looks calmer.

The old man steps back to a stool and sits. The cop removes his note pad. "Can you tell me what happened, Merian?"

I speak, though the cop has his back to me. "I was kidnapped and—"

"Shut the fuck up," the little cop yells and charges, ready to backhand me.

"Frank!" the big cop says, which, thank God, slows the little guy down.

The big cop points at me. "We'll get your statement in a minute."

He takes five minutes writing the old butler's story. When he's finished, the old man leaves the room, and the big cop turns to me. He's so tall, I have to crane my neck to see him, but I start in on my story. I get to the bullets flying over my head part, and his little buddy perk's up.

The big cop interrupts. "You're telling me the senator fired a gun in tour direction?"

"I don't think he fired the gun at me. Maybe one of his employees."

He's writing, but I can tell he's not believing me.

"I've got to deliver the necklace to the Stanford lab. It's critical."

"And this necklace," asks the big cop. "Where is it?"

"In this bag."

The cop rolls his eyes and looks at his partner, who is still holding the gun. "Frank, put that thing away."

The little cop lifts the gun slowly, as if the situation is still dangerous, eventually pointing the business end at the ceiling. He clicks the safety, then holsters it. He's been watching too many cop movies.

The big cop unzips the bag.

His eyes brighten when he sees the partial strand of beads. "Holy shit, you do have a necklace." He pulls the pound or so of gold out of the bag. His eyes are big. "It's a gold necklace too."

He fingers the four-inch disc and hefts its weight. "Man, this thing weighs a ton. Where did you get it?"

"I told you, my dead partner took it off a corpse in Brazil, and we've had nothing but trouble since that day. I've got to get this thing to the lab, because I think it has the original strain of Trillian."

The cop isn't listening, if he ever was. He looks at his buddy. "Would you look at this hunk of gold, Frank?"

Frank's eyes glisten. "We'll take this into evidence."

"Hey, that thing is mine," I say, though I already know my words are not being heard.

The cop folds the thick chain and slips the pendant into his pants pocket. "What would a bum like you be doing with something like. . ." His hands come out of his pocket and he lifts both of them up, palms facing me, showing me nothing is there. "We could take you in for trespassing, breaking and entering, and probably come up with a few other violations that would land you in our friendly jail for the weekend. Judge Jenkins processes criminal cases only on Mondays." He gives me a sheepish grin. "Or we could give you a ride down the hill out of our friendly little settlement and forget this whole incident."

"You don't understand, the pendant's been nothing but bad luck from the first day I set eyes on it."

The big cop's eyes brighten, then his face is gleeful. "What pendant?" He looks at his buddy.

He steps to me, gives me a boost to my feet, and both cops usher me through the big front door.

As we walk toward the car, he says, "What do you want to do, go to the station or to the edge of town?"

If I sit the weekend in the police station, I'll be in Trillian again, and it'll be another eight days before I'm well enough to do a thing. I have to get back to Serenity. "I'll go to the edge of town."

The big cop opens the door, puts his hand on my head, and pushes me gently into the back seat of the car. Once I'm in and situated, he says, "Thought you'd see things our way."

He closes my door, and both cops get in front. The big one calls in to dispatch, then replaces the mike.

In silence, he starts the car. We slowly drive around the circular driveway and out the gate.

The same limousine cruises past and I duck behind the seat until we get to the end of the block. I already know saying anything to these two would be utterly hopeless, so when I rise to look, the limo is gone, and we're leaving the hill behind us.

My two police thieves joke and goof all the way down the mountain. They unlock my handcuffs and let me off on El Camino Real. The big one says, "I'm sure you already know not to return up the hill or we'll be forced to take much harsher action." He looks into my eyes to make sure I'm listening. "That doesn't mean throwing you in jail, if you get my meaning."

I grimace. "That necklace is bad luck."

He leans down and gets into the passenger side of the car. He closes the door and the window rolls down. He pokes his head out. "We'll worry about the luck part. You worry about getting out of town."

The window rolls up, and the car pulls away from the curb. The car gets to the end of the block some fifty yards away, takes a long, slow, sweeping left, and with the force of a five-mile-an-hour roll, runs headlong into a telephone pole. The impact isn't enough to damage the car, but it rolls off the curb, then climbs back onto the sidewalk and re-strikes the pole. I run along the sidewalk until I'm even with the car. Both cops are lying forward, heads dropped in a sleeping angle, one on his chest, the other at a painful angle to one side.

I leap to the car as it nudges against the pole for the fifth or sixth time. I grab the door handle and open it. During the drop back off the cement sidewalk, I reach in and turn off the ignition. The idling engine dies.

The two cops' color is fine, but there's puke on the floor in front of the big one. It's a classic sign of the Trillian sickness, but I've never seen it work so fast.

I rifle the big cop's pockets, find the necklace, and close the door behind me. I walk fast down the street to distance myself from the mess, then a brilliant thought comes to me. I return to the car. I slide the driver over —thank God it's the little one— and get into the car. I start the engine, pull the car away from the pole and along a side street to an alley. I stop the car and drag the sleeping little cop out, then work up a sweat getting him into the back seat, where, after removing his shirt, I drop him face first onto the floor. I don his shirt and button it. Although it's a little tight, I get into the driver's seat, prop the big guy's head up, then wedge him against the door. I drop the shift into reverse and back out of the alley. I have to get to the Palo Alto lab first. I'll figure out a way to get Serenity later.

I drive five miles along El Camino Real and into the wooded and huge lawn of the Stanford campus.

Although few people are present on the sidewalks and streets, I drive up behind a young woman with long black hair. I pull to the opposite side of the road and roll my window down. "You know the way to the lab?"

She points in the opposite direction. "You have to get back onto the loop that goes around the campus. The lab is about halfway along the road, you can't miss it."

I thank her, make a U-turn, and follow her directions out to the loop.

I find the building and park the cruiser in the back of a dirt lot. Before I get out, I drop the big cop onto the front seat so he's lying comfortably. Once out, I lock the door and put the keys in my pocket.

I open the front door of the lab and smell a faint odor of ozone mixed with alcohol, or maybe some cleaning mixture to mop the floors.

I walk the long hall with my muddy pants and cop shirt. I probably look a sight, but I don't care. My job is to get the virus to the lab. Once that job is finished, all I want to do is get Serenity and go home.

Halfway along the hall I open a random door; The

lights are off. The second door nets a small Asian man typing on a computer. He glances in my direction when I step in, but quickly continues his work.

"I'm looking for the lab that's working on the Trillian virus."

Without missing a letter in his typing or looking up, he tilts his head slightly to the left. "Three doors down on the left."

Three rooms farther on, I open the door. The room is filled with more people than I've seen in one place since Trillian started.

I walk in and over to the solid layer of inch-thick Plexiglas. I have to rap on the clear plastic several times to get someone's attention. A young woman with dark brown hair glances up from her table then back to her work. I rap on the plastic again.

She huffs, pushes her office chair back, stands tall, marches up to the Plexiglas, puts one hand on her hip, gives me a stern look, and flips a switch. "Yes," she says with contempt, "is there something I can do for you?"

"I want to speak to someone about Trillian."

She shakes her head. "And just what do you have to say?"

"Can I speak to your manager or supervisor?"

She huffs, and stomps to the far end of the basketball court-sized room, mostly filled with computers and people using them. I watch her knock on a door on the far end of the hall, and a moment later she returns followed by a gray-haired gentleman in a tweed business suit and clashing blue tie. He's in his late fifties. He has a perfect set of teeth when he gives me a cautious smile. He flips the intercom switch. "Can I help you?"

I'm not sure how to approach the subject. Should I blurt my business out or be more discreet? Since all I have is the squawky speaker, I leap into a shortened version of my story. I get to the end and pull the necklace out of my pocket. I put it in front of him on the narrow counter.

His eyes get noticeably larger. "Where did you get this?"

"I just told you, in Brazil two years ago. I think it has the original virus."

"Drop it into the receiving tray."

I look at him cautiously. I've seen this look before. The cops had the glazed eyes. Cowboy also looked that way. Sam certainly had the gold fever when he found the pendant. He hasn't got the interest of a scientist wanting to find the cure for Trillian. It's greed. He sees only the gold.

"First, I want to talk to the head honcho. Until then, the necklace is not leaving my possession."

"Look here, young man."

I yell, "Now, you look here. I came all the way from Sacramento to deliver this thing into the right hands. You get me the big boss right now, or I'm out of here."

A heavy frown darkens his ruddy face. His wrinkled forehead bunches. "Don't go anywhere, son. I'll get Dr. Cusherman. He's head of the department."

"Fine," I say, slip the pendant into my pocket, and take a seat on one of the three chairs against the wall.

During the three-minute wait, a young woman keeps glancing in my direction, then back at her computer.

The gray-haired man in his tweed suit and ridiculous tie comes back across the room. He's escorting an older man with a golf shirt and a tan like he's just spent a month on a beach in Mexico. His belly protrudes far beyond the tight belt that holds his gray slacks and pushes hard against the stretched shirt.

He stops at the thick sheet of plastic and flips the switch. "I'm Dr. Cusherman. Brad here says you have something you want to show me."

I stand and pull the necklace from my pocket. I've already explained its origin to Blue Tie, so I'm not about to tell the story a second time.

The golf enthusiast's face blanches. "Where did you get that?"

"As I told him," I point at the neon blue tie, "I got it in Brazil a few years ago with my buddy. I'm almost sure this has the virus you're looking for."

He nods toward the wall to my right and repeats Blue Tie's request.

I say. "No! This necklace is not leaving my possession until I'm sure it's in the right hands, and certainly not until I have a signed receipt."

The old man says, "that's fair. How about laying it out on the counter in front of us here so we can have a closer look?"

He lets the switch go and says a staccato statement to Blue Tie, who runs across the room toward the offices in the back of the room.

I lay the necklace down and position each bead on the chain so the front is facing up. Dr. Cusherman leans down with his nose to the plastic and studies the disk.

In a moment, Blue Tie is back with a sheet of paper. They point out features on the necklace, then confer about what is on the paper.

Cusherman looks up. "This is the original necklace."

I roll my eyes. "What the fuck do you think I'm doing here? Jesus, for a bunch of Ph.D.'s, you guys are a bit dense."

He and Blue Tie get dark looks on their face. Finally Cusherman says, "We have to be sure."

"Sure? What do you mean sure? You mean you've had other people come in with huge gold necklaces with a wild story about the Amazon?"

"Well, no, but. . ." His words fade. A moment of silence passes before he says, "Can we study it closer?"

"That's why I'm here."

The doctor reaches under the counter and I hear a buzzing at the left of the waiting room. I look in the direction of the sound and see the heavy steel door ajar.

"Please come in, Mr. . ."

"Oakley," I say, snatching the necklace and walking to the door.

The doctor and Blue Tie meet me at the door and usher me, in a roundabout manner, to a back office. The doctor opens the door and follows me in. I sit on a mustard-colored leather chair.

Cusherman asks, "Where are you from? We've had a battalion of government agents looking for you. We tracked the necklace to some obscure city in Colombia, but then it vanished."

I roll my eyes. "That was two years ago. No one could figure out where I lived?"

He smiles and lights a cigarette, then offers me one.

I shake my head. "I have a place in Nevada City that used to belong to my uncle before he died. I guess I never got the paperwork transferred. I figured living out away from the chaos would be better for my health."

"Well," the doctor says after taking a drag from his cigarette. "You're here now, and that's all that counts."

The office door opens and Blue Tie steps in with a clear plastic box, then sets it on the desk between Cusherman and me.

The doctor looks at the box. "Would you be so kind as to put the necklace in the box for us?"

I look at him. "Sure, but I want a signed receipt first, with photos. This exchange has to be well documented, because when you're finished, I want the pendant back."

"Mr. Oakley, the fact is, you possess a stolen artifact from Brazil. It must be returned to its rightful owner after we're finished studying it."

I leap to my feet and go for the door. I'm at the door before anyone can move, but I look back once I've opened it. "That's fine, then I'll just take the pendant back to the people who kidnapped me earlier today."

"Okay, Mr. Oakley, okay, we'll give you a receipt and return it to you."

I still stand at the door ready to bolt, but I relax a little. "That's why I'm staying until you get a sample, then I'm taking it with me."

"Mr. Oakley, will you come back in here and sit down? We're the right people who should have this necklace to study, and you shouldn't worry about its fate. It's our problem from today on."

I slam the door behind me, and bolt for the front door. I'm halfway across the hall as Cusherman pleads, "Mr. Oakley? Please, Mr. Oakley, let's work something out."

As I reach the front door, a big security guard steps into the outer waiting room and looks at me through the Plexiglas. I spin and bolt back toward the doctor and his buddy. "You bastard," I say when I reach him. "I came here in good faith, and you turn on me like this." I point at the front door and the guard.

"We can't let you leave with the necklace, Mr. Oakley. We just can't let you leave. It's too important to national security."

"What the fuck are you talking about? You're just as greedy as the people in the mansion."

The cop opens the big steel door behind me, and I glance back. He slowly weaves his way through the computer desks and researchers who are all staring at me.

"The people in the mansion?" Cusherman asks.

"Serenity and I were kidnapped earlier by a limo, and they took us to La Honda to some brick mansion."

"Serenity? Mr. Oakley, you'd better come back into my office and tell me the whole story."

The cop has stopped twenty feet from me. "Do I have a choice?"

Cusherman gets a sad look on his wrinkled face. "I was hoping we didn't have to get to this, but I'm afraid you don't have much of a choice."

I can try to take the cop, but he's much too big. I shrug and follow the old man into his office.

When we're all seated with the cop standing at the door, Cusherman says, "How about putting the necklace in the box, Mr. Oakley?"

I sigh, pull the chain from my pocket, and place it in the open box.

Blue Tie snaps the lid shut and closes the latch. He picks the box up, but Cusherman waves him away. "Not now, Brad. We'll start later."

Blue Tie scowls, drops the box hard on the table, and

slams the door on his way out of the room.

Cusherman licks his lips, pulls the box toward him, and looks in one of the heavy plastic panels. "You don't know how long we've been looking for this."

"I'd say a few years."

"Ever since Trillian started." The doctor shakes the box to reposition a portion of the necklace. He stares in the box, studying each embossed inscription of the medallion.

"Will I get it back when you're finished?"

The old man looks up from his gaze at the necklace. "Out of the question."

He shifts his wrinkled face to look at the big security guard. "Ted, will you please escort our Mr. Oakley to the far outer limits of the campus?"

"Yes, Dr. Cusherman, sir." The man speaks with an exceptionally high voice which completely belies his size. He looks at me. "Are you ready?"

I glare at Cusherman. "Just be aware that the necklace has been nothing but bad luck for everyone who tries to possess it."

The old man gives me a greedy little snicker. "We'll just have to worry about that from now on, now won't we, Mr. Oakley?"

"Are you ready, sir?" the cop asks.

"No, I'm not ready. He just stole my necklace."

He looks at the doctor. "Sorry, Dr. Cusherman."

Without returning his attention to me, he slugs me in the stomach. I'm caught completely off guard. Although I'm still aware, I'm unable to do anything except be led, hobbling around the desks and computers with all of the staring researchers to the front door, then out to the cool afternoon air.

The cop is almost friendly. "Where is your car, sir?"

I don't want to admit that I stole a La Honda police cruiser. With effort and what little breath I've regained, I squeeze out a short sentence. "I took the bus."

"I'll give you a ride to the bus stop." He puts me in the back seat of his car and drives me to the edge of the campus.

By the time we get parked, I can talk. "Can you give me a ride to the train station?"

"Sure. I hope we have no hard feelings. I'm just doing my job. By the way, if you are the same Jason Oakley who wrote all those books, I'm a real fan. Your stories are great, especially Baker's Corner."

As he drives across the intersection, I look at him, "You didn't have to hit me so hard."

"Come on, Mr. Oakley, tell me you would have left the lab without putting up a fuss."

"Okay, I'll give you that."

"I hit you in the place of least damage. I could have pulled out my stick and whacked you but knowing who you are, I pulled my punch."

"I guess I'm grateful you're a fan."

When he reaches the station he gets out and opens my door. I get out and catch him hard in the soft spot just below his rib cage. It's the place where he hit me. He goes to his knees. I pull his personal voice unit from his shoulder so he can't call in.

"Okay, now we're even. I'm going to need to borrow your car for a while, though."

He lies writhing on the sidewalk, trying to catch his breath. I jump into his car and close the door. Just before I pull away, I roll the window down. "I hit you in the place of least damage."

I'm on El Camino Real in a minute. I backtrack my way south, then climb into the hills above Palo Alto. My only chance to get away with stealing two cop cars in one day is to move fast. The cop I left behind has probably found a phone, and I may be on the most wanted list already.

I wind my way higher into the hills until I come to a familiar street. The brick wall with its ornate steel gate is in front of me. They already know who I am and the element of surprise is gone. I have one chance to find Serenity and getting the hell out of here.

Chapter 10

Escape

I spot a loose brick hidden in the undergrowth. I pull the car over, and pick the brick up. I return to the car, backtrack along the street, then park looking directly at the tall gate. I pull off my belt and use it to tie the steering wheel to the emergency brake. I slam the brick against the accelerator pedal and the engine screams. I drop the lever into drive. The car lays a long strip of rubber and rockets for the gate. The speedometer reaches thirty. I apply the brake to keep from going too fast.

The gate is big and made of steel, but it's ornamental, not a barrier. The car approaches the gate. I open the door and roll onto the pavement. The car heads for the gate. I sit up, then stand. The car slams into the gate, shearing it from its hinges, then races up the long arched driveway. I step through the gate and slip into the forested part of the property. The car roars ever closer to the big house. I watch through the trees while the car digs long divots in the manicured lawn, then slams into a fifteen-foot-tall fountain, scattering pieces for fifty yards. The car sits with its nose pushing hard against the stone base and digs deep holes in the soft soil.

Three big goons run out of the house, guns drawn, fanning out. Cowboy cautiously steps to the driver's door, gun pointed at the window, then opens the door and turns the ignition off. When the car dies, I'm ten feet from the far side of the building. The comparative silence forces me to dive for a line of rose bushes and slip behind a small hedge bordering a walkway.

I go to the first window and pull my way up to the ledge to look in. It's a large ballroom with a cut crystal chandelier centerpiece. Serenity is sitting alone on a comfortable-looking settee. Five or six men are yelling around front.

No one is in the room with Serenity, so I tap on the glass. She looks in my direction, then leaps to her feet and runs to the window.

She unlatches the lock and pushes the window up. "Jason, how did. . ."

I put my forefinger to my lips and whisper, "We don't have much time."

She looks back toward the great hall with its carved statues, its polished dance floor and plush furniture, then pulls the window open farther. She climbs onto the ledge, slides the window back in place and leaps to the ground. I grab her hand and we retrace my steps across the open lawn into the narrow band of forest to the brick wall. A minute later, we slip unnoticed around the wall and through the twisted gate. I sprint across the street and run along the sidewalk as fast as I can drag her.

We run five minutes before she says, "I need to catch my breath."

"Let's get to the next corner, Serenity, then we'll take a break."

When we reach the corner, I pull her around the bend and search the street for some kind of protection. Three estates along the street sport large hedges instead of the normal rock or brick walls. Out of breath myself, I pull her behind a hedge and lean against a huge cypress tree. I put my hands on my knees and take deep breaths for a minute until my heart calms. When I look up, Serenity is lying on the lawn beside the tree. Our eyes meet. She laughs, not loud, but a gleeful snickering. I join her. When she calms, she says, "I thought you left me."

"I delivered the necklace, but I'm not sure it's going to help. Everyone who sees that damn thing gets greedy. First the cops, then the bastards in the lab stole it from me."

Serenity rises onto one elbow, still breathing hard. "Maybe that's the biggest curse."

"What's that?"

"Everyone gets greedy."

"You might have a point."

The long black limousine cruises by. I see it through the shrubbery, but there is no way they can see us. I duck behind the tree anyhow.

"What is it?" Serenity whispers.

My hand pushes down in the open air. "Get down."

She drops to her back and waits. "Is it them?"

I nod and watch them work their way down the hill.

"Lucky for us we're in a maze of streets and roads that honeycomb the neighborhood. They could look for days and still not cover all the little courts and alleys."

"What are we going to do now, Jason?"

I lift her to her feet. "First, we're getting off this hill, then I'd say it's time to eat, I'm starving."

She takes my hands. "The Senator fed me while you were gone. Where did you go, anyhow?"

I turn and start moving again. "I'll fill you in while we walk, but we keep a close eye out for the limo."

"Which way?" she asks.

I point at the bay ten miles to the east and a thousand feet below us.

We turn the first corner and I tell my story. She stops me often to ask questions about certain parts I've left out. By the time I get to taking the campus security car, we've passed through the exclusive neighborhoods into the plain old million-dollar tract houses. Hell, it's Palo Alto, for God's sake; even the little shacks are worth a million.

By late afternoon, we finally reach the train station. The limousine waits in the parking lot.

"I guess we take a city bus," I say while we step from behind a hedge then return to the main road. We walk two blocks to a bus stop and wait inside an abandoned paint store.

Twenty minutes later, a bus comes into view. Serenity rushes to the stop and puts her hand out.

When the bus pulls over with its air brakes hissing and the driver opens the door, we step in. I drop a pocketful of coins into the meter for both of us. "We're trying to get to the B.A.R.T. train station. Can you let us know when we are at the right stop?"

The driver, a jovial man in his forties, scratches a steel wool pad of carrot-colored hair and smiles. "Sure, buddy, it'll be in San Mateo, about ten miles."

"Thanks," I say, and we walk back on an empty bus. One person rides with us, and he's in a sleepy nod.

We sit together on the worn seat. Some teenager's initials are carved deeply into the hard plastic seat in front of us. I look out the window, but keys and knives have scratched the glass with every symbol of the tagger known to man. The bus is a mess, but no one is left to mind. It's obvious the damage was done years ago.

The bus gives us a start-and-stop jerky motion when it rolls on uneven pavement. It isn't a comfortable ride, but we do get away from the clutches of those greedy madmen, and I include the scientists in that mix. What they don't know is how much trouble that one little necklace will cause. Isn't the medallion the reason Sam bought the farm as I made my way back to the States? Wouldn't I have had a lot of explaining to do to his mother, if she'd only been around? Hadn't we been riding with that guy for twenty hours in the most grueling flight I'd ever taken?

The weather looked sour.

I nodded toward a gap in the huge clouds. "We flying over them?"

The pilot laughed. "No can do. We have to stay low. The military is waiting for us to show on their screen."

"What about these mountains all around us?"

He laughed again. "Oh, hell, those aren't mountains. They're just little mounds."

He pointed at the screen. "See that?"

I nodded.

"We've got our own little radar, and even in dense fog we can see everything for twenty miles."

I began to mistrust his radar when, out of the fog, a hill loomed to the right. He banked hard and missed the trees by ten feet.

I wanted him to land and let us out, but we were flying through dense jungle. Once in awhile I saw the river.

The maniac motioned over his shoulder to a plastic chest bolted behind the seat. "One of you get me a beer out of the ice chest."

I looked at Sam and shook my head, but he leaned back and pulled a beer from the case, popped the pull-tab, and handed it forward.

After he took his first sip, maybe half of the can, the pilot asked, "How come you two were in the airport?"

"Vacation," Sam yelled over the engine noise.

"People don't vacation in that part of the Amazon."

I yelled, "We got lost in the jungle, and an old native brought us out."

"Is that where you got the tattoos?" He pointed at my forehead, then banked the plane into another steep turn. He missed the top of a tree by mere feet, leaped over the ridge and down into another mist-filled valley.

"I don't know. I woke up one morning and the tattoo was there."

He looked at Sam's forehead. "You know what the symbol means?"

I shake my head.

He returned to piloting the plane and yelled over his shoulder. "The natives have an old legend in these parts about a pair of white men who will wreak havoc on the world and decimate the population of modern civilization. The local natives believe the world will leave them alone after these two idiots show up."

He looked at my forehead. "The sign means you two are the ones." He gave a bellowing laugh. "Can you imagine, you're the grim reapers of modern times? You guys'll send us back into the stone age."

I looked at Sam and he at me as the pilot dropped the plane into a steep glide toward earth. "Hang on, we've got a wild ride coming up."

Lucky my seat belt was tight because he dropped the plane to within a few feet of the surface of a lazy brown river and leveled out with the bottom of the plane almost skimming the water. His eyes darted to the mirror, then back to the business of flying. "We gotta follow this for awhile, then it's smooth sailing out to the gulf."

"The gulf?" I yelled over the screaming engines.

"Gulf of Mexico."

Sam Yelled, "my God, are we that far north?"

"It's still five or six hours."

The next second the plane banked around a sharp bend and almost ran into a huge mud slide. Massive trees and brush lie across the flatness of the water. "Holy shit," he yelled and pulled the plane up, chopping masses of leaves with the propellers. At the last possible second, when I was sure we were free, something on the plane snagged a limb and we spun out of control, heading for the mound of mud at a hundred fifty miles an hour.

"Jason," I hear from far, far away. "Jason." I realize I'm being shaken awake. I open my eyes as Serenity nudges my shoulder. "Jason, our stop is coming."

"I was telling you my story."

"You fell asleep. I didn't have the heart to wake you."

We stand as the bus halts next to the B.A.R.T. station.

Still in a daze, I walk to the front of the bus and step down through the folding doors to the pavement. I look around for the limo. It's not here.

When Serenity is out of the bus, the driver closes the door and pulls away. I take her hand. "Let's go in."

We walk into the station and she squeezes my hand. "It's a first, you know."

The automatic doors open, and we walk into the air-conditioned building. I look at her. "What's a first?"

She blushes and gets a dopey girlish look on her face. "I've taken your hand a few times, but this is the first time you took mine."

Women get a charge out of the weirdest things. It's a moment for her and there's no use in ruining it, so I smile, and we step up to the ticket machine. I pull out a five, feed it into the machine, and a ticket appears low on my left. I slip in a second five and Serenity's ticket spits out with a little beep.

We feed the tickets, walk through the gate, and climb a flight of stairs to the loading platform.

"What are we doing now?" Serenity asks.

"Let's go home."

"What about your car?"

We sit on a long concrete slab and I look along the tracks. "The car is probably a stripped hulk by now."

"It was a nice car."

The blinking digital sign tells us the next train will arrive in five minutes.

"It was just a car, nothing to get excited about. I'll turn it in to my insurance as stolen."

"Technically, your car is stolen, one piece at a time."

I rub my face, then massage the area around my eyes. It always helps me wake up. When I'm finished, I look at

Serenity. “You’re asking these questions for some reason. What do you have in mind?”

She pulls her purse into her lap and leans on it to get to eye level with me. “I’m thinking we still have three days left before you go into Trillian again. Now that your mission is complete, why don’t we spend a little time in the city? Maybe we could pick up some baby clothes or something.”

“Baby clothes? Isn’t it a little soon for baby clothes?”

She’s silent for a brief moment. “If I’m pregnant, then compared to San Francisco, Nevada City has little to offer maternity wise, so it’s probably a good idea.”

Looking for baby stuff is not exactly what I have in mind, but I see the determined look in her face. “Sure, let’s take BART to the city, get a room for the night, go on to Concord in the morning, and pick up a used car to get home. I know a place in Walnut Creek.”

Her face brightens. “I have a friend we can stay with tonight, if she is still here. We’ll call when we get into San Francisco.”

The train starts and stops in a slow progression on its way to the downtown area. In forty-five minutes, we come over the rise just beyond Brisbane and I see the sparkling brightness of San Francisco. The way the buildings look, I can easily pretend that the people are still there, the traffic is still a problem and the shops and restaurants are still open. When we get down onto the streets the reality of the human condition will slam me back into the present.

“The city looks so beautiful,” she says.

The train drops us into the station. We walk outside then up to the sidewalk. Few people are on the streets. Where a hundred cabs used to pass this corner every ten minutes, now we have to wait a half-hour before we see one. I step out halfway into the empty street and wave. Although the light is red against him, he cuts across the intersection, swings into the non-existent traffic, and parks next to our curb. I open the back door, and Serenity gets in. I follow and close the door.

"Where you going?" The little man looks at us with a two-day growth of a dark beard on his olive-skinned face. He looks Greek or Italian.

Serenity says, "Nordstrom's, if it's still open."

"It's about the only one." He makes a U-turn in the middle of the street and races through five red lights without even slowing to look for opposing traffic.

"How come you're still in business?" I ask. "Didn't Trillian affect you?"

He looks in his mirror. "Me and my two cousins trade shifts. I've got twenty-two hours before I go into the first phase, then Michael takes over. Me and David are single. Michael's wife takes care of us all."

Serenity sniggers. "That's a lot of work."

"I guess so, but we're a family, and it's what families do, isn't it?"

Serenity gives me a womanly smile.

The cabbie drops us at the front door of Nordstrom's. I give him a fifty, tell him to wait, and we step into what used to be a shopper's paradise.

What is left of the stock, though expertly displayed, leaves large gaps in clothes racks and wide stretches of empty floor space. The empty parts of the floor shows where merchandise used to be.

On the third floor, the maternity section is in the back, and Serenity piles baby clothes high on the counter before she's finished. I'm wondering how we can carry all of this crap to the B.A.R.T. station.

When she's finished and we're ready to pay, I take her aside away from the saleswoman. "Once we pay the bill, we must get back in the cab and disappear quickly."

"Oh Jason, what on earth for?"

"They'll track us by the use of my credit card. Because I pulled all of that stuff back in Palo Alto, I think the cops might be on the lookout for me. We use this card, and we have to get out of this area pronto, right?"

She gives me a worried look.

The saleswoman rings up our purchases and asks for our card. I say, "Can you bag everything first? Then we'll finalize the sale."

"Sure." She pulls out four big bags, loading each full, and half fills a fifth.

When she's finished, I ask, "Can we get someone to help us carry these down to the cab?"

She gives me a suspicious glare and calls for help.

A young man dressed in a Polo shirt that looks two sizes too small steps up to the counter.

"Mel, can you carry the bags downstairs to the front door?"

Without saying a word, he hefts three bags in one hand and two on the other and starts for the escalator. When he steps on the stairs and disappears, I hand the saleswoman the card.

"That'll be five hundred thirty-six dollars and fifteen cents." She hits the last key on the cash register and slides the card through the scanner.

I hear a beep that's not familiar. It's not the friendly little chirp, but a warning honk. She slides the card again, then looks at the screen, and her impassive, makeup-encrusted face frowns. She looks at the card, then at me.

"I'm sorry, Mr. Oakley, your card didn't go through and the bank has asked me to cut it up."

"Shit," I say as I grab Serenity's hand. I pull her away from the counter. We race for the escalator. I coax her down the three flights of moving stairs to the ground floor.

The hunk is standing at the front door, bags in hand. I pull Serenity past him and out to the waiting cab. I open the door and give her a push in. I jump in. I close the door and yell, "Get us out of here, quick."

The cabbie drops the shifter into drive and leaves a little rubber when he pulls away from the curb.

"Make a right at the next block."

The cab runs the red light to make the turn, and I see two cop cars race past us in a dash for the storefront.

"Take us to Market."

Serenity cuts in. "I thought we were going to Susan's house."

"It's too dangerous." I point at the cabbie, then put my index finger to my lips in a shush gesture.

He parks at the curb. When we get out, I tell him to keep the change. It's probably the best tip he's gotten in weeks. I grab Serenity's hand and drag her into McDonald's.

"I don't eat at these places," she says.

I'm staring out the dirty window, watching the cab disappear. When it's gone, I walk her back out to the street and stand peeking around the wall of the building until the cab makes a turn at the next corner.

"Come on," I say, "we've got to get to B.A.R.T." I grip her hand and pull her along, cross the empty street, and step onto the escalator going down into the bowels of Market Street. When we reach the bottom, I buy two tickets and push through the ticket shoot. We go down another long escalator to the Concord line.

The train is pulling to a stop. Serenity, two other people, and I step onto the one-car train. She and I sit at the far end of the car while the other two sit next to the door.

The train closes its doors and moves off along the singing tracks.

"Okay," Serenity speaks in an irritated voice. "We're on the train. Now, do you mind telling me what we're doing here?"

"I'll tell you, but you must keep your voice down."

She grimaces.

I lean toward her as the train drops into the tunnel. The pitch of the wheels on rail turns our train into a siren, and we both put our fingers in our ears to deaden the squeal. In five minutes, the train emerges from the depths of the bay and climbs high above the roads on a tram.

She whispers. "Okay, tell me what just happened back there."

I look at her. "When the young woman kept my card, the police were on to us. I don't know if you noticed, but two police cars were racing toward Nordstrom's when we pulled around the block in the cab. My guess was to arrest me."

"Arrest you? What on earth for?"

"Earlier today, I stole two cop cars, but my guess is they want me more for other reasons."

"Which reasons would that be?"

"Testing."

"Wouldn't you do anything to end this nightmare?"

"I wouldn't give up my freedom. They don't want to

just draw blood. They want to lock me up and study me. I don't think so."

She huffs and looks away.

"Look, Serenity, this isn't a virus like the scientists think."

She snaps her head. "You're so sure of yourself, aren't you, mister?"

"Trillian has cursed us, and I was the unfortunate sap who brought the thing out of obscurity. I told Sam to leave it alone, but he couldn't. He had to bring the necklace out of the jungle."

She looks out the window.

Chapter 11

Going Home

I feel for the long since faded tattoo. *It was still on my forehead when the plane hit the side of the hill.*

The dye still marked Sam and me when the drunken pilot got skewered through the chest by a tree branch. I rifled his wallet and found two hundred dollars. We untangled ourselves from the wreckage and half swam, half climbed our way upstream beside the slow-moving river.

The pilot was going upriver, so we simply continued, hoping some kind of civilization lay ahead.

For two days we saw no one while we climbed higher and higher up the stream. On the afternoon of the third day, we walked around a bend, and a half-naked young woman with long, black hair knelt at the water's edge washing clothes on the rocks. A three-year-old child was cavorting among the white granite boulders.

When she saw us, she pulled her top up, grabbed her child, and backed into the forest, leaving her clothes lying on the rocks. Where she disappeared, a well-marked trail led into the brush. We followed for a half-mile before signs of humanity showed along the trail. We stepped into the clearing of a small village. Only the dogs milled around looking to us for handouts.

After a thorough search, we came upon an old man who was too weak to leave his bed.

"Hello," I said, but he waved me off with one weak swipe of his gnarled hand.

"We're lost, Grandfather. Do you know the way to civilization?"

His speech was broken and he paused often, but he spoke English. "You must return the curse to the forest. Bury it deep in the ground."

I looked at Sam's frown and knew I'd never talk him into abandoning the pendant. I'd tried too many times.

"You have only one day," the old man said. "You must move fast, or you will fall prey to its powers. If you choose not to bury the curse, then climb to the top of our mountain." He pointed to his left. "You will find your city in the next valley." His hand dropped again to the bed, and he fell asleep.

Sam and I walked outside the hut and looked up through the clearing at an almost vertical assent to a raw stone peak.

Sam looked at me. "What did he mean when he said we have one day?"

I shrug.

We pulled strips of meat from a drying rack, left a badly scripted thank you note and a ten dollar bill. We started through the dense forest without a machete to clear our way. By evening, cut and scratched from the underbrush, we reached the rocky crags of the peaks and looked over another ridge at lights and the reflection of a long ribbon of railroad track leading down a wide river valley.

The next morning, both Sam and I got sick again. We blamed it on the old man. By noon, we couldn't move. We'd puked so many times, I was afraid we were dehydrated, a dangerous thing while deep in the forest. Sick as we were, we pushed down the backside of the mountain and reached the river by dark. Exhausted, we collapsed at the edge of the water and fought mosquitoes the entire night. By dawn, we were very sick. I could hardly raise my arm to wave at the unending stream of boats in the river.

By luck, a boat came close enough that I made an extreme effort to yell and wave it to stop. I remember little else until I found myself between clean sheets in a hospital bed with a matronly blonde standing over me. She had a pinched smile and a hurried manner. "How are you this fine morning, Mr. Oakley?"

"Where am I?"

"In the hospital. We've been concerned about you and your friend for a week. We weren't sure you were going to make it."

"A week?"

"Both of you have been in a coma these last five days. We thought it might be a snakebite, but we couldn't find any marks. This morning you awoke and seemed fine."

"Where is Sam?"

"Over here, buddy."

The nurse pulled back the white curtain dividing us.

I gave him a weak smile. "I guess we made it again."

"Luck of the Irish."

I crossed myself. "Bad luck of the Irish, I'd say."

The nurse rushed out of the room. Sam fished inside his hospital smock. The heavy pendant reflected its golden brilliance. Sam's eyes glistened. "Still got it, good buddy."

I rolled my eyes. "Would you get rid of that fucking pendant, Sam? Hasn't it brought us enough bad luck?"

"That's not true. Look where we are, resting in the lap of luxury. I'd say this is good luck."

"Sure," I said, "after crashing in a plane and having to traipse across half the continent."

He gave me a determined glare. "I'm getting this thing home and that's all there is to it."

The next morning, once I got my insurance to cover our stay and secured emergency funds from my bank, Sam and I walked out of the hospital and went directly to the train station.

When I came back from the ticket agent, I gave Sam the news. "The only trains going down the river this week are logging trains."

Sam, always the optimist, pointed down the track. "Let's hike to the first tight turn and hop a train as it slows."

Most of the day went by before we could jump a train loaded with huge mahogany logs strapped to flat cars. I was relieved. "Maybe this time we'll actually make our way home."

Sam smiled.

By nightfall, the train rumbled into a lumberyard.

We hopped off when it slowed to switch tracks. The city lights lay a few miles downhill with a harbor beyond.

We found our way out of the lumberyard and walked along badly rutted dirt roads to the center of town and rented a room.

The next morning, we attempted to find a ship to the States. Most of them were America bound, but booking passage on freighters was another trick indeed.

By noon, Sam got the idea of working our way back to the States, which was the only possible way to find passage. We presented ourselves to the ship steward and he belly laughed us right out of the office.

We went into a storage room, and Sam stripped another huge gold bead from the strand. He handed the bead to the steward. The man bit the gold, smiled, put it in his pocket and signed us on in engine maintenance.

What a mistake that turned out to be. I never worked so hard in my life, nor had I ever seen such a dangerous and polluted atmosphere.

Although moving south, the ship plugged on, getting ever closer to the west coast of America and our eventual release from bondage. On the fifth day, after we went through the Panama Canal and started on our way up the coast, we got sick again. On the sixth day the entire crew came down with the flu.

The ship dropped anchor in East Costa Rica and lay in a quiet harbor. Next thing I knew, Sam and I awoke dehydrated. As we searched for water and food, we discovered that the entire crew was dead.

After hours of maneuvering a lifeboat over the edge into the water, we were able to paddle into a small fishing village.

Chapter 12

Transportation

After two days of a Jason Oakley kind of adventure come to life, Serenity and I race to the BART station and get on a train headed for Concord. It's at the eastern end of the line in the Sacramento delta. On the single-car train with two other passengers, Serenity asks, "why the rush?"

I look at her. "Like I said, when I used my credit card, they were onto me. We had to get out of town."

After a moment's silence, she asks, "where are we going?"

I continue to look out the window. "Home, I hope."

In twenty minutes, when we come to the Concord station, I stand and slip my hand into hers. She walks with me to the door as the train comes to a stop. We step onto the platform like two high school sweethearts and walk down the defunct escalators. At the bottom, I lead her into the parking lot, and we wind through the lot as I search through windows of cars and trucks. We come to the end of the lot and walk across a wide boulevard void of traffic. In a store parking lot, I continue to look in cars until I find a green sedan. I take a quick glance around, drop to my knees in front of the car, search under the front bumper, and come out with a magnetic key box.

"Jason, what are you doing?"

I open the driver's door. "We need transportation, and I can't use my credit card any longer. This car might get us home."

I unlock the passenger door, and motion her in. I climb behind the steering wheel, insert the key and turn. The battery is dead.

"We'll have to get another car," she says.

"Not exactly." I release the emergency brake. "One of the criteria for finding a car was it had to be parked on a hill so we could roll it to a start. Close your door, and let's get going."

The car reluctantly begins a stiff, slow roll toward the bottom of the lot. Once it picks up a little speed, I pull the floor shift lever into gear with a loud grinding noise. The car bucks, and the engine rotates, but doesn't start. I push the clutch and the car rolls free and gains speed. At the last second before we reach the end of the parking lot, I release the clutch again. The engine spins wildly, but doesn't start. I come to a sliding halt in a parking place at the bottom of the lot. We get out.

"What do we do now?" She asks.

"We find another car at the top of a hill. Maybe the

gas is too old. Let's get some fresh gas first."

At the end of the boulevard, a Shell station is open. They get so little business, only two of the ten pumps are active. I pay cash for a can and a gallon of gas, then we continue our search, looking up toward the hills along streets and in abandoned parking lots. We come to a dusty-windowed video store with three filthy cars in front of the store. I peek in the window of car two, a maroon SUV, then climb under the front bumper and come out with a spare key. "Let's put in some gas and see what we have."

Once I unlock the doors, she settles into the dusty car while I pour the gas into the tank. I open the hood.

"What are you doing now?"

"Getting a little gas into the engine. It'll help get the car started."

We go through the same maneuver as before, rolling, then jerking the engine. The car starts on its first try. A long-forgotten CD fills the passenger compartment with an old blues song. The instant the surround sound music reaches my ears, I am transported back to the times before Trillian, when things seemed simple. All we had to do was get up in the morning and go to work.

I turn off the music.

She grimaces. "I want to hear that."

"Let's get this car in running shape, then we'll have plenty of time to listen to music. Right now, I need to hear the engine."

When the car warms up, I put it into gear. Although the car moves, it does so with a herky-jerky motion.

She gives me a worried face. "What's wrong?"

"We'll get to a station and put in some fresh gas, then

this thing will smooth out."

Although we pick up speed, the car sputters.

I pull into a car wash. "First thing we do is make this car look like we use it, or we'll get stopped the first time a cop sees us."

I pull into a stall. With the engine still running rough, I get out and drop quarters into the cashbox. The car wash looks like it hasn't been used since Trillian began, but the sprayer spits a few times then spurts a steady stream of water. We work for a half-hour, scrubbing with the brush, then spraying, and scrubbing again, to get rid of two years' worth of grime. Finally the car looks presentable.

"Can we vacuum it?" She asks. "It's pretty dusty in here."

I pull up to the vacuums, and the first one we try works fine. Serenity spends a few minutes sucking the layer of dust from every surface.

When the machine shuts off for the second time, she replaces the hose, and we get back into the car. I pull away from the lot. "Okay, we get some gas and we're off."

Continuing with the jerky motion of the car, I drive out onto the empty street and three blocks back to the Shell station. We fill the car up.

I pay, get back into the car and look at her. "I hope we don't have any problems, because I'm down to my last ten dollars."

She digs in her purse. "I have a few dollars. Let's spend my money on something to eat. I'm kind of hungry."

"What would we find to eat?"

She points behind us. "I saw a deli back where we found the car. I don't know if it's open, but we're in the city, and maybe some places still serve."

"Sounds good. Point the place out to me, and let's give it a try."

"Take us back to the video place. The deli's across the street."

A mile later the car is running better. I make a left past the video store. She points ahead and to the right. "Pull into the parking lot."

I drive up the small hill into the lot. The deli sign reads Gerivono's, and someone is inside. I park and keep the car idling. Although I see almost nothing in the store, the old man greets us with a big smile and a strong Italian accent. "Good afternoon, peoples. You wanta me to make you delicious sandwich?"

"Yes, please. I'd like a turkey on rye and a Coke."

His big smile turns down and his old man wrinkled eyes crunch. He shrugs his shoulders. "I'm a sorry, we only have salami and a some French rolls." He smiles. "I have a sliced pickles I have a been saving."

She says, "Salami would be wonderful. Do you have mustard?"

"Yes a ma'am. We get you all fixed up."

"Two sandwiches, then, if you please."

We pay him, take our sandwiches to the car, and drive away. She opens the butcher paper and gives me my first half.

We pull onto the freeway, and the car still sputters. I take my first bite. "This is great."

The car rolls along barely making the speed limit of fifty-five and much less on hills. With so little traffic, whatever speed we travel is not going to affect the rest of the world. We eat our sandwiches. I feel satisfied and safe for the first time since we ran out of gas in the city.

By the time we reach the Martinez Bridge, both of us realize almost at the same time that we spent our last dime at the deli and we have no bridge fare. I point at the glove box. "Look in there. Maybe there's quarters in the bottom."

She pulls out two-year-old receipts, owner's manuals, a stale pack of gum, tissue wipes, and a tube of melted lipstick. In the bottom, she finds two quarters and three pennies.

I slowly climb the hill approaching the bridge. "What about in the console between us?"

She searches the console and finds two dimes and a hair clip. I'm forced to put the car into the lowest gear to make the slow climb onto the bridge.

The car takes forever to reach the top, and I'm finally able to put it in a higher gear. I turn to Serenity. "We can't pay with anything but cash or they'll track us."

She brightens. "How about the ashtray? If this person didn't smoke, the ashtray could be the logical place." She hits a bonanza of quarters and dimes.

We pull into the bridge toll booth and hand the woman a fistful of quarters, then drive on.

Ten miles later, Highway 680 meets I-80 and I'm still amazed at the nonexistent traffic. In the four-mile stretch I see in front and behind us, there are two other cars, one following a mile behind, and one in the opposite lane of traffic. It doesn't bode well for what remains of humanity.

By the time we reach Fairfield, the engine has evened out.

Past Sacramento, in the vague distance, she points at

snow capped peaks. "The Sierras. We're almost home."

"Still sixty miles or so," I say. "Anything can happen. I really want to be home before I go into my next cycle."

When we climb our first hump into the foothills, I feel grateful for getting home in one piece, though I'm still not exactly home yet.

All along the I-80 corridor, once thriving businesses lie in dusty ruin, unoccupied, with faded signs, peeling paint, and broken windows. If there is one thing most distressing in this whole mess, it's the broken windows. If someone could fix the windows I would feel better.

We pass the Harley dealership, and I wonder if I can simply go in and pick out a bike. I've always wanted a fat boy. On a stupid whim, I exit at the Rocklin off ramp.

"Where are we going?" Serenity asks.

"Checking something out. It'll only be a minute."

I swing back onto the frontage road, drive a mile, and pull into the parking lot of the Rocklin Harley dealership. Of course all of the windows are broken. I pull into a parking place.

She grimaces. "Harley Davidson?"

I open the door. "A young man's fantasy. I always wanted one of these."

She gets out with me, and we walk, not through the two locked and intact glass doors, but around the side through the fifteen-foot-tall broken plate glass window.

The inside is strewn with shards of glass, random Harley emblem displays, a few torn T-shirts, but little else.

She shrugs. "What did you expect? These bikes were popular as hell."

I kick a shard of glass as we step toward the back of the store. Helmets and other accessories hang in racks against the wall. One jacket, a black leather with chrome studs and tassels, drapes unhindered on the wall. Above the breast pocket is the Harley symbol. I unleash it from the hanger and blow off the dust.

Serenity shakes her head. "The dust in this place makes me sneeze. I'll wait outside."

I call to her as she finds her way to the broken front window. "I'll only be another minute."

She raises one arm in a gesture of okay and disappears to the parking lot.

I slip the jacket on. It fits perfectly. I step up to a shattered dressing mirror and look through the foot-wide triangle attached to the frame. The jacket looks great.

A full-sized double-wing Harley insignia stretches across my shoulders.

I'm about to follow Serenity out of the store when I spot a small door with a sign above it that reads "Service."

Chapter 13

Grayson

I step through the door into the service center.

Six bikes are on stands all in some stage of repair. I stroll along the walk inspecting each one. I get to bike four and stumble back.

"Did you come to pick up your bike?" A tall, gray pony-tailed guy stands with a small chrome wrench in his greasy hands. He looks like he hasn't eaten in weeks.

"I was just looking."

"Because I couldn't get the parts yet, so it'll take another few days."

"I'm just looking."

"It's hard to find parts these days, but I'll try to have your bike out by the weekend."

I decide to play along. "I'm in no hurry. Take your time and do the job right."

He gives me a relieved smile, but says nothing else. He sits back on his mechanic's stool and continues to fiddle with the bike, though he's simply clinking the wrench on different parts of the bike. It's obvious he's spun a few gears.

I ask, "you ready for lunch?"

He says, "Lunch already? The day goes by so fast."

"Hey, I ordered takeout. Should be here soon. I'll go out front and check."

"Okay." He returns to his work, bending over and clicking his wrench.

I step through the service door and wind my way past rat-infested clothing, over discarded chrome bike parts, past empty display racks, through the broken plate glass window, and out to the car. "There's someone in there, and he's hungry. We got anything left of the sandwiches?"

"I couldn't eat all of mine." She digs in her big purse and pulls out the butcher-wrapped parcel. "Who is this person?"

"I don't know, but maybe he used to work here. The way he looks, I don't think he's left the place in a long time. He's a mess."

"Jesus, Jason, leave the man where he is, and let's get home."

I open the package and half of the sandwich is left. "I'll be back."

I pick my way to the back of the building. His name tag says Jim. "Hey, Jim, lunch is here." He stands. "I was getting kind of hungry, but I'm not Jim. I had to borrow his shirt. Mine kinda wore out."

He takes the sandwich, unwraps it, and wolfs the

entire thing in ten seconds. Mouth still full, he speaks through his chewing with an apologetic tone. "Guess I was hungry."

"I guess you were. How long have you been here?"

He swallows hard, his color returns, and he's more coherent. "I don't know, maybe a couple of days after Billy Black left. The owners left a month ago." He pauses to think. "Could have been longer. I can't remember."

"Billy Black took care of you during Trillian?"

He gives me a blank stare. "Trillian?"

"You know, the flu that's been going around."

"Me or Billy never got the flu. Billy's gone."

"You never got sick?"

"I don't remember much beyond last winter, but I got a cold this spring. Does that count?"

"Billy either?"

"He was lucky; he never even got a cold."

"How long ago did Billy leave?"

He gets a blank stare. His eyes look toward the ceiling like he's trying to find something in his mind. "I don't know for sure. I think it's been a few days, but it could be weeks, I can't tell anymore."

I put a hand out and grab his shoulder. "I know what you mean. I'm having a hard time keeping track of the days too."

I wait through a long silence before I ask, "What's your name?"

"Grayson. It's been awhile since I even said my name."

I put out my right hand to shake. He grasps mine with a limp, milquetoast grip, though his mechanic's calluses and grease-caked fingernails surprise me.

"I'm Jason Oakley."

His face tightens. "I remember. You're the writer."

I feel the embarrassment of being recognized again, then kick into the well-versed mode practiced at book signings, though I've done neither since coming back from the Amazon. "I wrote a couple of books."

His shell-shocked blank look brightens for a second. "You wrote Baker's Corner?"

"I guess that one put me on the map, but I'd published five before that."

"No kidding."

I smile.

"I remember Baker's Corner. It was a good story. I'd like to be a writer."

Muddle-brained a few moments ago, he's instantly normal. He's a regular bike mechanic doing his job and talking about my book. He goes through a few questions I've heard a hundred times about why I did this and what happened to that character, all of the questions I have no answers for, because I have no idea why I wrote the things I did, especially Baker's Corner.

I finally ask, "did you start writing?"

His face drops back into a, I-can't-figure-out-how-to-tie-my-shoelaces look. He lowers his head. "Well, no. I never could figure out how to start."

It's the first time I've heard that response. Usually, I hear, "Someday I'll start, or I started, but I got bogged down in the first ten pages, or I've got it all up here. I'm just waiting to get the time." Grayson hit the nail right on the old head. "I never could figure out how to start." It's the most honest sentence I've heard.

I want to give him some hints, help him in the first few lines, give him a short boost, but it's clear to see that he's dropped out of the moment of clarity and back into his shell-shocked stare.

"How are you doing, Grayson?" I snap my fingers in front of his face, but no one is home.

The sound of crunching glass echoes into the service center. "Jason?" Serenity's voice has a worried quality.

I raise my voice. "Back here, Serenity. I'm through the service door."

The crunching of glass shards gets noisier. Grayson sits back on his mechanic's stool, grabs a wrench, and starts in again, not fixing the bike, but simply touching each bolt or nut in a well-versed repetitive pattern.

Serenity pushes the swinging door open and steps in. "It's getting dark, Jason. It's kind of spooky sitting out there. Could we head for home soon?"

"Sure, Serenity. Give me another minute." I motion her toward me and she steps over. I turn to Grayson, pretending to adjust some hidden nut on the dust-riddled motorcycle. "Grayson, this is Serenity."

His face goes pink with embarrassment.

Serenity breaks the spell. "Hi, Grayson."

He nods, but doesn't speak. He touches the small wrench to each bolt, by now for the fifth revolution.

I place my hand on Serenity's small shoulder, and step her away from Grayson. As the repetitive tinkle of his wrench tradition continues, I bring my face in close to her and whisper. "He never caught Trillian."

Her face crinkles at the edge of her eyes. "So?"

"He's the only one I've met who isn't affected."

"And what do you have in mind?"

"His buddy took off a few days ago. If we leave him here, he's going to starve."

Her face gets a hard glare. "So you want to take him home like some lost puppy?" Her voice has raised a half octave with a razor-edged quality.

"Yes," I say with an air of finality. Maybe this conflict will be our first fight. I straighten and stand my ground, but add a pitch that may soften the blow a little. It's obvious she doesn't like the idea.

"For a few days until I contact the scientist. I'm sure they're going to want to study him."

Her face relaxes. "Will he want to be studied?"

"He's having a hard time focusing. I've seen this look on men who saw action in the Gulf Wars back when I was a kid. It's a kind of shell-shock. If we leave him here, he'll starve."

"We can't take him home with us. What if someone is taking care of him?"

"I guess a man named Billy Black was taking care of him, but Billy left."

"Oh, shit, Jason, we can't. . ."

I take her hand. "I'll contact the authorities in a day or so. I don't know why, but I think taking him with us is important. If I'm the one who brought this sickness down on humanity, then I think I've got to help with the cure."

She puffs, looks at Grayson who is nervously clinking his wrench, then turns back to me with resignation on her face. "It isn't what you said a few days ago when I could hardly get you to turn the necklace in."

"I've had a change of heart."

She takes a deep breath and gives me a dark frown. "Whatever."

She lets her breath out, and steps over to Grayson. "Would you like to come with us?"

He speaks with a distracted voice. "I'm okay here."

"Who will feed you?"

His face relaxes and the little wrench stops tapping.

"Can I take my tools and my motorcycle?"

Serenity looks at me, then over at Grayson. "We've got room for the tools, but we can't take the motorcycle."

"Oh," he says. The wrench begins its tapping again.

Serenity shrugs.

I turn to Grayson. "We'll come back in a few days with a truck and get your motorcycle."

Grayson stands, walks to the big red toolbox, opens a drawer here and there, removes a single tool from each drawer and places them one at a time in the pockets of his filthy coveralls. When he's found every tool he thinks he needs, he says to us, "Okay, I'm ready, but we'll come back for the motorcycle, right?"

"In a few days," I say, "but for the moment, let's take your coveralls off so they don't grease up the car."

He unbuttons the suit, and it's immediately obvious he's wearing nothing underneath as he strips to a pair of yellowed skivvies and filthy socks.

I think fast. "You wait right there, and I'll get you a change of clothes." I rush back into the showroom and rummage the shelves. A shirt and Harley sweats are easy to find. Socks and a pair of Harley boxer shorts take a little more time. In five minutes, I'm back with an armful of clothes and he dresses while Serenity still has her back to us.

The three of us, Grayson with his coveralls in hand, step through the door back into the showroom.

Grayson stops. "Wait, I've got to leave a message for Billy. He might come back."

While I was looking for something to dress Grayson, I spotted paper and a pen. I step to the desk and pull them out. "Write your note, Grayson, then let's get out of here. It's getting dark."

Grayson takes the pen, and in a scrawling backhand, something like I've seen on prescriptions at a doctor's office, he writes a fast note. "Where are we going?"

"Nevada City," Serenity says.

He signs it, folds the paper, and disappears into the service center. I follow and watch while he attaches the note to the clutch lever on the handlebars.

His eyes are bright again. "Okay, I'm ready."

We make our way to the car. He puts his filthy coveralls in the trunk, and I get him in the back seat. We have to open the windows to vent his body odor, but once on the freeway the air moves through enough that riding with him in the car is bearable. The guy is a mess.

The climb into the foothills is eventless. We stop for gas once we get off the freeway in Auburn.

Serenity and I get out of the car. I ask him, "you want anything to drink, Grayson?"

Serenity whispers, "We don't have any money."

I turn to Grayson. "Do you have any money?"

He gets out, opens the trunk, and digs into his coverall pocket, then hands me a crumpled wad of twenties. "Will this be enough?"

I take two twenties and go in to pay for the gas. When I return I have a quart bottle of Coke that I hand through the window.

Serenity comes close while I'm putting the gas in the tank. "He's pretty rank."

I whisper, "Smells like he hasn't taken a shower since Trillian started, but he'll clean up okay."

She smiles.

For a woman, she is more flexible than I'm used to.

I take an air freshener out of my pocket. "Bought this with some of his money."

Before I get back in the car, I look in the window. "Grayson, do you need to go to the bathroom? We've got forty-five minutes before we get to the house."

He looks innocently at me through the open window. "We going to your house?"

"Sure. We'll have something to eat there."

"No bathroom, but I'm hungry."

I climb into the car and start the engine. "Me too. We'll be there soon."

"Good, I'm hungry."

The guy is a few cans short of a six-pack.

We ride in silence for the half hour it takes to get to Grass Valley, then over the hill toward Nevada City, the whole time passing only three cars.

As we get to the Brunswick Basin, the shopping area for the two towns, I ask, "we need anything?"

Serenity says, "nothing that these sorry excuses for stores can provide. I'd love a Ben and Jerry's ice cream or a cup of real coffee."

I smile. "Maybe our buddy will provide some answers to get some things back on track, and you can have that Ben and Jerry's."

"If it were only true."

"Either way, he might be some help around the house once I go into my first phase."

"I wouldn't count on it."

We race past the Brunswick off ramp and climb out of the basin toward Nevada City. It feels good being back in my hometown. I missed the trees.

The freeway ends, and I go toward home. After five miles of curves, I turn onto my dirt driveway.

The final three hundred feet to my house and the peace and quiet of being home is good. I'm exhausted, and I feel the first tinges of Trillian. I wish I could have another day to enjoy my home before I get sick, but it's the way life is these days. I'll be sick in the morning and that's all there is to it.

I turn off the engine. The late afternoon silence drops in on us once we're out of the car. I stand and take in the sweet scent of the pines.

When Grayson gets out, I'm immediately reminded that he needs a shower. "Okay Grayson, you go get in the outdoor shower next to the stairs. There's plenty of shampoo and conditioner."

"I don't need a shower."

I look at him. "Trust me, you need a shower."

He gives me a puppydog look. "I'll take one in the morning."

"No problem, buddy. If you want to spend the night out here with the raccoons and bears, you can wait until morning, but you're not coming in the house until you've showered."

He looks at Serenity for help.

She scrunches up her face in a comical gesture. "Take a shower, Grayson. It'll be easier on all of us. We've got some fresh clothes when you finish."

"Okay," he says with a resigned huff.

Serenity goes up the stairs. "I'll get you a fresh towel some soap, and a washcloth."

Grayson strips the biker clothing and drops it on the deck I built ten years ago. I adjust the temperature of the water. Grayson gets in. I can tell I'm going to have to remind him how to take a shower. "Get the soap, good buddy. Now get some on the washcloth and scrub your whole body down. Lots of soap."

He's a lost cause. I eventually have to turn the water

off and help scrub him down. I squirt shampoo into his hair and scrub the lather in until he gets the message and starts rubbing himself. We have to rinse and soap three times with a lot of scrubbing in between, but he finally comes clean, and after a dollop of hair conditioner, he's squeaky clean.

I toss him a towel. "Come in the house when you're dry, and we'll get you something to wear."

"Okay, Jason."

I walk up the single flight of stairs and step into my house. Serenity is lighting a fire. It'll take a few hours to warm the house, so I turn on the oven and wash three potatoes, the only vegetable available these days. The oven will help warm the house.

I look at my answering machine and its fifty-seven messages. I assume they're all from other Trillian people looking for matches, so I ignore them.

I sit in my recliner and push the head support back until the footrest flips out. "It's good to be home."

Serenity sits in a kitchen chair. "This isn't quite my home yet, so I'm going to have to go in the morning to get some things. I assume you'd rather be sick here than at my house."

I take a moment to think. "Yes, here."

"You and Grayson will be on your own tomorrow while I tie up some loose ends at my house. There isn't enough room for both of you anyhow."

I get up, walk to the door, and open it. "Grayson, are you out there, buddy?"

"Yes, Jason," he says, with a chatter to his voice.

I step out the door and look down the steps. He's shivering, holding the towel.

"Go ahead and dry yourself, Grayson."

"Okay," he says, and dries his goose-bumped skin.

He's got the concentration of a three-year-old.

"Come up the stairs, Grayson, and into the house where it's warmer."

"Okay, Jason." He walks up the stairs and into the house. I close the door behind me and hand him a fresh T-shirt, then a pair of sweats and some socks. After he's dressed, I help him pull a brush through his tangled, straight hair.

Serenity grabs his hand. "Come on over here next to the oven, Grayson. It's warmer." She pulls him into the kitchen and holds his hands over one of the lit burners. It takes a moment for him to stop shivering.

"I'm thirsty," he says. "Can I have my Coca-Cola?"

I walk toward the front door. "I'll get the bottle from the car."

In the morning I awake with the feeling again. I race for the toilet and barely make it before I puke my guts out. I'm lying on the couch two hours later. Serenity gets up and comes downstairs. She looks concerned. "Jason, you okay?"

I'm feeling so sick I can hardly speak without wanting to puke. I'm on my back and wave a hand. My words are short and choppy. "I'm okay. Trillian again."

"Can I get you some tea?"

Knowing that the biggest killer is dehydration, I nod. "A gallon."

"Chamomile will settle your stomach."

"Cold mineral water in the fridge too."

She's halfway to the kitchen. "That too."

She draws some water, turns on the stove, then opens the refrigerator. In a second she's handing me a bottle of

Calistoga water, one of the last few from a twenty-case buyout I'd made two years ago.

The bubbly water settles my stomach, and I allow myself the luxury of sitting up. "I hate being sick."

Serenity sits on the little love seat across from me. "I so lucky I'm pregnant."

When the teakettle whistles, she races to the kitchen. In a moment she's back with a cup of tea and a fistful of saltine crackers. She sets the plate in front of me. "I know you don't feel like it, but these crackers have helped me, and you're going to need something."

The thought of eating gags me, and I almost race to the bathroom, but I'm able to contain my gorge and sip on the chamomile tea. It helps.

She stands. "Maybe I'll check on Grayson. He didn't look like he had enough sense left to know to get out of bed."

I smile and take another sip. I'm secure knowing that when I go into the third stage I'll be well cared for. With all of the dingbats and dipshits I've had in the past, this is a rare feeling.

We'd put Grayson in the cabin some ten yards away from the house. It has its own stove, toilet, and a small living area I'd set up for guests. It has never seen one guest since I took the place over.

Sam had been so fucking stubborn about keeping that pendant, even after so much bad luck had come our way getting out of the jungle. The plane wreck was one in a long string of bad luck scenarios. We were lucky we got out of that with our lives, much less with no major broken limbs. Had there been even a sprained toe we would have never made it. Sam never made it.

The ship load of dead sailors off the coast of Costa Rica was spooky enough, and it took us hours to drag a lifeboat to the edge of the ship, hook a boom to it, and drop it over the edge. When we boarded the thirty-foot steel boat, I pushed off in choppy waters while Sam pulled on the ten-foot long oars in a futile attempt to make our way toward shore. An hour later, we were a few hundred yards away from that doomed ship. Both Sam and I were exhausted. Blisters had formed on my hands. By mid afternoon something shifted, and we raced toward shore, ten yards with each paddle of the oars. I tried to steer toward the only beach, but the currents and our rotten luck would not let us make an easy landing.

The boat hit the first of the rocks and ripped a hole in the hull the size of my fist. We were still out a hundred yards from shore, and the waves were crashing with six-foot crests against jagged rocks. A surfer would know how to deal with the waves, but in a metal boat quickly filling with water, we had little choice. I screamed over the sound of the surf. "Swim for the sandbar." I pointed to the south a half mile away.

Another swell overtook us and swamped the boat. Sam and I swam parallel with the shore.

A minute after we were in the water —and thank God the water was warm— I lost sight of him. I battled my way south trying to stay far enough out to sea that I was not dashed against the rocks.

I must have been in the water for an hour before I saw the sand. I aligned with the center of the small beach, then stopped swimming and allowed myself to drift to shore. The swells turned to cresting waves, and I bodysurfed my way to a steep, pebbly beach. Finally, completely spent, I dragged myself above the water line and dropped face down on the black gravel.

The sun dropped below the horizon before I awoke.

I sat, looked up and down the coast, but didn't see Sam. After all we had been through, he couldn't just disappear, but then that damn pendant was gone, and I no longer had to deal with the horrible luck that followed it. Maybe it was at the bottom of the ocean where it could no longer give anyone any trouble. I hoped Sam wasn't down there too.

I stood and looked for something to eat. I hadn't had a thing since we'd left the ship.

The palms were laden with coconuts, and I combed the beach for fallen ones. Of course there was no way to open them. Where was my Swiss army knife when I needed it?"

After an extended search, I found a long, skinny seashell on the beach. I used the sharp end to pierce the three soft spots at the top of a coconut. I drank the milk of my first coconut since I was a kid. It was delicious. Since the water bottles went down with the lifeboat, the liquid was essential.

I'd slept in direct sun for most of the day, and the coconut milk also soothed my burns.

Higher on shore just inside the line of the jungle, I ran across a rock the size of one of my coconuts, and used it to slam the drained nut open. After ten tries the hull cracked. I used the same shell to dig out the meat and ate three coconuts. Dusk settled on the tropical beach as I laid under a palm, rested my head on a protruding root at the edge of the jungle, and fell into a deep sleep.

In the morning, though the sun was bright, the wind was whistling through the trees. The waves I thought were big yesterday had doubled in size and intensity. A surfer would have loved that beach.

With no idea which way to go, I trudged up the beach heading north because north is home, and every step I took got me that much closer.

The beach was small, so in less than a half-mile, I had climbed over the first of many rocky outcroppings. The crags got more intense, and I was forced to scale large walls of black rock to get to another short run of beach. At the far end of the fifth beach, I saw a speck on the sand. It was either human or a sea lion. Maybe Sam had washed up on the beach.

When I got close enough, Sam lay askew at the high water line. It was not a good sign.

When I got closer, he rose to a sitting position, and waved.

I stepped up to him. "Let's get rid of that fucking pendant."

In his ever-positive attitude, Sam laughed over the sound of the howling wind. "Jason, Jason, what the hell are you thinking? This thing is going to make us rich."

"That thing will be the death of us."

We'd been through that same argument so many times I didn't take my statement another word further.

I wake, get off the couch where I spent the night, and walk to the side door. I feel a bit better, so I'm taking advantage of the minor reprieve by going outside and walking the ten yards to my cabin. Grayson is in the cabin watching the white noise on my little television. Since Trillian, I've yet to find a working station. When I open the door, Grayson sits at rapt attention, staring at the snow. He turns to me with a blank stare.

I give him a smile. "You want some breakfast?"

He nods.

"Come over when you're ready."

I close the door and a sudden flush sneaks up on me before I can make it back to the side deck. I reach the rail and unload a small amount of acidic bile.

I leave a small pile on the ground next to my volunteer daffodils and slide slowly along the rail, onto the deck, ten paces to the back door and through before the next wave hits.

I'm on the couch dry puking into a pot Serenity gave me last night. God, I hate this sickness.

I guess Serenity has heard me because in a minute, wrapped in my robe, she feels my hot head. "You going to be okay, Jason?"

I nod and go into another bout of heaves. Luckily, this part of the sickness lasts only a few days. All I have to do is force enough liquid in me to hold for the next five days. Once I go into the final stage, I won't be able to take in nourishment or water.

Serenity hands me a glass of cold water and I take a drink. A hint of lemon and honey settles my stomach.

I have enough energy to take two more swallows, hand the glass back, then drop onto the couch. I lie prone and unmoving while Serenity cooks some breakfast for Grayson and tries to engage him in conversation. He speaks, but only when spoken to, and even then with one-sentence, choppy replies. I'm coherent enough to hear everything, but not strong enough to speak.

For two more days I get progressively worse, then the next thing I remember the day is dark and Serenity turns on lights. "Hey, Jason, you're back."

She hands me another glass of honey water, and I down it before my head falls back on the pillow.

"Think you can get something solid down?"

My mouth is too dry to speak, so I nod.

In a minute, she's back, carrying a piece of toast with blackberry jelly. I taste last summer's berries first and crunch the seeds between my teeth.

She hand-feeds me the bread until I no longer have strength to chew. I'm force-fed another glass of honey water, and everything goes blank until I awake in pitch black with the fire flickering shadows on the ceiling. I realize I'm home and safe with Serenity taking care of me. The blackness surrounds me again until I hear Grayson come in the back door. I assume it's morning; which morning I don't know, but I'm thirsty.

Serenity hands me a glass of water but I'm too weak to lift my hand. She dribbles the water into my open mouth and I gulp. When the glass is empty, I ask, "How long?" I want to ask how long have I been out and how long before I go into the next stage, the frightening catatonic one. She's anticipates my question. "This is your fifth day. Sometime later today you'll go in. Don't worry, though, both Grayson and I will take good care of you."

She looks up when Grayson's blank face peeks over the back of the couch. She puts one hand on his shoulder. "Right, Grayson?"

"Uh-huh," he says. It's the very last thing I remember before I drop into the long tunnel of confusion.

The next time I awake, it's dark, but I feel better. I float back into a lighter, dreaming sleep, unlike the deep sleep state of stage three, knowing that in the morning I will be back on my feet. God, I'm glad it's over.

In the morning I'm met with two happy faces, a full breakfast of eggs, the last of the toast, jam, and a slice of chicken breast, though it's more than a little tough.

Grayson

Although still shaky on my feet, I feel good enough to walk to the kitchen table and eat.

Grayson sits across from me. I look at him. "You don't get sick?"

"Don't think so."

Serenity sets a glass of water in front of me and puts one hand on my shoulder. "He's been just fine this whole last five days."

I look back at him. "Well, that's something."

Grayson gives me a shy grin. "Does it mean a good thing?"

"I don't know, but it's worth checking." I take my first bite of food in five days. Although my stomach is still queasy, I'm hungry beyond belief. From experience, I have to meter myself from wolfing the entire breakfast because I know I'll puke it up. I methodically chew, fully masticating each morsel so my stomach has time to prepare.

As usual, when coming out of Trillian, I barely finish a third of what's put in front of me, but I'm satisfied and feel stronger by the time I leave the table.

The day is sunny and warm, so I go outside and sit at the round outside table on the side deck. The birds are noisy, and the bugs buzz by, going in all directions on their appointed duties. It's good to be alive again.

Twenty minutes later, Serenity and Grayson come out and sit with me.

"So, Grayson, what do you think about meeting some research people and having them test you?"

"Research?"

"If you're not getting sick, then you have a chance to help the rest of us poor saps who get sick every five days. Maybe there's something in your makeup that knows how to fight this damn virus."

He looks nervous. "I don't know about research."

Serenity puts a hand on Grayson's shoulder. "While you were asleep, Grayson and I talked a lot about this. He remembers spending some time in a lab."

"I didn't like being there, Jason."

"Okay, buddy, I understand."

Serenity sits at the table. "I've been thinking about it, though. Maybe we could find a way to get the researchers some blood without them knowing who you are, like we could have the local hospital draw some blood and send it to the labs."

"Not too bad an idea. We could do the whole thing anonymously."

I look at Serenity. "Did you find a business card in my shirt?"

"I put it on your desk."

"Good, it's the research place at Stanford. They have the pendant; that is, if they're still alive."

Serenity goes into the house and comes back with the card.

It's white with smallish block letters. A phone number and the address of the lab line up under a man's name.

I snap the card between my fingers. "When we go into town, I'll call and set things up. I'm sure the hospital can draw the blood."

"Maybe you better draw the blood so there is no trace of who is where. I have a friend who works nights in the lab."

Grayson says, "I don't want to give my blood."

Serenity puts her hand on his. "Look, Grayson, it's no big deal, but it will mean so much to Jason and me."

"I don't like blood." His voice is shaky.

She squeezes his hand. "I'll be with you."

"You won't leave?"

"Nope."

Very slowly, with lots of feeling, he says, "Okay, draw blood for Serenity."

I look at him. "You'll be doing this for the good of the rest of the world too."

He lifts her hand and rubs it against his cheek. "For Serenity." His eyes are closed, so I take a quick glance at her. She shrugs.

After their special moment, I stand and walk toward the side door. "I'm going to take a shower. Maybe we'll go into town later."

The hot water feels great, and since it's been five days, my body is itchy from not being bathed. I'm lucky to have Serenity to take care of me. I stand under the cascade of water soaping myself with a rough washcloth and can't believe that in such a short time I actually have feelings for her. I've never had feelings for any woman so soon. Hell, it took six months of steady sex with Gloria before I felt a tinge of something for her. Another six months went by before I could say the word "love". Ten years ago, she left for another woman. We had four years, but the last two were pretty rocky.

In retrospect, her leaving was the best thing that ever happened to me, though at the time I was devastated. It changed my whole outlook on life, which shifted my writing style. Baker's Corner came out of the devastation that Gloria left in her wake, and hell, without Baker's Corner, I'd still be some two-bit struggling writer and waiting tables in town.

I let the water slosh in my open mouth, splash onto my face while I say a silent thank you to Gloria as I have done so many times. Even after so long, I still have a soft place in my heart for her. I wonder what she's doing now. I hope she's all right.

When I've rinsed, Serenity hands me a towel. "While you were sick, Grayson attached himself to me."

"I can tell. How are you doing?"

"Well, I'm glad you're awake. Maybe you can take him into town with you and give me a little time alone."

I dry my face and shoulders. "Sure, no problem. Has he been a pain?"

She gives me a soft smile. "No, far from it. He has a sweet nature. He's too needy, and I want a break."

"No problem. We'll get out of here in an hour."

"Thanks, Jason." She leans forward to give me a peck on the cheek. I turn my head and our lips meet for a second. She's startled and pulls back a little too quickly. Her face is pale, then pink. "Jason, I. . . well. . ."

"Don't worry, Serenity. The kiss was a small token of my appreciation for you taking care of me."

She's so flustered that she walks away, leaving me to dry and look at the hot tub. It's been broken for a year. The single little part to fix it is no longer manufactured.

I finish drying, and go upstairs and into the house.

Grayson is helping Serenity in the kitchen. I dress with clothes she put out for me. I like having a woman around again. How long has it been, maybe before Trillian? Sure there were a few short flings and then all of the women caretakers after Trillian, but they never stayed for more time than it took to complete their agreement. They saw me through the third stage, but I was never around. Most left on the day of my appointed awakening.

Those arrangements were hollow and unrewarding. It's been too long since I felt anything for a woman, or she for me. Maybe this isn't that feeling; I can't tell, it's been so long. At the least we're committed to one another for the next nine months and then during lactation. Children reared during this period will not have breast weaning traumas when they get older.

I put on my clothes and step into the kitchen where Grayson hovers over Serenity. "How about you and I go into town today, good buddy?"

He says, "I'll stay here."

"Let's you and I go into town and give Serenity some time to herself."

Grayson looks at her.

She takes his hand. "Go into town, Grayson. I need some downtime."

He looks hurt. "If you say so, Serenity."

For a few seconds I think he's going to sulk all the way into town, but his expression shifts, and the excited Grayson emerges. "Can we get some Coca-Cola?"

"If they have some. Things have been a little shaky in the grocery department lately."

"That's okay with me."

By the time I've fully dressed, combed my hair, and fed our cat, Grayson is chomping at the bit to get going. Almost like a child, he asks a steady stream of questions, first about town, then about the stores in town, then about feeding cats, and in his excitement, he fires questions until I'm about ready to strangle him.

When we get into the car, I plug a CD into the stereo and turn up the sound to drown him out.

The six miles into town gives us three songs from Van the man and an old Beatles tune, "When I'm Sixty-four."

By the time I'm off the empty freeway, I've turned the music off and Grayson has calmed. I ask him a simple question, ready to turn the music on again if he starts running at the mouth. "Where did you live before you were at the Harley shop?"

He takes a long time to answer. "I don't remember much before. Maybe I lived in Roseville, but I'm not sure. I might have been in a hospital."

"How did you end up at the dealership?"

"I used to go to the shop every day; I know that for sure."

"On a Harley?"

"No."

"What do you remember before Trillian?"

He looks out the window. "I remember my mother and my sister. They both died. I had to bury them in the back yard because no one was around to help. His voice chokes. "I remember my dog, but he died a long time ago."

He's still looking out of the window. I turn into a parking place and kill the engine. "What was his name?"

His eyes glaze. Tears are ready to run down his cheek. "I don't remember."

I give him a moment to compose himself, then I open the door and get out of the car. He gets out with me, and we walk together into the barren store.

"Oh, look, Jason, they have Coca-Cola." He runs up to a tier of big, dusty plastic bottles stacked into a pyramid. "Can I get three?"

I grab a shopping cart. "Get five, if you want."

"Really?" He looks at the stack, then at me, then grabs his first one from the center of the carefully stacked pyramid. Twenty or thirty plastic bottles crash to the floor and roll out away from the display in all directions.

I don't even try to reproduce the stack, but simply

pile the bottles next to the display. Grayson chooses the five best ones, though they're all the same.

When he puts them in the shopping cart, I push it to the measly vegetable section. I find limp greens, an endless supply of potatoes, a few wormy apples from last season, and some local mushrooms that look more dangerous than edible.

We come to the end of the depressingly empty section and discover a small display of thin baby asparagus.

I push the cart to the counter. I look around as if I'm readying myself to steal them. The sign above them says "local asparagus, eight dollars a pound." Their price is highway robbery, but I don't care, I stack three big bundles into a plastic bag and place them on the upper tray, where kids sometime sit in the cart.

I find other spring surprises, but the asparagus is the delight of the day. In less than twenty minutes, Grayson and I are walking out of the store and loading the two bags into the back seat of the car.

"Can I have one of the Cokes now?" He's acting child-like again.

"Probably not a good idea, Grayson. They got pretty shook up when the display fell."

He gives me a sly smile. "All except the one I picked: That one."

"How do you know which one it is?"

He shrugs, "I know."

"Hey, who am I to say no? You do what you want, just open it out here, before you get into the car."

He snatches the bottle and cracks the seal. I step back, but the bottle gives a slight hiss and settles down into a few bubbles. He smiles and lifts the bottle to his lips, then takes a long drink. When he's finished, he belches.

"I love Coca-Cola."

"That's obvious. Let's get into the car, we still have the post office to deal with."

He gets in and places the huge bottle between his thighs. He buckles his seat belt, and we drive out of the parking lot, through the lights at the corner, and onto the freeway going back to Nevada City.

I pull off of the empty freeway and go up the hill toward town. Not one car is parked along the streets nor one person walking along the sidewalks. I drop into a momentary depression. I caused it all. How does a person live with this?

By the time I make a right onto Coyote Street and drive the single block to the post office, my cloud of responsibility has dissipated a little.

When I park, Grayson takes another long drink and expels another childish belch. I look at him. "You want to wait here in the car?"

He opens the door. "I'll come in."

Grayson and I walk into the empty post office. I go to my mailbox and pull out the standard handful of bills and a very small envelope addressed to me in a flowing script, I can hardly read.

I look close at the cancellation and read: Newport Richie, Florida.

I open the frayed edge of the envelope. A small card slides out with a hand-painted watercolor of a small fishing boat bellied halfway upon a white sandy beach. The white sand fades off the edge of the card.

In the same careful scripting, I read: "Hope you are still okay. I survived Trillian by luck and found myself here in Florida. Please send me a note if you are still all right. Everyone else is no longer around." On the bottom, of the letter it's signed, "Sylvia."

It's my younger sister. My eyes fill with tears, and I'm forced to wipe them three times before we get to the front door.

I reach to push the door open. A man who has his back to me checking his box spins and blocks the door. He has a black suit and black tie like he's going to church. His face is freshly shaven, though he'll have a five o'clock shadow by noon. "Are you Jason Oakley?" He speaks in a demanding, cop-like tone.

I'm ready to deny, but Grayson pipes up. "Yep, he's Jason, all right. He's my friend."

The man ignores Grayson and continues to block the door. His arm swings from under his jacket, and he has something shiny pointing at me. I don't take the time to figure out what he has. I drop low and give him a body slam. I've had enough of those spooky bastards.

Air belches out of his mouth. I spin away and rotate out the door. I give a last-second glance and see that he's going down. I wave Grayson to follow. He's a little slow on the uptake, but he finally moves. I face a second man with a pistol directed at my right eye.

I put my hands out and drop my mail.

"Cowboy?"

He gives me a cat-eating-the-canary grin. "Hi there, Mr. Oakley. We've been looking for you."

I'm positive he's not going to shoot me by accident so I relax my stance a little. "What do you want?"

He swings the gun away from Grayson to me. "The pendant. Where's the pendant?"

"I gave it to the researchers at Stanford."

"We checked. The people who are left never saw it."

"Who's left?"

"The building burned to the ground. Not many got out alive."

I shake my head. "I don't know why you want the pendant. That thing has brought everyone horrible luck."

"Where is it?"

"Probably melted in the fire, at least I hope."

I'm trying to think of a way to get out of this when Grayson, in a lightning-quick move, drops to one hand and slides toward Cowboy. He kicks both feet out and clips Cowboy behind the knees. The gun goes off with a deafening thunder, but the barrel is pointed toward the sky. Cowboy flips onto his back, bangs his head, and drops the gun. In the half second it takes for all this to happen, Grayson has the pistol and points it expertly at the door. The guy inside, who is almost to his feet, stops before he reaches the door. Grayson motions him to come out. The pudgy man cautiously opens the door. Grayson speaks in a voice I've never heard. "Give me your gun, those cuffs of yours, and the keys."

The guy complies.

Grayson drags Cowboy to the newspaper rack, pulls his arm through the rack and clips the cuffs to his wrist. "Cuff yourself to him."

Grayson steps back, and we watch pudgy bend down and snap the cuffs into place around his right wrist. Grayson checks the cuff tightness then pockets both sets of keys. One at a time he pulls the clip from each gun, opens the slide, ejects the one shell in the chamber, locks the gun in the open position, then slams it to the pavement, bending the slide sideways by a quarter inch. He says, "let's get out of here."

We get into the car like nothing happened and drive away.

We reach the top of the hill. "Grayson, where in hell did you learn how to do that stuff?"

He's lost his no-nonsense manner and is back to his childishness. "I don't know, Jason. I don't remember."

I pull up and stop at the crossing of Highway 49. I don't even know why I stop. I look both ways out of habit and pull across the highway. I shift into second and say, "I knew the person in the cowboy hat. Met him last week in Menlo Park. He works for some senator or something."

Grayson is taking a long pull on his bottle of Coke. He says nothing.

I drive the windy road a mile to the top of the hill, before Grayson says, "I know him too."

"You know him?"

"Him and his cowboy hat."

"Holy shit, Grayson, you do get around."

"I can't remember how I know him. . ." His voice fades.

We drive in silent introspection for a mile. "Someone knows the town I live in and that someone wants me. We have to be extra careful."

By the time we reach the house, Grayson has finished the bottle of Coke and belched a dozen times. I park, and we get out of the car. "Grayson, can you take this grocery bag into the house?"

He takes the bag and leaps the steps two at a time, then opens the door and disappears inside. I follow and put my bag of groceries on the kitchen table.

"Where's Serenity?" Grayson asks.

"I don't know, buddy, I just got home myself. Maybe look up in the garden. Women like gardens on sunny days like today."

He sets the bag on the table and disappears out the side door, leaving me to put the groceries away. A few minutes later he and Serenity come in the house. She gives me a peck on the cheek. "Grayson said you got into a little skirmish."

I put the limp carrots in the vegetable crisper and speak with my back to her. "And you'll never guess who was there."

"You mean you knew him?"

I close the door. "Cowboy."

"From San Francisco?"

"The very one."

She sits at the table. "What would he be doing up here?"

"Looking for me. The guy had a gun."

She grimaces. "Those bastards can't leave us alone?"

I sit across from her. "He thinks I still have the pendant. The research building at Stanford burned to the ground."

"That pendant is incredibly unlucky."

I look at Grayson, who stands behind Serenity. "You remember anything more about Cowboy?"

"Only that he was nice and he liked to kill people. It was a long time ago."

"Whoever it is, they're much too close. I'm glad this car isn't registered to me, they'd be driving down the driveway right this minute."

Serenity fiddles with a pencil. "We have to go into town once in awhile. If these people are around, how are we going to do that?"

"I have six months of storage food. It's spring, and the garden will produce something soon. Maybe we could get my neighbors to pick up some things."

Grayson pulls a chair next to Serenity. “I like Coca-Cola?”

She looks at him. “You like Coke.”

He smiles wide like he’s got all of his marbles and he’s faking it.

“One thing for sure, soon we’ve got to get some blood drawn from you and send it to the research people. The lab in Stanford no longer exists. I think the next closest one is in Phoenix.”

It’s Serenity’s turn to act childlike. Her eyebrows rise. She gets a goofy look on her face. “Let’s take a road trip to Phoenix.”

“Out of the question.”

“We could get out of the house while Cowboy is looking for you. It’s only a matter of time before he figures out where you live.”

“Have you ever driven to Phoenix?”

She shakes her head and hair cascades in a mass of curls.

“It’s a long way and a lot of gas. I don’t even know if gas stations in the desert are still open. I’d hate to get half way and run out.”

I know I’m reaching for reasons why we shouldn’t go, and the gas problem is a shaky one at best, but I don’t feel like wasting my five days of coherence on a long hot push to Phoenix, Arizona.

Serenity nods toward Grayson. “Is there another way to get his blood to Phoenix? Maybe the research labs want some other things from him.”

“They have all kinds of ways to store blood,” I answer, but I realize I’m a little too fast on the uptake. I’m just a little too eager not to go.

“Look,” I say, “the truth is, sitting in some car driving

across the desert is not my idea of fun."

Serenity smiles like she has me cornered. "Maybe we could wait until you're in the catatonic state, and we'll find a motor home so you can be comfortable, then Grayson and I will drive. By the time you wake up, we'll be in Phoenix. We could hang around in the desert for a week until you go back in, then I'll drive home."

"You got the whole thing planned, don't you?"

She gives me a Cheshire cat smile. "What's left of my family lives in Phoenix. I'd love to see them again."

I look at Grayson. "What do you think about this?"

Grayson grins. "I've never been to Phoenix."

"Oh, you're a lot of help." It's my last defensive move in a discussion I know I'll eventually not win. "Whatever happens, we have four-and-a-half remaining days before I get sick again. Let's think about it. For now, I want to sit in my garden, take hikes in the woods, maybe lie on my favorite rocks at the river, and enjoy what's left of my pittance of an existence."

Serenity crinkles her face. "Oh, poor Jason," she says in a mocking tone. "Let's go to the garden."

The garden, with baby squash, immature lettuce, the almost ready radishes, and the corn that just sprouted, gives me a special kind of solace. Although I hate gardening, it's a necessary evil these days. I lie directly on the earth smelling the mustiness of freshly turned soil and pine trees, while I listen to Serenity turning shovels of dirt, preparing another plot for more vegetables to eat later this summer.

"Why do you think they still want me even after I gave the pendant to Stanford?"

Serenity pushes her shovel into the earth. "You did mess up the senator's front yard. Maybe he's still pissed."

Grayson is raking the clods smooth behind Serenity. "Cowboy is bad."

A series of cotton-ball clouds slowly plod their way across what little sky the forest allows. The sun peeks from behind one and instantly the air warms.

"What if I just called and asked why they want me?"

Serenity stops shoveling. Small beads of sweat trickle down the side of her face. She wipes them with her sleeve. "You certainly don't want to call from here. Maybe we go down the hill a bit."

"Good idea. How about in the morning? We'll go to the Five-Mile House. There's a phone next to the store. That way I don't have to drive through town at all."

I put my hands behind my head and feel the earth under me. I study the clouds again in silence while Serenity and Grayson make shovel and rake noises.

Serenity speaks. "When do you write?"

Her words are like a gun going off in my head. I have a response, but no words form in my mouth. I lift upon one elbow and look at her.

She says, "I mean, I've been with you a week or so, and I haven't seen you in front of the computer. Isn't writing what you do for a living?" She's nervous. "I've read all of your published novels and they're great. Why aren't you writing any longer?"

I lie back on the earth and speak to the clouds. "I'm taking a break."

"For how long?"

I look at her. "What's it to you?"

"Just wonder how a writer writes."

I look back at the clouds in silence. "I haven't written a word since Trillian began."

Grayson stops raking. "You're not writing?"

I look at him and huff. "Not you too, Grayson."

He gets embarrassed and returns to his raking.

I sit up on the plot of soil and look at the two of them. "When I used to write I had to get a rhythm. I needed a few weeks of writing every day to get into the groove, then I could write my best stuff.

"Baker's Corner happened in a three-month frenzy of writing four or five hours every day. I wrote the first draft while I lived in the south of France.

"Trillian constantly disrupts my process. I get a rhythm going, then get sick again. I can't even look at a keyboard for ten days. Once I'm out of the sleeping state, I'm so glad to be alive and have so little time before the next cycle begins, I don't want to waste a minute."

Serenity stops and leans on her shovel. "What are you doing this very minute?"

"What do you mean?"

She pushes the shovel into the loamy soil and pulls up another spade full of dirt, but she doesn't answer.

"What do you mean, Serenity?"

"Hell, Jason, you have this gift, and I can't believe you're going to let your talent go to waste because," and the next few words she says with a sarcastic whine, "you can't get fully into the groove."

"That's a hell of a thing to say."

"It's a hell of a thing to waste a talent like yours just because a little flu takes some of your attention."

"I told you, I can't concentrate."

Her shoveling doubles. "Sounds like an excuse."

I get up and take a step toward her, huff and leave the garden, slamming the gate. I walk down the path to the house. Grayson whispers, forgetting that in this silence even a whisper can be heard. "Little bit touchy."

Serenity snickers, which angers me more.

By the time I've reached the house I'm doubly pissed, and I look for something to throw or break to relieve the rage, but I find nothing I can't live without. In a moment, I've calmed enough to sit. For some reason, I sit at my desk in my big executive chair and lean back, looking out the window at the forest.

Why can't I write?

The question rattles around in my head for about ten minutes until something clicks, like a light turning on. It's a small wattage light, but it's on.

Maybe what I need is a different way of writing. I do miss writing, and I remember feeling so much better about myself when I wrote every day. What happened? Why did I stop?

Chapter 14

Contact

The phone rings. I'm sure it's one more desperate person wanting someone to fill in for them before they go into the third stage. For some reason, I pick up the phone. "I'm no longer in the cycle." I long ago dispensed with any formal hello of civility with phone conversations. The phone these days is used only for finding a caregiver. I can't remember the last time I got a social call or even a business call. A call from a telemarketer would be a change of pace.

I get ready to hang the phone up. I have it halfway to the receiver when a coarse, gravely voice speaks. "What are you doing about Cowboy?"

I look at the phone, then slowly return it to my ear.

"What cowboy?"

"The one who's been chasing you all over creation."

"How do you know about him?"

"We know a lot of things. For instance, Cowboy and his buddy are on their way to your house."

I look out the window at the driveway. "How do you know?"

"Don't worry how we know. You have ten minutes. I suggest you get in your car right now and get the hell out of there."

"Who are you?"

"Jason!" The voice is demanding. "Don't worry about that stuff. We can work out the particulars later. If you don't believe me, get yourself, Serenity, and Grayson in your car and drive out to Bloomfield Road. Park your car in a hidden place and wait for Cowboy to drive past in his black Suburban. When he passes, drive into town, and we'll meet you at the fire station at the bottom of Coyote."

"Who are you and what do you want?"

The line is dead for a moment, then the gravely voice says, "Bring your computer and your guitar."

"My guitar?" I scream into the phone. "What the hell for?"

I hear the click of the line and the phone is dead.

How does he know about Cowboy and my guitar? No one knows about my guitar. I play it only at home when I'm alone.

I grab my guitar and put it in the case. I unplug my laptop and slide it into its case, then take both to the car. I start the engine and drive around to the garden at the top of the property. Serenity and Grayson rise from a kneeling position when I park the car. "We've got to go."

"Go where?" Serenity asks.

"Cowboy is on his way."

Grayson pales and grabs Serenity's hand. "We got to go, Serenity. We got to go now. Cowboy is trouble."

She yanks herself away from Grayson's grip and puts one hand on her hip. "Just hold on a minute. How do you know he's coming?"

"I just got a phone call. There's no time, Serenity. We have to go now."

Grayson grabs her hand again, and she reluctantly allows him to pull her out of the garden to the car. When both of them are in the back seat, I slam my door and back the hundred yards along my driveway to the pavement. I don't have time to turn around.

I race to Bloomfield and turn toward town. I speed a few hundred yards and turn onto Douglas, then park behind a huge madrone tree. I get out of the car and step around the tree. The moment I position myself, a black Suburban with two police cars trailing slides past and disappears. I see the white cowboy hat in the driver's seat.

I wait another thirty seconds, then get back in my car and drive toward town.

"Where are we going?" Serenity asks.

"To meet the person who called and warned us."

I'm trying to go slow enough not to draw attention to myself, but the speedometer keeps creeping up to forty-five and fifty in a thirty-five zone. My wheels squeal around a tight turn. Serenity gasps. "You've got to slow down, Jason, or we're never going to get into town."

I let my foot off the gas and coast down to thirty-five.

She leans forward. "What happened back there?"

I tell both of them about the phone call and where

we are supposed to meet. By the time we start down the hill on Coyote Street, I've given them everything I know.

The fire station comes into view, and a junky-looking red pickup sits facing the road. A tall young man with a heavy plaid shirt and Levis stands next to the truck and nods to me. I stop. He pokes his head in the shotgun window. "We're going to Penn Valley, then about five miles out a dirt road. You got enough gas?"

I look at my gauge. "I'm full."

"Okay then, follow me."

"Where are we going?" I ask.

He smiles. "To meet Philip, of course."

"Philip? Who is Philip?"

"The voice on the phone. Everything will be explained when we get there." He walks fast-paced to his truck, gets in and pulls onto the road. We get on the freeway, drive through Nevada City, Grass Valley, then make a right onto the Marysville Freeway.

Ten miles later, we go right toward Lake Wildwood and over the small dam. He makes a left onto a dusty road and drives a few miles until we make a left onto little more than a cow path.

Serenity speaks from the back seat. "Take it easy, Jason, I'm feeling sick."

I point out the window. "I'm trying to keep up with this maniac."

"You've got to slow down or I'm going to puke all over your car."

I open her window and let my foot off the gas, glad to be going slower myself. The truck leaps out ahead, then disappears over the next rise. I hope there are no turns.

"Thanks, Jason," Serenity says.

We drive for another mile or two until we come to

an arch made of coarse stone. On top is an eagle or osprey nest made from large sticks. I approach and a large bird rises into the air over the car, but I can't see more than a glimpse of color. We go under the arch and Grayson points through the windshield. "The bird circles overhead. It's a good sign."

We drive over a short hill overlooking a mile-long valley scattered with oak trees, a dozen houses and a small lake centered in the valley. A population of people mill about like worker ants on an anthill.

The dirt path leisurely meanders to the pond, then to an area with thirty or forty cars parked haphazardly under massive oak trees.

I park next to the truck, and the young man stands next to the bed of the truck talking to a portly young woman. I turn the engine off. He and the young woman walk to the car. I open the door.

The young woman puts her hand out to shake, and I respond. She takes my hand with a tight grip like a man. "I'm Sonya. Welcome to Canyon Ranch."

"I'm Jason Oak—"

"Yes, we know. You're Jason Oakley."

She bends low and looks inside the car. "Please, get out, and let's go meet Philip. We've all been waiting for you."

As Serenity and Grayson find their way out of the car, I get out and shake hands with the kid.

Serenity speaks with a cautious tone. "Where did you all come from?"

The young man speaks. "There were only a few people here before Trillian, but we've been coming here one or two at a time from all over the country."

Serenity waves one arm. "Why are you here?"

Sonya speaks. "Considering how things are, wouldn't we be better off to band together to help one another, rather than try to live this virus out separately? At any given time a third of this population is sick. A second third is caring for them, and the rest get to live their lives without the worry of trying to find a caretaker."

"But how—"

The young woman's face lights. "Let's go meet Philip. He can explain things much better." She leads us across the parking lot, up a slight rise to a large ranch house with a full veranda. The building looks as though it was originally here while the other structures have a newer look in style and materials.

When we climb the three steps onto the porch, two thick construction types open the front door and burst onto the deck deep in conversation. They walk past us without even noticing we're here. Sonya opens the screen and ushers us into the building with its worn hardwood floors and furniture placed in a large living room, not with an aesthetic concern but more as a conference room or place where groups of people gather. The room is slightly dusty, but neat and clean, typical of a ranch house. The six couches positioned in a large circle fill one whole side of the room, with a massive roll-top desk in one corner. A slight, blonde woman in her thirties sits in front of a computer typing. She doesn't look up.

A middle-aged man stops sweeping and looks at us. He puts the broom against the wall, walks over, and puts his right hand out. "Jason Oakley, I am so glad to meet you. I've read all of your books."

I shake his hand and look at Sonya. She points at Serenity. "Serenity, this is Philip Moorly."

He shakes her hand and smiles. "We've heard so

much about the both of you."

"How could you?" I ask. "We met a week ago."

He doesn't answer, but turns to Grayson. "But you, Grayson, are the surprise of the week. Where did you come from, and how did you happen to not get affected by Trillian?"

Grayson gives him a confused look.

After a silence, I ask, "how do you know about us?"

Philip smiles. "Lucky for you, we have little birdies everywhere. Cowboy has caused a lot of trouble in the few days he's been in our neighborhood, but don't worry, we've got a whole team of people on him."

"How do you know about Cowboy?" I ask.

"We have ways. For now, though, let's leave such unpleasant subjects behind us. I want to show you around. Maybe if you like the place, you might want to stay. We don't have many writers, especially ones as good as you."

He leads us into a full restaurant-style kitchen. Five men and two women are stirring pots, frying vegetables, chopping onions, and doing all the things necessary to prepare for a large meal. The smell is intoxicating.

Philip yells over the noise of pots being washed, skillets being positioned, oven doors opening and closing. "We're cooking the evening meal for a hundred seventy-five people. This is Martha."

A woman with a freshly stained white bib looks up from chopping fresh mushrooms and nods.

I say, "I haven't seen an edible mushroom in a year."

She smiles. "These are Morel mushrooms. Not many, but they're good." In a second she is back to her work.

Philip grabs a freshly-baked dinner muffin from a cooling plate and leads us out the back door. He breaks it in half and offers it to me.

"I just ate."

Grayson takes it and we go through the back door. The din of the kitchen fades, and the sounds of birds and a distant chain saw settle in the air.

I say, "Kinda noisy in there."

Philip takes a bite of the muffin and talks while chewing. "Martha would kill me if she knew I took this."

He leads us across the veranda and down the back steps. "The barn has chickens and stalls for milking the six cows who are lactating these days. We've got five more calves ready to come out, then we will have plenty of milk for cooking and making cheese. Martha is great at making cheese."

Serenity waves her hand around the property. "Where did all of this come from?"

Philip walks sideways for a few paces. "The Olsen family had everything together when we started coming here after Trillian started. All we did was expand on the concept to accommodate the influx of people."

Serenity asks, "how come I've never heard of you? I know every corner of this county."

Philip's smile is wide. "We knew we'd better be quiet about what we're doing or we'd have the whole damn county moving in. Not that we don't accept anyone who has a skill we can use. We just have to go slowly or risk being overwhelmed by a population explosion. Most of us come from other areas. We have to be discerning."

Philip leads past the barn to a long narrow structure, newly built that resembles an army barracks. It has a single door at either end and a string of windows along both walls.

He opens the door with a gentlemanly swagger and

has Serenity go in first. Grayson and I follow.

"This is the infirmary."

He doesn't need to speak. Beds are lined up along both walls with a patient in each one. "This part of the whole thing has been the hardest to stay ahead of, but in a year and a half, I think we finally have a handle on it."

He looks at Grayson. "We're going to draw some blood from you and study why you're not affected by Trillian."

Grayson turns pale. "Blood?"

"Not now. When you're ready."

Grayson's face relaxes, and he gives Philip a tentative smile.

Philip leads us along the corridor past fifty beds. Ten attendants casually move from patient to patient.

Philip points at a boy of ten lying curled under a single sheet. "Sometimes we actually get a medical case other than Trillian, and we have to call in Doc Benson. This child came down with something two days ago, and it isn't Trillian. Benson says he has a lung infection. We're keeping an eye on him."

Philip moves down the aisle and we follow, looking at pale-faced flu victims in varying stages of the illness. We get to the far end. Philip opens the back door and we step out into the sun. "All of us end up there for two-thirds of our lives. I wish we could've found you before you gave the pendant to that money-grubbing research guy in Palo Alto."

I look at Philip. "Money-grubbing?"

"His research building burned to the ground because he wanted to sell the pendant. Can you believe he was selling it?"

"Who would buy such a thing?"

Philip stops. "The thing's made of gold. Anyone who sees only the gold would covet your pendant."

I give him a wry smile. "Whenever anyone touches it, their lives turn to shit."

"I know."

"How is it that you know so much about everyone?"

He walks toward an ancient oak with a small cabin nestled under its branches. With his back to me, he says, "We have a secret weapon."

"Secret weapon?" Serenity asks.

Philip puts up his hand, and extended a halt gesture. "In a minute."

He marches us to the small cabin. He sits us on three of the four wooden folding chairs on the porch. "She'll be out in a moment."

He goes inside and I look at Serenity, who raises her eyebrows. I glance at Grayson, and he shrugs.

Chapter 15

Mother Louanne

A minute later the door opens. Philip ushers a woman out who looks older than any human I've ever met. Her almost nonexistent silver hair is tangled like she just got out of bed. Her face is filled with wrinkles. Her lips look chapped, and she smiles with no teeth. Philip steps her slowly to the one padded rocking chair and helps her sit.

With an air of reverence, Philip introduces me. "Mother Louanne, I would like you to—"

She waves one shriveled arm. "No need introducing these three, Philip." She speaks with a Texas drawl. "We know who they are., Jason We've been waiting for y'all for quite some time. I couldn't figure out why you hadn't come clear to me, but the moment you walked into the motorcycle shop, I knew why."

She looks at Grayson. "Son, you're the surprise. I'm glad to have you with us."

"Thank you, ma'am," Grayson says in a southern slur I've never heard. "I'm glad to finally be here. I knew I belonged somewhere, I just didn't know where."

The old woman cackles. "You belong here, boy."

In a whisper, Grayson says, "Yes, I know, but do I have to give blood?"

"You don't have to do anything you don't want to."

He flushes and smiles. "That's good."

She puts an arthritic gnarled hand on his knee. "Billy Black will come visit in your dreams, I promise."

Grayson immediately tears up. With a quivering chin, he says, "Really? I miss him terribly."

"You just wait, son. He'll be a visiting soon."

The old woman turns to Serenity. "You're going to have a baby girl?"

Serenity's face flushes. "I think so."

The old woman's wrinkles are more noticeable when she smiles. "You got the sight, girl. All you need to do is trust what you see. Come visit me every day, and we can talk about where you might take your gift."

Serenity has a frightened, wide-eyed stare. "We're going back, aren't we? We're going back to our normal life. I want to go back."

Philip puts a hand on her shoulder, which calms her. "You can't go back."

Serenity breaks into a long shudder, then lets loose a deep, long sigh. She puts her face in her hands and asks through them, "Why?"

"Because Cowboy is after all of you, and he isn't too friendly, now is he?"

Grayson speaks. "Cowboy wants us dead."

Serenity takes her tear-streaked face from her hands and looks at Grayson. "How do you know that for sure?"

The old woman speaks with a soft, reassuring voice. "Because I've seen him. He doesn't want any of you to live."

Philip, who is the only one standing, opens his arms. "Thanks to Mother Louanne, we have a place set aside for you three. In a few weeks we can send someone back to your house to get some of your essentials, but for now you'd better stay with us."

I look up at Philip. "A place?"

He smiles. "We knew you would be coming, so we've had time to prepare. You three are celebrities of sorts, so we all got together and built you a house. It's not much, but you'll find it cute and secluded." He looks directly at me. "So you can write. I can't wait to read your next book."

"Oh, that," I say.

Philip gets a quick worried look. "You did bring your computer?"

"I've got it."

"Okay, then, there shouldn't be a problem."

I don't say anything. He looks so excited, I don't want to disappoint him.

He looks at Serenity. "Wanta have a look at your new digs?"

She sighs. "That would be nice."

Philip points toward a rise with blackberry bushes at the top. "Okay, then let's go see what we have."

The old woman speaks in a soft voice. "Y'all may want to leave our ranch, but I warn you that Cowboy is determined. I can feel him. Maybe you better wait until

I can't feel him any longer."

We all shake hands with Mother Louanne and step off of the porch, then walk toward the blackberries. We veer to the right of the bush and go around the east side of the huge patch.

Philip turns to me. "We saved this bush because the berries are thumb size. They'll be ripe in a month."

In among the thorns, thousands of immature pink berries dot the solid green of the bush.

We skirt the bush and take a well-beaten path to the top of the rise. I look back, and we can't be more than fifteen feet higher than the rest of the settlement. I look forward. In the distance, under a large valley oak, a smallish ranch-style house stands overlooking the pond. It's nothing fancy, but well built with a sense of design. A long porch roof stretches along the entire front of the house which gives it a casual feel. Maybe it has two bedrooms, not big, but then my house isn't too big, either.

Philip asks, "what do you think?"

"This is for us?"

"Mother Louanne thought you were going to arrive last winter. The place has been sitting vacant since December. We all got kind of worried that she was losing her touch."

"Actually, last December I was about ready to move into town. It would have been so much easier, with gas being tight and all, but I just couldn't get the energy or time. The flu kept knocking me down, and finding someone to care for me took most of my time."

As we step onto the porch and out of the sun, Philip says, "She was right. Damn, that woman has not missed a beat since she got here."

He rushes ahead of me and opens the door, ushering all three of us into the small living room. A soft yellow couch with matching recliner is positioned around a glass coffee table. Philip points at a small stereo with a collection of a hundred CDs neatly stacked on end in the corner of the room. "We tried to guess your taste but, just in case, we have more in storage for you to choose from."

I give the stack a short glance and walk toward what would normally be the kitchen. When I go through the door I see that it's a bedroom, with lace pillows on a king-size bed and a mirrored dressing vanity with a collection of facial products lined on top of the cabinet. The curtains are matching lace, and the window overlooks the berry patch.

Philip walks in behind us. "Your bedroom, Serenity, though none of this is cast in concrete. If you don't like it, we have plenty of other furnishings to choose from."

She grins, stretches her arms out and spins slowly one revolution. "It's exactly what I'd have chosen." She steps through a side door. "And a bathroom, too. This couldn't be better."

Philip says, "your bedroom and study is through here." He takes three steps and opens a second door, then motions for me to follow.

The room is decorated with a chocolate leather love seat and a long walnut desk polished to perfection. A Tiffany-styled stained glass lamp sits atop the desk. A brown leather executive chair faces the desk, with a small hand-carved wooden sign. My name is carved into it. I pick up the small placard.

"We thought this might suit you for writing. We could pull a bed in here if you two sleep separate, but

Mother Louanne said you sleep together, so we didn't bother."

Serenity looks shy. "I guess we're sleeping together these days."

I drop onto the love seat and settle in. "Yes, I guess we do, don't we?"

"Great," Philip says. "Then we don't need to change much."

I say, "looks pretty good to me."

Grayson gets a lost look and stands against the wall. In a soft voice, he says. "What about me?"

Philip snickers. "We knew you were coming too, Grayson, though not until lately. We have something especially for you."

I stand. "Where's the kitchen?"

He smiles. "We all eat together. The kitchen is at the main building. Martha oversees the food, and you'll be glad she does. She's an amazing chef, top shelf, like eating at a fancy restaurant every night, and each meal is a complete surprise too. She's great."

He leads us back into the living room to a small bar with a bottle of my all-time favorite, Jack Daniels. "You have a small refrigerator here behind the bar to keep soft drinks, beer and snacks, but other than that, all of the snack food is in the big refrigerators next to the kitchen. Not as big a selection as the old days, but Martha makes up for any shortage with quality. There's always more than enough to eat and plenty of leftovers for lunch the next day."

"But. . . but I want to be with Serenity." Grayson looks like he's almost ready to cry.

Philip gives me a short look of surprise, then looks at Grayson. "The place we have for you, buddy, is far better than this boring little two bedroom. How about I show it to you and let you decide?"

Grayson's face doesn't change expression, but he acquiesces. "Okay."

Philip motions all of us to follow. He leads us out of the house, around back, to the far side of the old oak, where a small boxy building stands. It's the size of a three-car garage and just as interesting. The front of the building has a large bay steel roll-up door.

Philip grabs the door and pulls it up into a pocket. A one-car garage with workbenches and a full-size red Snap-On tool box sits in the middle of the room. Next to the toolbox on a jack stand sits the same Harley that Grayson was working on when I met him. His eyes light up. He rushes in and hugs the tank of the machine.

When he's finished, he picks a wrench from the box, sits on the mechanic's stool, and taps on various parts of the bike. It's a ritual he has done for a long time.

Philip whispers to me. "Jack and Tony were down in Roseville the other day. They picked up the bike and all the equipment."

Serenity puts her hand on his forearm. "How did you know?"

"Mother Louanne. She knows everything."

Philip says to Grayson. "Hey, buddy, that door leads to a nice bedroom for you."

With tears in his eyes, Grayson stops tinkering and looks at us. "I'll stay here, if that's okay, Serenity. I can come visit."

Serenity snickers. "Sure, Grayson. No problem. You can come over to the house anytime."

He continues tapping the other parts with a wrench.

Philip says, "You'll hear the dinner bell in an hour or

so, Grayson. Come to the main hall, okay?"

"Sure, Philip. I'll come."

The three of us walk around the side of the building. Philip puts his hand on my shoulder. "I had a hard time believing Mother Louanne but, damn, Grayson took to the bike like ducks to water."

"Tell me, Philip," I say while we walk out into the sun and take a slow saunter toward the big pond. "Wouldn't it be better to have Grayson at a research facility where they can do more in-depth tests on him? I mean, he's immune to Trillian. He's the only one I know."

Philip says, "my fear is they'll lock him up in some room and not let him live his life. I don't think that's fair. Our research people here are working with a lab in Phoenix. I think together we can study Grayson without disrupting his life."

Serenity says, "Whatever kind of life that is, tapping a musical tune out on some macho motorcycle that'll never run."

Philip stops walking. "Maybe just tunes to you and me, but it makes him happy. We also have Dr. Jeffries on property. He's a clinical psychologist. Maybe he can help Grayson."

I say, "Maybe, but I have to warn you. Grayson knew how to fight his way out of a tight situation the other day when Cowboy had us cornered. Grayson took care of Cowboy with a professional effectiveness I couldn't believe. Also Grayson knows Cowboy personally."

"Yes, we know. Mother Louanne gave us an update. It's where Grayson lost his center."

"What's that?" Serenity asks.

"He was some kind of C.I.A. operative when Trillian struck. We think they tested something new on him. It worked, but it left him muddled. Mother Louanne says he escaped the lab. Dr. Jeffries thinks he's in some kind of limbo."

"Where does the motorcycles come in?" I ask.

"That, we don't know."

Philip restarts our tour of the ranch. He points at the water. "The pond is spring fed and gives us all of the water we need to feed the livestock and grow a killer garden. We are low enough in elevation that we get vegetables all year."

"Where is the garden?" Serenity asks.

"Just over the rise." He glances at Serenity. "You want to see it?"

"Yes, of course. Gardening to me is like tapping out tunes on a motorcycle is to Grayson."

We walk another fifty yards and come over the rise to three acres of lush, green garden with a small four-foot fence.

Serenity gasps, "Oh, my God, that's beautiful."

Always concerned with the practical, I ask, "How do you keep the deer out with that dinky fence?"

Philip points high above the fence once we come to one of the three gates. "The fence posts are fourteen feet high, and the string at the top confuses the deer enough that they never jump over."

"No kidding?"

Philip opens the gate and ushers us in. "It's early in the season, but by midsummer this garden has amazing crops."

Most of the beds are dotted with baby plants. I can identify squash, tomatoes, string beans on poles, and bush beans. There are myriad plants I don't recognize.

Serenity saunters through the garden oohing and

ahhing. She looks at each bed. Philip and I haven't moved from the gate.

She asks, "do you have fruit trees?"

"Some older trees, mostly fig and almond. We put in a new orchard this last spring; apple, cherry, some apricot, and peach."

Serenity has a soft voice as she picks some leaves off of a plant. "That's good. Is someone growing herbs?"

Philip shrugs. "I couldn't tell you. I'm not much of a gardener, myself. At dinner you'll meet Yulanda. She's the garden manager. That woman loves gardens."

Philip looks at his watch. "In fact, the bell will be going off any moment. Maybe we should work our way back and meet the rest of the family. They've been looking forward to meeting you."

I walk out of the garden with Philip. Serenity calls from inside a short patch of green tomatoes. "I'll be there in a moment. I want to sit in the garden for awhile."

"We'll see you there," I say.

Philip whispers, "Never much into gardens myself."

We step shoulder to shoulder. "Me neither."

We walk a hundred steps in silence, then Philip springs the ever-constant question. "What's your next book about?"

I feel embarrassed. "I don't have a next one at the moment. Trillian threw my rhythm off."

I hear genuine disappointment in his voice. "Oh, I'm sorry to hear that."

I need to say something in my defense. "I did start a piece yesterday, but I'm in the early stages. I never know if it's going to go anywhere. I've had hundreds of false starts over the years."

"Hey, a start is a start. Maybe being here will spark

your writing. It's either write or work in the garden."

"I'll write. I swear, I'll write."

He snickers. We walk on in silence around the pond and move toward the main house as a bell chimes six times.

He says, "ah, yes, dinner is ready."

We reach the house, and a stream of people work their way in from various areas on the farm. They look like cattle coming in for the evening milking, but I say nothing.

We step onto the veranda and through the front door. We're the first in the big hall, which has lines of extremely narrow tables, each with light peach cloths to match the paint on the walls. Ten place settings run down the center of the tables with ten custom-looking chairs on each side. The forks, knives, and spoons have a Danish design that lends class to the table setting, but no plates. The wine glasses are fragile crystal standing next to a peach candle between each setting.

I say, "except for the narrow tables, this is like fancy dining."

Philip grins. "It is fancy dining."

"Where did you get all of the equipment?"

He leads me to a table and motions for me to sit in the middle, then sits directly across from me. Serenity comes in the door and sits beside me as the first person of a long line of people steps into the room.

Philip gives me a curious smile. He picks up a wine glass. "We got these in Sacramento. Because of the radical reduction of population, we found hundreds of closed restaurants, hardware stores, clothing stores, auto dealers, you name it. When they went out of business, most stores simply were abandoned, sometimes without even locking the doors. If the doors were locked, vandals finished the job. We make forays into Sacramento once a week and harvest what is needed here on the farm."

"Isn't that stealing?"

"Yes, I guess it is, but there would be no other way to attain these things, mostly because the supply houses are also abandoned. We certainly have the money to pay for what we need, there just isn't anyone around to collect. We tried many times in the early days."

I pick up a fork and look at it. "Things certainly did change once Sam and I brought the pendant back."

"Too bad we didn't get to you a few days earlier. Our research team could have used your pendant."

"You wouldn't have wanted it around. The thing has a streak of bad luck a mile wide. I'm positive it got through the fire in Palo Alto. It always seems to get through every disaster."

"Still, with the pure virus we could have made major headway."

I don't want to tell him, so I change the subject. "How come the tables are so narrow, and why only one place setting?"

He gives me a secret smile and puts up one finger. "In a few minutes."

Thirty or forty people of varying ages and ethnic backgrounds are in the room, with more filing in. They sit across from one another and pull up to the table. I notice their knees are forced to touch. Maybe not forced, because they pull up extra close so their knees interlock.

An older woman takes a seat next to Philip, sitting across from Serenity. Others fill in the rest of the table. Both Serenity and I are positioned with room for our opposites, but I can hardly reach the table.

Philip's smile widens and his crow's-feet eyes crinkle. His lids narrow. "Don't see how you're going to eat sitting back so far."

I slide my chair up an inch or so. "There's no room."

"Guess you're going to have to touch knee to knee."

I feel my face flush.

"Look, Jason, we designed these tables specifically so people have to physically connect. It's more than okay with me, in fact, I demand that you touch knees with me."

The older woman pulls back a lock of silver-gray hair. "We all had to get used to touching at one time or another. It's a little nerve-wracking at first, but now I love connecting with a new person each night at dinner. It's so much more intimate, don't you think?"

Serenity pulls her chair closer to the table and meshes her knees with the woman. "I'm Serenity." She puts out her hand to shake.

The woman gives her a movie star smile. "I'm Marya." She shakes Serenity's hand, then holds it out to shake mine. "You're Jason Oakley."

I'm forced to pull my chair in closer to shake her hand, and my knees touch Philip's.

"You'll get used to it," Philip says, "especially once we start eating."

I pull my hand away from Marya and look at Philip. "What do you mean?"

He grins again when I look along the table. Everyone is smiling at me. "What?"

"The food will be out soon."

As if timed, he says the last word, the door to the kitchen bursts open, and seven people file out each with a tray of four plates. They quickly spread out and serve separate tables. Another seven hurry around with large pitchers of a burgundy liquid, filling glasses. I get the feeling it's not wine. A young man with a small goatee steps up to our table and sets an extra large dish in front of Serenity and Marya, then three more along the length of the table. Once he has set the dishes in their place, he races back to the kitchen.

I look at the dish in front of Serenity; I have never seen more artistically designed creations with such simple things as broccoli, carrots, a sprinkling of peas, and a large portion of the leg and thigh of a chicken. A light creamy sauce dribbles over the meat with a small sprinkling of minced almonds. Atop the chicken sits a long, narrow spire of something like jicama radish. The dish looks right out of a cooking magazine.

In less than a minute, the overly-large plates line up along the center of each table, and everyone cheers when Martha steps into the room. Applause fills the room when she sits at the table with the waiters.

Because I'm in a strange situation, I wait for someone else to make the first move.

Philip stands, picks up his glass, then lifts it into the air. "To a bountiful harvest and to our three new guests." He and close to two hundred people lift their glasses high, then a strange thing happens. Philip sits and offers the glass to me. I reach out to take it, and he shakes his head. "I offer this drink to you."

I look about, and everyone is drinking while the opposite person is holding the glass. I take a sip, and the juice, maybe blackberry with some grape, slithers down my chin. Philip slides a cloth napkin under my chin and wipes the spillage. "Want another, or shall we eat?"

I look at Serenity and she at me, then I notice our

whole table is looking at us, not directly, but looking just the same.

Philip picks up his fork. "Which do you want to taste first?"

I'm so confused, I can't answer. I shrug.

He dips the fork into the vegetables. "How about some carrots? Martha does wonders with carrots." He stabs a single carrot spire and lifts it to my mouth. I take a bite, and the taste is like nothing I've ever eaten.

"What did I tell you? Isn't she a wonder?"

"Yes, this is good."

"What next?"

I'm getting the hang of it, so I say, "Maybe some chicken."

Philip slips the knife out and slices off a small piece of chicken. He puts it into my mouth. The spices and succulent quality of the meat make the piece melt. I chew, but I almost don't have to. "Oh, this is great."

"We're lucky to have Martha, aren't we?"

"Oh, yes, very."

He stabs another bite of something I don't recognize, maybe chutney.

Serenity breaks into a sob.

I look at her, and tears are rolling down her face.

I put my hand on her shoulder. "Are you okay?"

Her head bobs. She tries to say a word through her crying. "This. . . this. . . is so special." Her tears well up again.

The woman sitting across from her, with tears in her eyes, sets her fork down and reaches over to hold Serenity's hand. "It's okay, honey, I did the same thing when I first got here. I hadn't been fed since I was a young child, and all of the memories flooded back."

Now that I think about it, this does feel like when my mother fed me in the high chair. But for me, mom wasn't a good memory. She resented me. Feedings were traumatic events. I quickly learned to feed myself.

When Serenity calms, Marya releases her hand and picks up the fork again. She spears an asparagus and sloshes it into a dinky bowl of melted butter, then points it at Serenity who opens her mouth.

I look around the room and feel the gentle quality of the entire room feeding one another. I look back at Philip and he slides another bite into my mouth. While chewing, I ask, "Why?"

He stabs the asparagus. "In the early days, just after Trillian, when there were only a few of us, we realized the only way to survive was to pool our energies. At first every person scrambled around attempting to get their needs taken care of, but one day Bill and Louise came to Mother Louanne with an idea. They said it might be better if we shifted from everyone trying to get their individual needs met to making certain that everyone's needs automatically were met so worry was no longer an issue.

"It took a month, because around here everything takes forever. We agreed and implemented the hospital program for third-stage flu. In those days, before the infirmary was built, hospital happened right here in this hall."

He slides a spear in the butter, then into my mouth, and I happily chew. He continues. "Once the pressure of Trillian was no longer an issue, and our group was able to relax. Another of our elders, Sadie, came up with a second idea to extend the help to second-stage Trillian sufferers. The idea was so successful, more suggestions came forward that extended into everyday life. We found we were creating a new type of community. The way it was before Trillian never fed the soul. The nuclear family model has been bankrupt for a century, and it was time to find a new approach."

He slices a piece of chicken and puts it in my mouth. While I chew, I ask, "When do you get fed?"

He smiles. "That's good. You're catching on. The new approach is to be concerned about your neighbor more than yourself."

"So, when do you get fed?"

"When you're finished, I eat. Martha will bring out another dish so someone else can feed me. This method does two things; brings us together, and forces us to slow down. Better for the digestion, you know."

He butters a piece of thick-sliced dark bread and positions it across the table so I can take a bite. "In a sense, Trillian has been a gift to our little community. It's made us slow down and notice each other."

"Another bite of that incredible bread, please."

He picks the bread up and slips it over to my mouth.

I take a bite and chew for a moment, then ask, "Who came up with the narrow table idea?"

He sets the bread down and picks up the fork. "Actually, Martha was the genius with that one. While working in restaurants, she noticed that each little group was completely separate from one another. People never extended themselves any further than a slight nod or a few words, but mostly they blocked the rest of the restaurant out of their little worlds. Martha's idea was to force us to interact." Philip searches the room, and points at a smallish man sitting behind him. "Frank came up with the idea of making the tables narrower, so we all had to touch one another. It's the biggest bugaboo in our culture, don't you think?"

I chew another bite of the chutney.

"I don't know where it came from, but touching one another, especially knee touching, was one of our biggest hurdles. It took three months to make a decision to even cut a single table down. Everyone had to rotate to that table a few times before we decided it was the best thing anyone had come up with to that point."

"To that point. You mean there's more?"

His ever-present smile widens. "Oh, yes, Jason, there is more, much more. For right now, though, let's get through the food part." He stabs another vegetable. I happily take the morsel and bite into a scrumptious zucchini, maybe my least favorite in the vegetable family.

In another ten minutes, I take a last bite, and a waiter is at the table to take my dish away. In a moment, he sets a repeat of my meal in front of us.

"Okay," Philip pulls back from the table and gets up. "It's time to switch."

I'm ready to feed him, but he stands and moves down the same side of the table four positions. A young woman with long, black hair and skin like porcelain sits in his place. She can't be twenty-five. She slides in close, and her small knees interlock with mine. She extends her hand. "I'm Catherine Bonner."

I grasp her little hand and try not to squeeze for fear that I'll break every bone in her bird-like fingers. "I'm Jas—"

"Yes, I know, your Jason Oakley, the author. I've read every one of your books at least three times. I like Baker's Corner the very best."

"Thank you. I think it's my best piece so far too."

We release hands. I pick up the fork. "What would you like first?"

"I want to know what you're working on, but I'll take a bite of the chicken as a close second."

I put the first piece into her mouth. I realize how awkward I feel feeding someone else and also how intimate it is. Serenity, next to me, giggles as she feeds a bent old man who looks like he hasn't shaven for a week.

After Catherine chews the first bite, she asks, "So, what are you working on?"

It's hard for me to admit, but I finally give her a lame explanation: "Trillian kind of knocked the creative juices out of me. To tell the truth, I haven't had time to write."

Her doll face drops into a frown. "But how could you stop? You're such a great writer."

"I don't know how. I spent most of my last few years surviving Trillian. There was little time left. Serenity is pregnant now, so maybe I'll have more time."

The girl looks at Serenity, then back at me. "If you stay, you'll have lots of time. We help each other around here, which frees up more time than you can believe."

I scoop some vegetables and direct them to her petite mouth. She opens and receives the bite. I'm sure Serenity isn't exactly feeling the same, feeding the old man, but sitting so close to and feeding the exotic young woman is almost sexual, though I say nothing.

"Why did everyone switch?" I ask.

She finishes the bite, motions for another bite of chicken, then answers. "The sitting close and sharing food part was firmly in place before I got here. I think it was Jacob." She nods at the old man sitting next to her. "He suggested that we switch so the person being fed didn't feel beholden to the person feeding. What we were attempting was to learn to receive without having to pay back. By then, a bunch of old traditional ways had been broken, and most of us were up to trying new things more readily. We took less than a week to implement the trading-places thing."

I cut a piece of chicken, slather it in the sauce, lift it to her mouth and wipe the slight dribble from under her lip.

"So, receiving is the issue here?"

She chews the bite in a dainty manner, swallows, and says, "Receiving is one of a human's biggest problems. The next step in our evolutionary process is to learn how to give, but so few of us know how to receive."

"You might have a point." I put a spear of asparagus in her mouth. I wipe her chin again and feel stupid that I can't aim better.

She chews and swallows, then says, "I'm much too young to come up with something so profound, but I like the concept, don't you?"

"Now that I think of it, receiving is probably the hardest thing for me. It's easy feeding you, well. . . besides getting all of the food in your mouth that is, but I felt uncomfortable getting fed by Philip."

She giggles, and her simple little snicker, with us sitting across from one another, knees interlocked, makes me fall in love with her. I feel intimate, like the act of feeding her is sexual, and it's the best sex I ever had. I don't say anything, of course.

"Receiving is the hardest thing for me too," she says, this time with her mouth still chewing the asparagus.

We sit in silence. I put three more bites of food in her mouth. She asks, "So, maybe you have a story in mind?"

"I started something the other day, but I never know

if it's anything worth finishing."

She finishes. "Where do your ideas come from?"

I stab a piece of zucchini and lift the morsel to her mouth. This time I have the napkin ready. "I don't know. They just come to me out of the blue, and I write them down. Sometimes I don't get to the idea for years. Some ideas I know I'll never get to, but I write them all down."

We finish with her plate, and after the waiter takes the dishes, she leans in close and gives me a shy look and squeezes my knees with hers, though I'm sure it's not intentional. "You have to acclimate to our new environment for a week or so, but when you're ready, could I have a cuddle date?" She blushes, pushes back her chair, stands, nods, then goes toward the kitchen.

The old man gives me a big grin. "A cuddle date with Catherine. Consider yourself lucky. She never asks anyone, though all of the young men ask her all the time."

Serenity puts a last forkful of chicken in his mouth and asks, "What's a cuddle date?"

His smile widens. "You'll have to let Philip fill you in. I'm an old man. I don't know much about such things."

He takes a last bite of asparagus, reaches over, and puts his gnarled hand on Serenity's. "Thank you. Being fed by you was a real treat." He stands and hobbles his way out of the hall.

A few other older people stand and work their way out of the main hall before Martha stands and clinks a spoon against her crystal goblet loud enough that I'm sure she'll break it. The hall gets quiet. She looks around the room. "I'll take you, Jack, Mary, Sylvia," and she runs through a list of twenty people in the room. "I'll also take you, Jason Oakley."

When she's finished, Philip stands and swings one

arm toward her with his palm open and up, like he's presenting someone. "Thank you once again, Martha."

The room breaks into a roar of applause and cheers. Her face reddens, and she sits among her minions in embarrassed silence.

When the room calms, people file out of the hall and I ask Philip. "What was I chosen for?"

"Kitchen detail all three meals tomorrow. Personally, I thought it was a little too soon to put you to work, but around here, when the subject is food, what Martha says pretty much goes."

Immediately, I want to complain that I only have a few days of freedom before I go back into Trillian, but I catch myself when I remember everyone has a few days. "What time do I start?"

"Four o'clock. Don't worry, Martha has someone wake you so you don't have to keep track of time."

Philip walks both Serenity and me outside as the kitchen crew swarms around the tables picking up the last vestiges of dinner and folding tables and chairs.

"What happens when Martha gets sick?"

"Joanne takes over. During those rare occasions when both Joanne and Martha are in the cycle at the same time, yours truly becomes chef. I can pull a meal or two off, but I'm not that good."

Philip strolls us back to our home over the rise and away from the noise of most of the ranch.

Chapter 16

Cuddle Date

When we reach our small veranda, I ask, "what's a 'cuddle date'?"

"Where did you get that?"

"Catherine asked me for a cuddle date."

Philip's right bushy eyebrow raises. "Catherine asked you for a cuddle date?"

I nod.

His voice has a jovial quality. "Well, that's a first."

"What do you mean?"

"She's normally hounded for cuddle dates, especially from all of the young men. I don't remember the last time she accepted one."

"What is a cuddle date?"

"First, Jason, you must be aware just how much of an honor she has placed on you."

Serenity looks at Philip and puts her right hand on her hip. Her head cocks slightly to the right. "Tell us what a cuddle date is."

Philip snickers.

I feel Serenity's hackles rise.

"I'm an old man. I need to get off of my feet. Can we sit in the chairs here so I can tell you and take some of the pressure off my knees?"

Serenity stomps across the small veranda, sits in the far chair, and crosses her arms in front of her, certainly not in a relaxed manner.

Philip sits and pulls his chair around to face both of us. When he speaks, he leans forward and puts both his elbows on his knees. "We realized quickly that there was sexual tension here on the farm. People lost friends and family members in the early days, and there was still an uncertainty through the whole affair. Life was tentative and fragile. Most people simply didn't want to be alone. Promiscuous sex was a problem, and we weren't sure how to contain it. The one thing we knew was it would rip our community apart. Girlfriends and husbands alike were screwing like rabbits, and the jealousy quotient was high.

"Martha brought the cuddle date into the circle, and after we tried it —and it took awhile to catch on— the problems surrounding sexual issues dropped radically."

"What is a cuddle date?" I cut in.

Philip raised one hand with his first finger extended. "Give me a moment to fill you in on the background."

I nod and lean forward like Philip, elbows on knees.

"Not that sex is a bad thing, but what emerged was

most people have some kind of trauma around sex. Women have sexual issues ranging from harassment in the workplace to the extreme of molestation when they were young. Ninety percent of the female population has been molested. Even if one is generous and cuts that statistic in half, far too many women have sexual trauma in their past."

Serenity says, "I was molested by my uncle when I was ten."

I look at her but don't say anything.

Philip puts a hand on her hand. "Case in point."

Even if I did have something like that in my past, I would never openly admit it. Serenity gains another notch of my respect.

Philip goes on. "Men, on the other hand, have the ongoing trauma of being rejected by females. We have all been horribly abused by women when it comes to sex and mostly the lack thereof."

I humph and nod.

"So we needed to find a way to heal the emerging traumas in our community before we could actually step into healing with one another. Without the healing, the community was destine to fall apart.

"Martha suggested the cuddle date, and once we implemented the concept, a shift took place. Like eating from the narrow tables with knees touching, it helped in the healing."

I'm getting antsy because he's telling history, but not explaining what it is.

He leans back in the chair. "The cuddle date is simple. Two people who feel like they want to spend intimate time make a date to spend the night together."

"What?" Serenity says loud.

Philip laughs. "A woman's first reaction."

She tries for a smile, but isn't successful.

"The clear agreement —and you have to understand there can be no wiggle room in this area because we're talking about healing the old wounds instead of inflicting more— the solid agreement is that while these two people are together for the night, or in some cases a few nights, there is to be no sex, no mention of sex, not even any sexual tingley feelings."

"Well," I say, "that's impossible, don't you think?"

Philip smiles. "Not as hard as you might think."

"I don't get it. If two people are attracted to one another, how can sex be taken out of the equation?"

She leaps into the conversation with a demanding voice. "So you're attracted to her?"

"Well, of course I am. She is beautiful and—"

Philip puts up one hand. "You two have just proven what happens when sex enters the picture." He looks at Serenity. "Now, take your jealousy or insecurity and imagine the two people sitting across the dinner table from one another, knees interlocked, feeding each other. How do you feel now?"

"I don't have to imagine, it just happened." Serenity says. "I felt a twinge of jealousy, but only a twinge, but sleeping together is different."

"How different?" Philip asks.

Serenity holds up her hand, fingers splayed. She drops one finger. "You have two hundred people around to keep things from getting out of hand."

"What if there was a guarantee that things would not get out of hand?"

Serenity's hand disappears into her lap. "Don't things always get out of hand."

"Imagine it doesn't."

She thinks for a moment, then her eyes brighten. "Then all that is left is me sleeping alone, and now that I've gotten used to Jason, I'd hate not having him there."

Philip grins. "But other than missing him, with those parameters, would the cuddle date be okay?"

"Yes, barely."

He turns to me. "A cuddle date is just that. You leave any sexual desire behind. There is no place for even an inkling of sex because most people here are engaging in cuddle dates not as intimate recreation, but a conscious attempt to heal old wounds inflicted, more often than not, during childhood."

I say, "Don't know if I could not have sexual desire. I'm not wired that way."

Philip shakes his head slowly. "Yes, of course there will be those feelings; the only thing you can't do is act on them, not even slightly."

"That's asking a lot of a man whose typical sexual wound is never getting enough sex."

He shifts in his chair and crosses one knee over the other. "Is it not getting enough sex, or not getting enough intimacy?"

"For me it's sex."

"Most men give the same answer before they spend the night with a woman without sex."

"Trust me," I say, "I have spent many nights with a woman without sex."

"Okay, let me be more specific. He spends the night with a woman where the possibility of sex is nonexistent. His choice, not him being the victim of a woman's choice."

I put both hands to the sides of my temples and

rub. "Oh, that is a hard statement to comprehend. How would no sex ever be my choice? Better yet, when has it ever been my choice? Women have total control in that arena, and my experience is they wield their power with a heavy hand."

Sernity gets a hurt expression. "I've never done that."

With my hands still on my temples, I turn toward her. "Well, of course not, we've known each other two weeks. There hasn't been time for you to begin the painfully slow process of shutting down. Let's talk again in six months when the romance has waned and we're a little bored with one another."

"How could you say something so hurtful? I have never acted like that."

Philip puts both of his hands up like a traffic cop. We both stop. He drops his hands and looks directly at me. "What Jason said is the classic male wound. Whether you would do such a thing or not is not the point. He feels that way, and those feelings may have some basis in his past. although you want them to go away and prove him wrong, his feelings are valid."

She spits out the next sentence. "What do you mean, valid? His statement is so wrong, even I can't believe he said it."

Philip, in a patient, slow execution of words, says, "Wrong or right, Jason's view of his world is valid for him. He has an opinion, and he has a right to his opinion. You have your own opinions, and you have a right to yours."

"You don't get it, Philip. Jason's opinion is wrong. The fact is that I would—"

Philip holds up one hand again and cuts her off. "It's not a fact, because you have no idea what is going to happen in six months. It's your opinion. Jason has an opinion and so do you, and both of you have a right to your opinions."

Her voice raises and she speaks in a demanding tone. "He has no right to his opinion if it affects me."

Philip shifts his halt hand motion to a single index finger held up. "He has a right to his opinion whoever it affects, because his opinion is his. He owns it. He has no right, however, to force his opinion on you."

Philip makes his point eloquently and with just the right amount of force. I could never go into this kind of discussion without either shutting up or going ballistic. I want to scream that I do have a right to my opinion. Not an angry scream, but one of joy and exuberance, because I've never been able to have an opposing opinion with any woman worth her salt.

I say nothing, though, because I'm in guy heaven watching this man expertly maneuver his way around her rock-solid factual-sounding statements.

After a minute of the back and forth, the solid place inside of her that will not move, begins to melt. I witness this happen for the first time in my miserable life. A man can actually change the opinion of a strong woman. Philip is inspiring.

When he makes his last statement, and it's strong enough and with no holes, I see her resolve crumble. Oh, what I would give to record this conversation so I could play it back later to see how to accomplish such a feat. Philip is a man among men.

When she crumbles, she does not with the crashing of her walls of fact, but with a narrow opening in her resolve. Only a chink, but it's the first I've seen.

"Okay," she says, "maybe I see your point. Maybe he has an opinion, and maybe his opinion might be in conflict with mine, and there can be no fact in something that might or might not happen in six months."

Philip smiles, and I feel him relax for the first time in five minutes. "And he has a right to his opinion."

"Yes, okay, he has a right."

"Even if it conflicts with yours."

"Yes, yes, but I feel constrained by this."

Philip sighs. "Yes, I know. Most of the women in this compound feel the same way. Maybe it's a female thing to feel constrained by male opinion."

We all look toward the road. A big, black SUV barrels down the dirt trail kicking a dust cloud high into the air.

Philip stands with a worried frown. "Cowboy."

"Yes," I say. "I recognize the car. But how did he find us so quickly?"

Philip says, "The bigger question is how did he come within five miles of this place without Mother Louanne knowing. She knows everything."

Philip points at the front door. "When Cowboy goes over the rise, get in the house and stay there until I come get you."

The car drops behind the hill.

"Okay, go into the house now." Philip leaps off the porch, then runs toward the main house. He gets ten yards. I open the front door and look back. The big black car cuts across the open field and heads for our cabin.

We step inside. I look back and see Cowboy through the windshield. His face is contorted with determination. I close the door. I look through the lacy curtain of the side window.

"What do we do now?" Serenity moans. Her face is white.

"Lie on the floor in front of the couch."

She doesn't move.

I yell, "Do it, now!"

She drops out of sight.

I look out the window. The car speeds past Philip, missing him by inches, rolls another twenty yards to the house, and slides to a stop. The doors open. Cowboy leaps out of the car and runs to the veranda. I see an automatic pistol in his hand, maybe an Uzi. When he's out of sight, I leap for the front of the couch myself, lie next to Serenity, and whisper in her ear. "He's here. Don't make a sound."

The loud bark of an automatic weapon splits the air with a fast dozen bullets. The front door explodes. Although the door is still on its hinges, the latch and lock are gone. The door casually swings open and rests against the wall.

"Oh my God, Jason, what—"

I put my hand over her mouth and press hard. The boot steps of Cowboy's long stride vibrates the entire house. Three strides, and he's inside; two more, and he's standing over us. I look up and see the business end of the pistol pointed directly at my head. Beyond the barrel of the pistol, Cowboy's lean, angry face turns into a sardonic grin. "Found you, didn't I? Where's the pendant?"

Serenity is pushing herself under the couch, though there is less than two inches between it and the floor. The couch rises while she wiggles farther under.

"I told you, I gave it to the researchers."

"Why don't I believe you?"

"Believe me, because it's true."

He glares down the barrel of his gun. He swings the pistol to the right. He fires. I see the flash. I feel the bullet sing past me and slam into the floor. It's one inch from my head.

"You've got one more try."

"I gave it to the—"

A second shot rings out. I feel a searing pain in my right thigh. I scream from the pain. "I did, I swear."

Cowboy points the gun at my other thigh. Something crashes through the window. It lands hard on the side of Cowboy's head. He slumps to the floor.

I scramble forward and pull the pistol from his grip.

Grayson's voice rings out. "You okay, Jason?"

I yell back, "He shot me, but you got him just right. He's out."

Footsteps rush the front door. I direct the gun toward the door.

Philip and Grayson step into view. I lower the gun.

Four or five other men rush into the room, and one has Cowboy lashed tight in ten seconds.

Philip steps up to me. "Jason, you've been shot."

I look down at the small puncture wound in my leg and the dribbles of blood running down my leg. Everything goes brilliant white.

I remember nothing until I awake in a hospital bed with a bunch of catatonic patients.

I look out the widow, and it's either late night or early morning. The sky outside of the small row of windows is marbled with puffy clouds turned bright pink. The sky behind is a gray of dawn or dusk, I'm not sure.

I look about my bed and find a buzzer. I push the button, and a small red light blinks next to my thumb.

In a moment, an older woman with dyed red hair and an inch of gray at her roots steps up to my bed. Her crooked smile reveals a dentist's nightmare of teeth, but her smile is gentle. "How are we this morning, Mr. Oakley?"

"Jason," I say. "Call me Jason."

She tries my name almost silently. "Jason."

"I'm thirsty."

"Sure Mr. Oak. . . I mean Jason." She moves away, her wide hips rotating wildly.

When she returns with a pitcher of water and a glass, she pours a half glass for me.

I drink the contents in a single gulp.

She pours the second without saying anything, and I drink.

"How long have I been out?"

With the pitcher in hand she steps to the end of my bed, picks up the clipboard, and studies it. "I just came on duty, but according to your chart, yesterday afternoon. They pulled a bullet out of your leg last night."

"What happened to Cowboy?"

"Cowboy?"

"The guy who shot me."

"Oh, him. Well your little adventure has raised quite a stir around here."

"Is everyone else okay?"

"Heavens, yes, Mr. Oakley; everyone is fine. Your friend Grayson beaned him with a rock of all things. We signed him up for softball."

"Serenity, is she all right?"

"A few scrapes on her back and neck from the couch. Otherwise, she is fine."

"Where is Cowboy now?"

She gives me a sheepish smile. The next few words she says in a whisper. "He's asleep in the bed next to you."

"Next to me?"

"There were only two beds available. This week's always busy with Trillian."

"Oh great, he can carry out his plans without even getting out of bed."

"We used his handcuffs to attach him to a steel pipe. It's a little awkward for him, but I don't think he'll be bothering you, unless he can yell you dead. I don't think he'll be in any shape once he awakes anyhow. Your buddy Grayson beaned him pretty hard. He's been out since it happened. He'll be okay, but he's going to have one hell of a headache when he comes around. We put three stitches in his temple."

"Chained to the wall?"

"Safe and sound."

"Okay, I guess I can relax."

She leans forward, tucks the pure white sheet up to my chin, and pats my shoulder. "Go back to sleep, Mr. Oakley, you'll be fine. Philip has the gun stored where even I couldn't find it, and I'm the biggest snoop there is."

She walks out of my little cloth-walled cubical, and pulls my curtain farther around to close me off. At the last second, she pokes her head back in the six-inch opening. "Get some sleep, Mr. Oakley. We'll have you back on your feet in no time."

I want to respond, but I feel more tired than I ever have in my life. My eyelids are heavy, and the room disappears into a soft pillow of darkness.

I awake in the middle of the night as someone grabs my wrist in a rough manner with meat-hook hands. A small flashlight is pointed at my chest. My tongue is thick. "Can I have some water?"

The voice is baritone. He tries to whisper, but no matter how quiet he tries, his voice has enough power to carry across the meadow. "When I finish checking your pulse, Mr. Oakley."

I lie silent for a moment until he releases my wrist. I hear the clink of glass followed by the splash of water. He hands me a large glass. "Just put it on the counter when you're finished."

"Thank you," I say and drink. He exits my cubicle. I watch the flashlight beam bounce ghostlike through the curtain, while he checks on the next patient. I set the glass down and everything goes fuzzy again.

In the morning, the long hall is a flurry of activity. Carts roll down the center of the hall. Boots and squeaky tennis shoes traipse across the waxy floor. I hear clinks of glass and ceramic and the sound of people waking up with morning greetings.

When the activity gets to my little cubicle, a large black man pushes my curtain open. He smiles without saying a word, flips a switch to raise the back of my bed, then picks up a tray of food and slides it into my lap.

I look sleepily at scrambled eggs with a single piece of bacon and two slices of toast. A glass of orange liquid sits at the corner of the tray, though I have a sneaking suspicion it's not orange juice.

I pick up the glass and the young man stops me. "I'll feed you, Mr. Oakley." He puts the glass to my lips and it is orange juice. He sets the glass down and reaches high to close me in. "Don't close the curtains," I say. "Could you open them more so I can see where I am?"

He smiles and pushes them back on the rail. The rest of the room has maybe fifty beds with a dozen people sitting up, being fed their breakfast. The remainder lie in reclined positions with gray faces. It looks like they're in the sleeping phase.

I recognize the long face of Cowboy with a white turban wrapped around his head. He lies next to me with one arm awkwardly attached to the wall.

The young man shovels some fluffy scrambled eggs that taste so fresh the chicken must have laid them this morning. The toast is fresh baked, and the single strip of bacon doesn't have the usual preservative taste that comes with most bacon. Breakfast is as good as last night's dinner.

I'm halfway through my meal when Serenity steps in and walks the long hall to my bed. She sits beside me and takes my spoon. "How are you, Jason?"

The young man nods and leaves without a word.

"My leg hurts, but otherwise I feel pretty good."

She gives me a bite. While I chew, she says, "I guess the carpenters are repairing yesterday's damage." She nods in Cowboy's direction. "I swear, it amazes me how much plaster and wood chips were scattered."

"How's Grayson doing?"

She spoons another bite. "He's back to tinkering with his Harley, so it's hard to tell. I'm not sure bringing the bike here was such a good idea."

Before I take the bite, I whisper, "The old woman thinks so, and it looks like most everyone around here follows her lead."

"I noticed."

I half chew the eggs and talk with the bite in my mouth. "I trust her judgment. Maybe there is some kind of calming affect the bike has on Grayson. Maybe he'll need the bike to break through the shell."

She picks up the one piece of bacon. "Maybe."

I take a second bite, and realize I haven't had bacon since Trillian began. While I chew and savor the flavor, Serenity says, "Doc says for you to stay down for the rest of the day, then tomorrow you can move around."

"Oh great, I'm going to spend my third day here. Just about the time I'm ready to get up, I'm going to be sick again."

She glides a piece of toast to my lips. "Oh, quit your complaining. You could be dead."

I chew. "Guess we're pretty lucky."

I hear rustling from Cowboy's bed and turn when he lets out a moan. His free hand rubs the bandaged part of his temple. His eyes open. He looks about, then rests his stare on me. At the same time, he realizes he's handcuffed to the pipe. "How long have I been out?"

Serenity snorts with disgust. I answer. "Almost a day."

"What happened?"

In a spiteful voice, Serenity spits the words. "What happened is you almost killed us, you bastard. If Grayson didn't have such a good throwing arm, we'd probably be in the morgue."

He speaks apologetically. "It wasn't personal."

She sets the plate down on my lap and glares. "I don't know anything more personal, you sick fuck. What gives you the right to think you can take our lives and not even have enough feelings to make it personal? I can't believe that—"

"Serenity," I say. "We have to be more constructive."

She has fire in her eyes. "Maybe we shoot him in the leg and threaten his life and see how impersonal he thinks it is."

She's building to some level of a frenzy, the extreme

of which I'm not sure. I also know I've got to disarm this situation before she throws my food at him. In a calm voice, I ask, "why are you chasing us?"

His face relaxes. "My boss wants the pendant."

Serenity starts in again. "You mean to tell me that just because that fat bastard senator of yours wants that stupid pendant—"

"Serenity!"

She asks, "what?"

"Slow down a little. I've got some questions, and I want them answered before you start shooting."

While the plate of food continues to sit on my lap, she scoops another bite of eggs. I take the bite, but at the same time look at Cowboy. "Why does he want the pendant? Doesn't he know how much bad luck goes with that thing? Every time I even look at the pendant my day turns to crap. Everything around me falls apart, and it takes longer than forever for the curse to dissipate. I was glad to hand the thing over to the researchers."

"So, the researchers have it?"

Serenity barks. "Along with your blind murderous tendencies, I guess you don't listen too well, do you?"

I put my hand on her forearm and squeeze slightly. She has rage in her eyes. She throws up her hands and gets to her feet. "I can't stand this. You'll have to feed yourself." She stomps down the long hall. She reaches the door as it opens and stops her headlong stride as a young woman steps in carrying a tray. Serenity stomps out of the room and slams the door behind her. The young woman tentatively steps along the aisle toward us. When she gets close, I realize it's Catherine, the woman who asked for the cuddle date. She looks at Cowboy. "You aren't going to hurt me, are you?"

He shakes his head.

She sits next to him on the bed. "I'm here to feed you."

"I'm feeling pretty good, missy. I can feed myself."

She gives him a patient smile. "It's not how we do things around here. Plus, it looks like one of your hands is busy." She picks up the spoon and scoops some eggs.

"I don't want—" He doesn't get a chance to finish his sentence as she slides the bite between his tight, narrow lips. He chews and lets out a hum of satisfaction.

I reach for my fork. Catherine stands quickly, then takes it from my hand. "It's not the way we do things around here, Mr. Oakley."

She shovels the last of the eggs. Before I take the bite, I say, "call me Jason."

"Jason," she whispers. "Jason," she repeats louder.

I take the bite and look at Cowboy. "Why does your senator want me dead?"

Catherine leans back toward Cowboy and scoops another bite of his eggs.

He takes the bite. "I never said he wanted you dead."

"Okay, you're not going to implicate him, I totally understand, but I still don't understand why someone would want me dead instead of simply taking the pendant and going about their business."

Catherine picks up the last bite of toast and puts it in my mouth.

I look at Cowboy, but he's not saying.

"This is not a courtroom here. I just need to know."

"You wrecked his fountain."

"His fountain?" I involuntarily scream the words. "He wants me dead because I wrecked his fountain?"

He nods.

"Do you know how twisted that sound? He wants to end a human life because of some concrete object?"

Cowboy whispers, "Italian marble."

"Oh, excuse me, marble. The thing I can't believe is you were willing to do it. Where is your humanity?"

Cowboy gives me a patriotic smile and salutes. "I'm C.I.A. and I do what my government tells me to do. It's for the good of the country."

I want to get out of my bed and throttle the bastard, but my leg is stiff.

"Do you think murdering me is good for your country?"

Cowboy's salute drops, and he speaks in a mechanical voice. "I'm not paid to think."

"Holy shit," I say. "Is this what it has all gotten to? A bunch of thugs doing the bidding of a completely disconnected human being who thinks a fountain is more important than a human life?"

Cowboy doesn't answer.

I slide the curtain forward so I can no longer see him. I close my eyes and try to calm myself. Eventually I fall asleep.

I must have been out for awhile, because when I awake it's dark. I hear the door slam and lean forward to see Philip and a big bouncer type walking toward me. Philip pushes a wheelchair along the hall. He reaches my bed and opens my curtain back to the wall exposing Cowboy once again. "Have you two met?"

My face prunes. "Yes, Philip, we've met. Now can you pull the curtain back to where it was?"

He grins. "Let's get you out of this bed. Doc wants you to get up and around in time for dinner."

I see his offer as a way to get clear of the depressing

catatonic ward and away from the murdering psychotic in the bed next to me. "My leg is pretty stiff."

"We'll be careful."

Philip helps me to the edge of the bed, then gently onto my one good leg and lowers me to the seat of the chair. A metallic attachment folds out to support my leg in an extended position. Philip slides a pillow under my leg and straps my ankle to the support. "How's that? You comfortable?"

I nod but don't say anything.

He looks at Cowboy. "Doc wants you to come to dinner in the big hall."

"I'm not hungry."

Philip has the key out and looks at the cuffs. "Sorry, doctor's orders. It's for your own good. You're not going to give me any trouble now, are you?"

Cowboy shakes his head. Philip loosens the cuffs. In a surprising move, faster than I could have imagined, Philip swings Cowboy's arm over and attaches the cuff to, of all things, my wheelchair.

"What the hell?" I yell. "I don't want him connected to my chair."

Philip gives me a pinched smile. "Mother Louanne ordered this."

"I don't care if the President ordered it, disconnect him from my chair."

Philip's forehead furrows. "Around here we listen to Mother Louanne. She's got the sight, you know."

Philip slides past my chair and steps out into the aisle. "I expect you'll act like a gentleman and bring Jason to dinner in a few minutes."

Cowboy's his face is twisted into a macabre glare. He starts to speak, but Philip cuts him off. "You two are going to have to figure this one out." He walks toward the door.

Cowboy yells. "But I don't want to do. . ." His voice fades when Philip raises his hand and shakes his index finger. Philip reaches the door and exits the building.

The cuffs jangle behind me, then everything goes quiet. I turn, but because of the position of my leg, I can't rotate enough to see Cowboy head on. He sits at the side of the bed one arm extended to my chair.

After a minute, I say, "I don't know about you, but I'm hungry."

Cowboy doesn't say a word. He stands, puts his hat on, and pushes my chair out to the center of the hall. He directs my chair past two staring nurses. We must look a sight, both of us in hospital gowns and cowboy with his hat.

He blocks the door open and pushes me down the long wheelchair ramp, then asks, "Which way?"

I have nothing to say to him, so I point to our right at the old farmhouse.

Slowly we work our way over rough terrain and up to the porch. A young blonde girl bounds out of the hall to the edge of the porch and points to the right. "There's a ramp around back. Hurry, we're all waiting."

Cowboy pushes me past azaleas and tulips, around the weeping willow, and along a gravel path to the back of the house and up a wheelchair ramp. We're on the porch, and I feel him hesitate. He could push me off and down ten feet to the ground. If I land right, with the weight of the chair on top of me, I'd break my neck for sure, but he doesn't push me over maybe because he'd have to follow me down. He pushes me along the veranda around to the front door. The young girl opens the door, and Cowboy guides me into a packed room with expectant faces. The girl directs us to the end of a table next to Philip. A big bouncer sort stands next to Philip, not in any threatening stance, but simply a presence. Philip unlocks the cuff and transfers Cowboy's hand to the metal chair, then pulls a second set of cuffs up and attaches Cowboy's left hand. Once the cuffs are in place, the bouncer type wanders back to a table behind me. Cowboy lifts his hands to the extent of the cuffs. "How am I supposed to eat?"

Philip smiles. "Jason here is going to feed you."

"What?" I scream much louder than I want.

Philip looks at me. "Mother Louanne."

I want to cuss, but the room is so quiet my one yelled word is enough.

Philip rotates my wheelchair and positions me so I can grab the spoon. I pick it up. The room applauds, then the evening meal is delivered by seven different people than last night.

Cowboy doesn't want to be fed by me as much as I don't want to feed him, but reluctantly, once he sees that everyone else is being fed by a neighbor, he allows into his mouth my first forkful of a lamb stew with new potatoes. His reluctant expression shifts to a surprised awe. His face brightens into a delighted grin. When he's finished chewing and swallows, he looks at me before he takes the next bite. "This is delicious."

"If it's anything like last night's I can believe you."

"I'm serious. I've never tasted anything so good."

He finishes the bite, and I shovel in another.

Ten minutes later my bowl is finished, and I sit in awkward anticipation of being disconnected from the spooky bastard.

Philip finally stands while the rest of the room plays musical chairs. He leads Serenity to our table and sits her down across from Cowboy. He unbuckles the right handcuff and puts both of his hands on the table, leaning low enough to look Cowboy in the eyes. "This is no place to cause trouble. If you even think you are going to be a problem, tell me now."

Cowboy gives him a secret smile. "I just ate the best meal I've had since Trillian began. I still have my job to do, but I promise I won't do anything here."

Philip says, "that's good, Cowboy, because you're going to feed Serenity."

Cowboy's face blanches. He looks at Serenity. He points his finger at her, not in an accusatory manner, but more like a question. "You're Serenity?"

She rolls her eyes. "What? You want to kill me, but you don't even know my name? I can't believe you men. You can't—"

"Serenity." Philip says in a less than friendly tone.

She stops and looks at him. "What?"

"This is a time to be constructive. We are attempting to heal the gap between his thoughts and his heart."

Her angry face relaxes a little while the second bowl of stew is delivered. Philip sits next to Cowboy and feeds me.

The first bite of stew lands in her mouth. Serenity's face relaxes. The rest of the meal is handled in culinary bliss. My taste buds explode with each bite. The bowl is finished much too quickly, and when Philip spoons the last of the juice, I'm full but because it's so good, I want more.

Once the meal is over, the traditional applause fills the room. Even Cowboy gets in on the cheer. For a second his frightening stone face softens. He claps. The lines in his cheeks relax, and he looks ten years younger.

As the second team comes into play to clean up the mess, people stand, talking to one another, and slowly mill toward the front door. In five minutes Serenity, Cowboy, Philip, the bouncer, and I are the only ones left in the big room. Philip grabs my wheelchair and faces me toward the door. I hear the handcuffs ratchet against the metal of my chair. I look back, and Cowboy is standing behind me attached to my chair again.

I look at Philip when he speaks. “Cowboy here is going to get you to your house.”

“Serenity can do it. I don’t like his mannerisms, and I certainly don’t like his eventual intent.”

Philip says, “Cowboy’s pushing you.”

I don’t answer. The wheelchair begins the journey out the door and along the veranda to the ramp.

Once we’re on the gravel drive, with Serenity and Philip in tow, Cowboy pushes me along the path into the darkening sky with not a cloud in sight.

“Sure is a beautiful night,” Philip says as though Cowboy is one of the strollers rather than a cold-blooded murderer. I myself can’t get past the fact that if it hadn’t been for Grayson, both Serenity and I would be dead. I ask Philip, “Where’s Grayson? I didn’t see him at dinner.”

Philip gets a worried expression. “We let him stay with the motorcycle. What happened yesterday sent him deeper into his own little world. I think we’re going to have a job on our hands pulling him out. For now, he’s happy tinkering with his motorcycle.”

“He’s okay, though?”

“Oh sure, he’s physically fine, but we thought the best thing for Grayson is not to see Cowboy right away.”

"Grayson used to be one of the best," Cowboy says.

"The best what?" I speak with an impatient snap to my voice when the wheelchair bogs down in a sandy area. Philip has to help get me through.

We're back on solid ground and Cowboy answers. "The best C.I.A. agent. He could go into a situation and root out the problem, then take care of it without a big mess. He was legendary."

"Take care of it?" Serenity asks. "You mean like kill someone?" Her voice is not accusatory but curious.

Cowboy doesn't answer.

When we reach the three steps of the porch, Cowboy pulls me up without much effort.

We go inside of the house and Philip takes out the keys. "You going to be good?"

Cowboy nods toward our bouncer. "Do I have a choice?"

Philip unlatches one arm from the wheelchair, then re-snaps the cuffs to himself. He unhooks the second set of cuffs and smiles at Cowboy. He throws the keys to me. "Insurance."

Cowboy gives him a pinched smile.

"Let's show you where you're going to sleep."

I'm expecting Philip to turn him toward the front door, but he walks directly for the spare bedroom. "Hold on there," I yell. "Wait just a damn minute."

Philip opens the door. "Mother Louanne."

"I don't think so. He tried to kill me. Do you think I'm going to be able to sleep knowing he's in the next room?"

Philip points into the room. "We had some special bolts installed so he can't leave."

He walks Cowboy into the bedroom, and I follow.

"Look, Philip, locked up or not, I'm not inclined to have a murderer as my guest."

"Mother Louanne wants it this way, and to tell you the truth, I have to agree with her."

I look at two steel hand-wrought eyebolts that pierce the wall on each side of the single bed. Two chrome-plated chains hang from the bolts with a large ring on the end of each. Philip has Cowboy sit on the bed. He snakes the open pair of cuffs around the ring and snaps them closed. He puts out his hand toward me, palm up, and I reluctantly drop the keys in his palm. He has Cowboy lie on the bed, unleashes himself, then snaps the second pair of cuffs to the second chain.

He looks at Cowboy. "We really tried to make you comfortable. Let me know in the morning if the chain is too short, and we'll have someone add some lengths."

Cowboy stretches both arms to his chest. "I've been in worse."

"Good." Philip tosses the keys to me again. "Have him push you to breakfast in the morning."

"Jesus, Philip, how can...?" I don't finish my sentence. I already know everything has been decided. Short of sleeping somewhere else, I'm stuck with this situation.

Philip and Serenity help me get into bed. I'm very tired and fall asleep with Philip and Serenity talking softly on the verandah.

In the morning, the tricky maneuver of reattaching Cowboy to my wheelchair is accomplished with Serenity and Cowboy's help.

My leg is sore, but it feels better than yesterday.

Breakfast is a more casual affair, though the same tradition is practiced of feeding someone else. People wander in and out. If there is an odd person, either one feeds two, or the person waits for a match to arrive.

Although I do so with reluctance, I'm forced to feed Cowboy, who is double locked to a chair. Serenity feeds a young man on the construction crew.

Breakfast is over and the young man steps up to me with an embarrassed nervousness. "You're Jason Oakley, the writer?"

I nod, never sure what to do in these situations.

"I've read all of your books. I'm Jacob Severson." He puts out a tentative hand. I reach up and grab his coarse hand and shake. "Glad to meet you."

Once we release hands, he gets a shy smile. "I was just wondering. . . Well. . . When is your next book coming out?"

It's my turn to be embarrassed. I still have fans and more than my share on the ranch. What do I say? Except for short starts and stops, I haven't sat in front of the computer for more than a year. "It'll be awhile yet, son. Things have slowed way down since Trillian."

"I know," he says. "But in some ways that's not a bad thing."

I smile. "Maybe you have a point."

He gives me a short bow. "I've got to get to work. Thanks for talking to me." He races out the front door.

Philip pulls out the keys. He unlocks one of Cowboy's hands and clips the handcuff to my chair. "How was breakfast?"

I'm distracted and give him a vague answer.

With his right hand latched to my chair and Philip working on the second handcuff, Cowboy says, "You're Jason Oakley? The writer Jason Oakley?"

I look at him. "Trust me, it ain't no big deal."

His expression shifts. He gets a gleeful grin. His

straight, movie star teeth show for the first time, but his face is pale, like he's seen a ghost. "You're the writer?"

He's asked the question one too many times. He's starting to get obnoxious. "Yes, I'm the writer."

"Baker's Corner?"

"Yes, Baker's Corner."

Philip has yet to make the final reconnect of Cowboy to my chair. "I almost killed you. Hey, Baker's Corner was the best book I ever read and, shit, I almost killed the best living writer I know. I feel like John Wilkes Booth and Lincoln. I feel like a traitor."

I'm not sure if I thank him for his compliment or for not killing me. I'm already anticipating the battery of questions almost everyone asks, especially about Baker's Corner. "What happened to Penny, the waitress? Where did the horse go? Whose car went over the cliff into the Dead Sea?"

These are all questions I get asked a lot that I have no answers for. I'm just the writer; I have no idea why things happen in my books, nor do I know anything beyond the story itself. People act as if it was a story about me.

With his free hand, Cowboy rubs from his forehead to his chin twice. I already see the question forming. "How do you write?"

"What?"

"How do you come up with all of your great ideas?"

I've never had the question put to me in such a strange way. My pat answer is not there. I flounder for five seconds trying to find an answer. Why couldn't he just ask about Penny or the horse like everyone else?

"I just write. I don't know where it comes from."

His face has a curious expression, like he's waiting for the formula. "I mean, how does everything fit in your brain to come out that way?"

"I don't understand."

"Like there's a sequence of events your brain already knows about?"

It's my turn to be nervous. "I don't know. I simply sit down every day, and a few hours later something is typed on the computer screen. Often I have no idea what I wrote. All I know is what I want the next scene to look like."

"I almost killed you," he whispers. I see the pain in his face. "I didn't even know who you were."

"So, you're not going to try to kill me again?"

"Well, I don't know. It is my job."

"Jesus Christ," I scream.

He gets a big grin. "I was just kidding. It's an old C.I.A. joke."

I let out a breath I think I've been holding since he drove through the field the other day and blasted his way into my house.

"So you're not going to kill me?"

He gives me a serious expression. "You're Jason Oakley. In my book, you're a national treasure. I should be protecting you."

In a mousy voice even I can't believe, I ask again. "You're not going to kill me?"

"No!" His voice is forceful and firm.

I lean back in my chair, and a flush of relief wells up in my throat. I choke on relief and start to cry. I'm embarrassed.

Cowboy puts his hand on my shoulder and says, "Hey, Mr. Oakley, I am sorry for all of this."

He uses my surname out of respect, and my tears turn to full-blown bawling.

At this second, I feel the first tinge of flu symptoms but I ignore them. I concentrate on the relief.

I calm to sniffles. Philip takes Cowboy's free hand and snaps the cuffs in place on the far side of the handlebars. "You're still on probation. You act like a gentleman, and maybe in a week or two, if you want, you can either leave or become a member of our community. We could use a good security person to keep out people like you."

Cowboy laughs.

"For now, Jason is in your charge. By the looks of him, he's ready to go into the first stage, so you're going to have a lot on your hands during the next week."

As if timed with Philip's last word, my breakfast comes up and spews out over the table and onto the floor. If it weren't such a common experience these days I'd be embarrassed, but we've all been there, and it is the first sign of what is to come for the next ten days.

"I don't feel good," I say.

One of the attendants comes out with a wet towel, a dustpan and bucket of water.

I look at him when he begins the job of cleaning the mess up. "Sorry, kid."

"No problem, Mr. Oakley, we do it all the time."

"I guess you're right. Sorry anyhow."

He stops shoveling the mess into the dustpan and smiles. "No big deal."

Philip puts a hand on my forehead and speaks to Cowboy. "This guy is burning up. I say we get him to the ward."

Cowboy moves me toward the front of the building. Serenity rushes ahead and opens the door as Cowboy pushes me through and to the wheelchair ramp, then along the gravel driveway.

"I don't feel good." It's all I can say.

Serenity and Philip get me to a hospital bed and lying flat. My head is swimming. I don't know which part I hate most, this first part when I'm sick or when I go away and come back five days later.

While Philip reconnects Cowboy to the pipe with one handcuff, my mind drifts back to Sam and the first days, bringing the scourge of humanity back from the jungle.

I tried to talk Sam out of removing the gold chain from the ancient bones of the corpse, but I couldn't persuade him.

We almost died during our first Trillian journey on the boat and woke up a number of times over the next few weeks while working our way back to America, always ending up with dead people around us.

I recall the ship, the long walk up the beach of Costa Rica, seeing the village far to the north, and how we didn't have the energy to make the journey. I remember my first puke onto the sand, a warning that Trillian was about to take over for the third time since Sam had found the fucking pendant and how that idiot was so taken by the gold and its possible riches.

We awoke the next morning in a small grass hut. I was lying on a mat on soft sand. I looked out the small opening as a young woman bent to enter, her chocolate breasts showed as her body contorted to fit into the hut. She carried two bowls. I hadn't seen a nearly-naked woman during the entire six weeks we'd been gone. Normally my attention would have been piqued, but in my sickness all I could do was give her a glance before my energy ran out, and my head dropped onto the velvety fur of some dead jungle animal.

She spoke in a soft voice, but I didn't recognize the dialect, then she sat cross-legged, her full womaness exposed under the short grass skirt. Dark fur covered most of her triangle of love, but a hint of her pink lips peeked out. I wanted to look more carefully but I had no energy. She sat in front of me and spooned a fishy soup to my weak lips. I tried to take in the soup but succeeded in lapping up a tenth of what she offered. The rest spilled onto the grass mat.

I looked at Sam. Other than a slight wheeze during his exhale, he looked dead.

The vision of the young woman sitting fully exposed carried me into the darkness, a darkness I was getting used to.

When I awoke, Sam was up and grinning. "I don't know what the fuck is going on, Jason, but I feel great. The entire village is sick, but I feel great."

I sat up. "I'm hungry and thirsty."

He handed me a gourd of liquid. "It was hanging on one of the huts. It's a little stronger than water, but it tastes pretty good."

I put the gourd to my lips and took a drink of a slightly bitter liquid with an alcohol bite.

Sam handed me a thin slab of jerky. "Found this meat on the drying racks."

"You just took it?"

He got a sheepish grin. "Well, everyone in this village is sick. There was no one around to ask, plus I can't understand them."

"It's the pendant, Sam."

"Jesus, Jason, how many times have we been over this? The pendant has nothing to do with anything."

He was right, we'd talked about it too many times. I

was not going to dissuade him, so what was the use?

I changed the subject. "It looks like we have five days before the sickness returns. I suggest we get going."

A man who didn't have a clue about direction, Sam asked, "You got any idea which way?"

"I'd say continue north up the beach until we find some kind of civilization."

Sam said, "I packed some of the jerky, and I got an extra gourd of the booze. I'm ready to go when you are."

I took a small bite of the tough meat. "I still need water."

Sam got to his feet. "Back in a minute."

When he returned he carried a fat skin that looked like the stomach of an animal. He handed it to me, and I pointed the spout at my mouth. The water had an odd, metallic taste, but it was water, and I drank the entire bag.

With the village down sick, not knowing most of them were destined to die, Sam and I left a twenty for the food and walked north up the never-ending beach. With nothing but the remains of the jerky and coconuts, we trudged on for two days, until we came around a bend and saw our first sign of civilization. It was a thirty-foot-tall sign in Spanish, painted high on a cliff directly on the stone, declaring the beach as private. It wasn't exactly the greeting I was looking for, but it did indicate that we were close. By evening, we stumbled into a small port village at the mouth of a wide river with a much larger city on the opposite shore.

After a day of somber non-communication, Sam looked gleeful. Our pace picked up when we stepped off the beach and walked into town. Sam slapped me on the back. "I say we get a room, get cleaned up, eat, and find a way out of here in the morning."

"A room sounds great. A shower sounds unbelievable, but we don't have much money."

He reached in his pocket and pulled out a wad of cash. "Found this on one of the dead sailors on the ship."

I shook my head.

We ran across a small bakery, got a skinny loaf of bread and feasted on it. We booked a room in a small hotel.

A little Mayan-looking man with high cheekbones, beady solid black eyes, and working hands was able to communicate with us in Sam's serviceable Spanish. He gave us a room with twin beds overlooking the coast. I'd spent so much time on that particular coast I didn't want to look at it another minute.

I dropped onto the bed. Neither Sam nor I awoke until late the next morning when a large shipping vessel blew its horn.

My eyes flew open. I sat up not knowing where I was. Sam snored in the bed next to me. I stood, walked into the bathroom, and puked in the sink. It was the first sign of that sickness coming to haunt me again.

An hour later, Sam raced for the bathroom in a repeat performance, and we spent the rest of the day prone.

Later that night, Sam was able to make his way to the front desk and order food and hire someone to attend to us. I remembered little for the next few days, and the world went black for what seemed like forever.

When I awoke, Sam was putting on freshly pressed pants, a perfumed T-shirt, and new socks. He looked at me with a grin. "I feel like a million bucks. Whatcha say we go find something to eat, then get the hell out of this town and go home?"

I took a shower, brushed my hair and slipped on my worn hiking boots. "Maybe we can take a taxi across the river, get a flight to a bigger city, then take a jet home. Sound about right to you?"

Sam bent down. "We still have to get passports and more money. I'm down to a few bucks." Sam tied his boots. "I'm tired of the tropics." He hoisted his little knapsack. "I don't know about you, but I'm starved."

We walked along the concrete stairs, made our way to the center of town, and found a small restaurant that was almost empty. I ordered something with eggs.

While we waited for the order to arrive, Sam called a taxi from the city, and in a half hour the cab whisked us over the steel bridge and into the city, where we spent the day going from one line to another until we had passports once again. The final cab took us to the airport north of town.

When we got out, Sam said, "I want a commercial flight with comfortable seats. No more drug runners, because I'm not ending up crashed in the jungle again."

Getting a flight to San Jose, Costa Rica, took a few hours of waiting and paying an outrageous amount of money. I thanked my lucky stars that one of my credit cards was attached to my key ring. It was a smaller version but it worked. By nightfall we stood on the tarmac of San Jose, Costa Rica. I wanted it to be San Jose, California.

By the next morning, rather than wait three days for the only flight to America, we jumped on a commercial flight that hopped up the coast of Costa Rica to Cartago, Quezaltenango, Guatemala, moving one fly-by-night airport at a time, ever closer to our destination.

We landed in the Mexican town of Puerto Vallarta, and were fed through a random check system. Sam was forced to empty his pockets, remove all his jewelry, and had his bags searched. It had to happen eventually, but Mexico was not the place.

In ten minutes, a young Mexican soldier with a large-caliber weapon pointed his gun at Sam and led him into a back room. I stood helpless as the door closed.

Twenty minutes later, Sam walked out of the room with a scowl on his face. "They got the pendant."

"Well, of course they got the pendant, Sam. It wasn't yours in the first place."

He sat next to me in an uncomfortable airport seat. "But they just took it. The captain put it in his pocket and acted like nothing happened."

I patted his shoulder. "Good riddance. That pendant was nothing but bad luck from the moment you found it."

Sam wasn't listening. He was already scheming a way to get the pendant back.

I snapped my fingers. "Sam, stop worrying about that pendant. We've got a plane to catch."

He had a determined glare. "I ain't going anywhere. That captain's not getting it."

"Sam, I don't know if you've noticed, but they've got guns, and I don't think they have any qualms about using them. At the very least you'll end up in some Mexican jail."

Sam wasn't listening.

I grabbed him by the shoulder. Although his eyes were looking in my direction, his focus was twenty yards due south, behind the cheap wooden door.

I shook him harder. "Sam."

His gaze broke. "I'm getting it back."

I dropped my hands from his shoulder. "Fuck, Sam,

I can't believe you're serious. Even if you succeed in getting that thing back, do you think for one minute they'll let you get on the plane?"

"I'm not getting on the plane."

I stood quickly and grabbed my bag. "If you don't get on with me now, you're on your own, because I'm out of here."

I hoped he would stand with me and traipse to the far end of the airport where the passengers were boarding, but he said, "I'm staying."

"Sam, what the fuck do you think you're doing?"

"Getting my property back."

"You idiot, I'm not hanging around for this. If you want to get yourself arrested, then go right ahead. I'm getting on the plane with or without you."

He looked at me with his familiar stare of resolve. "I'm getting my pendant, then I'll go."

I shook my head and walked toward the tarmac.

Maybe I should have tried harder. Maybe I should have stayed. I got on the plane, always expecting he'd come to his senses at the last second. The plane doors closed and it taxied to the runway. I wanted to get off, find him and kidnap him, but it was too late.

The plane rocketed into the air, and by noon the next day I was in Los Angeles. I'd been gone almost two months.

My eyes open to see the starched white sheets of the hospital bed. Cowboy sits in a chair next to my bed, one arm handcuffed to the pipe against the wall.

"How are you doing, Mr. Oakley?"

"Call me Jason."

He gives a smile. "I never saw just how close a person

comes to death. I mean, I've certainly been there so many times I can't count, but I've never seen it in anyone else."

My mouth is dry and it's hard to speak. "Can I have some water?"

Cowboy pours a glass from a clear plastic pitcher and hands it to me, then sits hard on his chair. His face looks pale. "Guess I'm getting sick again. Last night it started. Damn, I hate this flu."

I drain the glass and hand it back for more. "How did you get away with never attending anyone?"

"C.I.A. has its perks. They always had someone to take care of me."

"And you never had to take care of anyone else?"

"Not until the last ten days."

"Man, no wonder you're so spooky."

He looks hurt, but doesn't say anything. He changes the subject. "They say the pendant is the key to finding a cure to this cursed sickness."

I drain the second glass. "Looks to me like you need to get prone. You're looking pretty green around the gills."

He rattles the cuffs. "I can't reach the bed. Philip got sidetracked with some emergency this morning, and I haven't seen him all day."

"Did you get fed?"

He looks like he's ready to puke with the mention of food. "Couldn't eat if I did. I just want to lie down."

Although I'm still a little weak in the knees, I slide out of bed and, in bare feet, push his bed around sideways almost pinning him to the wall. "Climb aboard, and I'll get you comfortable."

He sits on the side of the bed and removes his boots, then lies flat with his arm extended to the water pipe. I push the bed in next to the wall. Cowboy drops into a deep sleep almost immediately.

A young man with short-cropped hair opens the door, steps into the long hall and slowly works his way toward us, checking on each catatonic or, like Cowboy, each second-stage patient. He looks at the rotated bed. "How are you doing, Mr. Oakley?"

"Oh, I'm fine, but I think our prisoner needs his cuffs removed. Is Philip around?"

The kid, with his pimply face and his little red goatee, looks at Cowboy. "When I'm finished with my rounds I'll go find Philip. I'll be about fifteen minutes."

"I gather he's real busy today. Maybe you can get the keys to these cuffs."

"No problem, Mr. Oakley. Give me a few minutes to finish."

The kid continues checking the remaining fifty or sixty patients. I lie back on my bed. I feel much better, but Trillian always leaves me weak for a few hours once it goes into remission.

Fifteen minutes later, the kid disappears, then returns holding the keys up like some trophy fish. "Philip said to be careful with the Cowboy."

"I think we'll have to be careful with him in ten days. For now, the guy is down for the count."

The kid looks at Cowboy, who is the common color of a Trillian victim. "I guess you can't fake the green color, can you?"

I shrug.

He hands me the keys, and I unlock Cowboy's cuff. His arm drops limp onto the bed, and I pull it around to a comfortable position. "Help me push this bed back."

The kid grabs the rail and pulls the bed into its

regular position, then picks up the chart at the end of the bed. He pulls a pen from his pocket and places a few marks on the chart, then looks up at me. "We mark what day he goes down so we know when he'll wake up."

"So you can put the cuffs back on?"

"More so we can have someone here to feed him and give him some water, but in this case, the cuffs would probably be a good idea too."

"I'm hungry."

He gives me a pinched grimace. "We had Cowboy care for you while you were down but we now need the bed. Can I get someone to bring you something to eat at your house?"

"That would be nice."

The kid walks to the door, opens it and disappears.

I get dressed and work my way back to the cabin. No one is home, so I sit at my desk and stare out the window.

Fifteen minutes later a knock comes at the front door. I yell to come in. A dark-haired teenager walks in with a platter, sets it on the desk beside my computer and removes the metal dome to reveal scrambled eggs with two pieces of toast.

I pick up the spoon. He smiles and takes the spoon from me, then dips for a bite of a white pudding. The food is great. I taste some hidden spice in the eggs that makes them exotic. The bread is freshly baked and the jam is peach. I'm sure it was harvested and preserved from this property last summer.

I eat slowly and when I'm done, I feel better.

He packs the dishes and walks to the door. Before he opens it, he asks, "You wrote Baker's Corner?"

"That's me, though I wrote other books too."

The kid shakes his head. "I know, I read the others

too, but Baker's Corner changed the way I think. I know you wrote it five years before Trillian, but how did you know what was going to happen?"

"I didn't know. I was just writing a story."

He grabs the knob of the door. "It was a good book. I hope you got something else coming." He closes the door behind him.

I want to say I don't have anything else because I haven't been writing, but he's gone before I can answer.

I notice my laptop for the first time. It's plugged in and waiting. I open the lid and turn it on.

When the screen becomes active, I open my files, and six unfinished novels stare at me. Except for the short bout a few days ago, I haven't looked at them in two years, not since I got the package from Sam. Why did I stop?

I click the file Flat Rock Mountain, and my very first attempt at a goofy story opens. I scroll down to page seventy-seven, and there it is, the last word I wrote. We lived in a different world when I typed those last few letters: Sam and I were planning on going to Brazil. We all lived in a world of abundance: food, movies, green lawns, barbecues, book signings, concerts, hobnobbing with the elite, limos. I had no worries once Baker's Corner came out. I'd made the big time, and the world was in my back pocket. I could do no wrong. I saw my world from the point of view of my next book because I had become a commodity. I was in demand, and price was not an issue. Hollywood was working on making a movie out of Baker's Corner. I had already banked my check for two million from the movie rights alone. After twenty years of abject poverty, I was living on easy street. Then I went to Brazil and the whole thing came crumbling down on me like a house of cards.

I look at the last word, and many memories of the good life flood in. I'd made it, only to cause the entire world to collapse around me.

Before the banks crashed, I was able to pull out a pittance of the cash, and I've been living on that for two years.

I look at the last word I typed two years ago and don't even recognize the thought. I have to spell it out letter for letter before I can pronounce it: "Home." I read the whole sentence. "Sundog walked in the dark to Billy's home." It looks like a complete sentence, but I'll be damned if I can figure out where I was going. I go back a half page and read the incomplete sentences, misspelled words, incorrect grammar, skipping over the incomprehensible parts of a first draft. I reach the end at the word "Home," and I type a new word tentatively, "again," then put a period. It's frightening to end a sentence so soon after so long, but I do, and I wait for the next sentence to emerge. When it does, I type in the next sentence in a slow, methodical manner, strike the period, and look at the line with wonder. I type the next sentence, then the next, and in a few moments my hands are flying over the keyboard. I don't know where I'm going, just trusting that I'll get there.

In a half hour, the computer screen flips over to page seventy-eight. I continue.

Serenity steps into my room as my mind becomes muddled from seeing too many keystrokes, too many words on the screen. I look at the page count at the bottom of the screen, and I'm on page eighty-four. Not bad for a first time back in the saddle.

"Jason?" she asks.

I look up.

She's smiling. "What are you doing?"

"Writing."

Her grin widens into the goofy face that I've become accustomed to. "Like, writing a book?"

I nod and close the screen. The computer gives a little beep, then goes silent.

"Jason, that's great. I was hoping you'd start again. I mean, you're such a great writer and all, it's such a waste." She steps around behind me and puts her hands on my shoulders. "Can I read some of it?"

"Sorry, I don't show anyone raw work. I have to edit the mess a few times before it's presentable."

"Okay," she says. I feel her disappointment.

"Nothing personal, Serenity. The way I write is so sloppy, you wouldn't be able to read it if you wanted to. You'd get bogged down on the first sentence with some unrecognizably misspelled word that would change the entire meaning of the sentence. I understand it because I know where I'm going, but you would be lost."

"Maybe you could edit it real quick."

I look at her. "I never edit until I've finished writing the entire piece. If I'd written a five-page vignette, then I'd love to go back and retrace it, but so far I'm on page eight-five, and I know it'll be much longer."

Her face has a disappointed look but she manages to crack a smile. "Okay."

I take both of her hands in mine. "There are parts I feel so good about I want to share them, but today's session was a warm-up. It's okay, but nothing real exciting."

"Does it feel good to be back?"

"Oh, yes. I had a hard time getting started again, but

once I was going, I felt great."

"I'm glad for you, and I think your fans will be glad too."

I still have her hands, and I squeeze. "Serenity, for now you can't tell anyone I'm writing again. It's still not real. I'm so new and raw that too much outside pressure could stop me."

She shakes her head. "Never thought I'd be around the creative types, I always attracted construction workers. Don't get me wrong, I like your approach to life, but you creative types are a sensitive lot."

"Writing is a sensitive process. If even one of my little foibles is tweaked in the slightest, my editor stuff kicks in and says I'm really no good, and who am I trying to fool?"

She steps back a few feet, pulls out a folding chair, and sits facing me. "I don't understand. You're such a great writer. How could you ever think such a thing?"

I point at my chest. "In here I don't think I'm that good. If I keep trying, I may be acceptable someday, but I am far from good."

"Really?"

"Yes, really. A part of me would give the whole thing up for that reason alone. It just may be the part that stopped me from my writing these last two years. That, and feeling so guilty for trashing civilization."

She takes my hands. "You didn't bring the pendant back, Sam did."

My face drops. I fight the depression just millimeters under my skin. "I didn't do anything to stop him."

"You did plenty."

"But not nearly enough." My tears break cover and one rolls down my cheek. I try to mop it before Serenity notices, but more follow, and too soon I'm into a full-blown cry.

She stands, leans in close to hug me, but I fend her off. "No, not now."

Through the waterworks, I see her confused face. She sits back down and folds her hands in front of her.

Crying for me never gets louder than a few whimpers with a lot of choked up snorting and sniffling, but it's more than I've done in a long time. Although I'm anxious while I'm crying, once I'm finished, I feel better.

Serenity has found some tissues and hands me two. I take them and blow my nose. "I feel like the cause of the whole thing and I don't know what to do."

Women are intuitive during these times. Another guy would try to talk me out of my feelings by giving me a hundred reasons why I wasn't the cause. Hell, I'd do the same thing in this case, but Serenity simply sits looking at me with big brown eyes. I lament being the cause of Trillian and how much weight that sentence carries. When I'm finished, she gives me a motherly look.

I break all my rules and read a short piece from what I just wrote. When I'm finished, I look at her. "It wasn't a great piece of writing, but I'm a bit rusty."

She shakes her head, I believe because she agrees maybe a little too much. "Jason, what you just wrote, raw as it is far exceeds most of the garbage out there, including the big writers."

I don't know how my mind twists people's words. Maybe I can't hear praise, or I don't want to hear the good people say about me, but I'm thinking she said I wrote garbage, and the funny part is I agree.

"It needs a lot of cleaning up." I'm not defending myself, more like giving her a reason why I'm wasting my time with the written word.

She leans down and looks up into my downcast eyes. “Jason, I don’t think you heard me.”

I look at her. “I heard you all right, but once the structure is cleaned up, it’ll be better.”

She shakes her head. “I didn’t say that.”

I’m still looking at her face expecting that she maybe meant to emphasize the word “garbage”. I’m ready to get a little angry that she can’t at least be a little more supportive, but I hold my tongue and wait for the ax to fall.

She smiles and articulates the next sentence slowly with lots of clear emphasis on each word: “I said your writing today is better than most of the garbage out there.”

The only words I hear are, “garbage out there”. “Yes, I know, but I can clean it up.”

She slides her chair forward enough to grab my hands. “Listen carefully, Jason. I want you to hear my sentence.” She repeats the same sentence three times before I hear the word “better,” but I don’t believe her. I finally put the entire sentence together and actually hear that she is paying me a compliment. My first thought is she is trying to bolster my fragile little writer ego. With stumbling disconnected words, I tell her she doesn’t have to be nice.

Her face gets a little red. She lets go of my hands, reaches up, and lifts my chin so I have to look her in the eyes again. “Jason, your writing is great.”

I don’t know why I’m feeling so raw this morning. I don’t know how this woman keeps bringing my rawness out, but when I hear her for the first time and I’m actually able to take the words in, I drop my face into my hands and burst into tears, no pansy-assed whimpering and sniveling this time. I burst into a full-out bawling cry, tears running down my face, nose dripping, running out of air because I forget to breathe, and I go for five forever minutes. She's holding my hands, sitting close, but doesn't try to come closer. If she did, I'd push her away. How are women so intuitive?

When I can speak, and it takes awhile after I stop crying, I look at her through bleary eyes. "I. . . I thought you said. . ."

"I didn't," she says. "I said you are great."

I could easily leap headlong back into another crying jag, but my body feels purged, and I don't have any more tears in me. I take a deep breath. "I never felt like all of the honors for Baker's Corner were warranted. It's such a trite piece of writing."

She squeezes my hands. "It was a great piece of writing. You were able to tap into the future. I don't know how you did it, but you wrote about what was going to happen, like you already knew Trillian was coming."

"Or did I create Trillian? God, the question boggles the mind."

The front stairs make the creaking sound of someone approaching; the sound of heavy boots clump onto the deck and take two steps to the front door. The screen opens and two short, soft knocks sound through the house. I turn to Serenity. "You get it. I'm not ready for company."

She stands and leaves my office.

As the computer screen goes dark for the second time today on my first day back in the saddle, I hear her high-pitched voice in a friendly tone, then a deep male voice as the door opens and closes. Boots clump across the floor. A chair slides across the floor. I hear the clinking of the teapot. Water is being drawn from the faucet.

I stand, go to the bathroom, and toss some water in my face. I look in the mirror. My face is still red and flushed. My eyes look like I'm hung over. The water helps, but not much.

I take a breath, step out of the bathroom, open the office door, and walk along the short hall to the kitchen. My leg is still stiff, but it feels much better. "Grayson, how are you doing, buddy?"

He has a worried look. "Oh, I'm okay, I guess."

The teakettle whistles. Serenity gets up. "You want tea, Jason?"

"Sure." I look at Grayson. "What's up?"

Grayson's face gets a concerned frown. "Oh, I was just worried about Cowboy. I went to the ward to visit him, and he's still out. I must have thrown the rock a little too hard."

I laugh. I can't believe how easy it is to laugh after all of that crying. "No, good buddy, he's just fine. He went down with the flu."

"Then it's not because I hit him with the rock? I had no choice, you know. I could have found a smaller rock but there wasn't time."

"Hey, you hit him with a rock that was just the right size."

Grayson's furrowed brow smooths a bit. His little-boy face turns to more of a man. He gives me a tentative smile. "I guess I was worried I'd hurt him maybe a little too much."

I point at Serenity and myself. "Grayson, you saved our lives, that's the very first thing to consider. Cowboy was hell-bent on killing us. The second thing is he was up and about for three days. You weren't around, but Philip locked him to my wheelchair and forced him to push me around for two days before he got sick."

Grayson's face brightens. "Pushed you around? I'll bet he hated that."

I snort. "At first he hated it, but once he realized I wrote his favorite book, he had a change of heart."

Serenity pours each of us a cup of tea.

We sit in silence until Grayson turns to her. "I've been busy with my motorcycle, and I guess I've kind of neglected you."

A grin spreads across her face. "Oh, don't you worry about that, Grayson. I've been kind of worried about you these last few days. I've got so much to do now that we are all working together on this farm."

"I just didn't want you to think I was ignoring you."

She stands, puts her arms around him, and kisses his three-day-old bearded cheek. "I never thought for one minute that you were ignoring me, Grayson."

He blushes when she smooches his cheek longer than necessary. Even I'd feel a little nervous.

She sits, then picks up her tea and takes a sip. The room drops into a comfortable silence.

Eventually, I ask, "So, how's the bike coming?"

His face is embarrassed again. He fiddles with his spoon. "Tell you the truth, Jason, I don't know anything about bikes. I'd like to get that one running, but I wouldn't know a tire from a tank. The last few days I've been thinking. I realize that fiddling with the bike all this last year has been something to keep me from being frightened. I was alone a long time before Billy showed up. Once he left, I was more nervous, you know. I had to get used to being by myself again. That was the hardest."

I say, "It's hard to feel alone here."

His grin widens. "Being here is like being in a candy store of humanity. I love being around all these people, and all of them are so nice. Dr. Jeffries has been talking to me these last few days, and I've been remembering things about my past. Cowboy is a part of my past, though I still don't know how. I had a wife but she died during the first wave of the flu. I don't remember much before."

Serenity leans forward and puts her hand on his arm. "Things like that come in small amounts. If you want to remember, keep at it, and eventually everything will come back."

"I want to remember." He gets a pained look. "I miss my wife."

Serenity squeezes.

Grayson looks at her. "Did you have a husband?"

"Yes, and now he's gone. I think it's why everyone out in the world seems like the walking dead."

"Why's that?" I ask.

"Because we all have someone close we're mourning, and yet there's no room to mourn because everyone is trying to survive. Maybe here there will be enough time and support."

"Oh, right." Grayson perks up after a half minute of silent introspection. "I almost forgot; Philip wants to see you, Jason. He's at the stables." Grayson points to the eastern end of the lake.

"What does he want?"

"I don't know. I was walking over here. He poked his head out of the barn and told me to get you."

"He wants me right now?"

"He didn't say, but he acted like it was important."

I stand and walk toward the door.

Serenity asks, "You going to walk on your hurt leg?"

I open the door. "My leg is still stiff, but Doc says exercise is good. I'll take a short walk around the lake."

She has a concerned look. "Jason, you just got shot."

I let the screen door close and walk to the edge of the porch. "The steps are the hardest," I say over my back. "I'll be all right once I'm on level ground."

Leaning heavily on the rail, I navigate the three steps, land on the earth, and follow the far left of the three beaten paths leading away from our little house. In a minute the lake comes into view. Although I'm walking downhill I feel exhausted already, so once I'm out of sight of Serenity, who I know is standing on the porch watching, I find a small park bench under a peach tree and sit for a moment. One would think that a bullet wound that left so little damage wouldn't cause such problems with stamina.

After a five-minute rest, I take the next leg of my journey to the shore of the pond, then follow the small path. By the time I've reached the barn I've rested twice.

I walk into the sweet smell of hay and horse manure. "Philip?"

His voice comes from the far end of the barn. "In here, Jason." I work my way past an old tractor with a big hay rake. The walls are filled with horse saddles, blankets, shoeing equipment, and ropes in large and small coils. I walk by each stall, and a horse pokes its head through the half-door to greet me. I've never been much of a horse person, so I ignore them and find my way back to the far right stall.

When I look in the stall, Philip is on his knees

attending to a large horse lying on its side. He has his head next to the horse's belly, listening for something. He speaks to the young man stroking the horse's head. "She ate something, and she's bloated. Let's keep an eye on her, but I think she'll be all right by tomorrow."

I ask, "You wanted to talk to me?"

Philip stands, dusts off his hands and knees, motions for me to follow, and walks me out of the stall, then through the back door of the barn. "Let's go to the edge of the lake where we can be private."

A hundred paces later we stand on the edge of the pond. A fish leaps out of the water, snaps an insect, then plops back into the lake, breaking the calm surface with ringlets of waves.

Philip says, "Doc Jeffries has been seeing Grayson."

"Grayson told me."

"In the few days you've been here, Grayson is acting a little more put together. I'm not sure if it's the visits to Jeffries or simply being around people who aren't so caught up in trying to survive."

I pick up a flat rock the size of a silver dollar, lean low to the water's edge, and skip the rock across the quiet surface. The rock bounces on the water ten or fifteen times before it finally sinks.

Philip grins and picks up his own rock. "Not bad, but you're dealing with a pro."

He swings his arm in a long arc and lets the rock loose a few inches from the water. It leaps out, takes the first skip, goes airborne again for three or four yards, kisses the water, and leaps into the air. On the third contact with the water the rock is twenty yards out as it continues to spiral and skip. I try to count skips as I did when I was a kid, but the rock ends its journey by spinning on top of the water like a Frisbee, maintaining momentum and pushing water ahead like a little motorboat. When the stone finally drops below the surface, both Philip and I look at one another. I yell, "Wow, you're good!"

His face is flushed with the innocent look of a ten-year-old. He laughs and points at the remaining ripples from the rock. "I never did one that good before."

I scrounge around the shore for another flat rock and both of us are back in our youth, to the innocent days, making a contest of the simple act of throwing rocks into calm water.

We toss five or six rocks each before Philip says, "You know, Doc Jeffries is a hypnotherapist."

"No kidding. You want me to get hypnotherapy or something?"

He snickers. "No. Doc's been working with Grayson. Jeffries put Grayson under the other day while you were in the third stage."

"Just spit it out, Philip. I'm not going to bite."

He stammers. "Well. . . Grayson is. . . or was, C.I.A."

"Yes, I pretty much guessed. He knew Cowboy, and he handled himself a little too well at the post office last week."

"What came out in the session was that Grayson was in an experiment without his knowledge."

I pick up another flat rock, toss it into the air like flipping a coin and catch it. "I wouldn't put anything past those spooky bastards to experiment on their own."

Philip puts his hand on my shoulder like he's going to steady me. "Grayson doesn't have a natural immunity to Trillian. He was inoculated."

"No shit."

"It came out in the therapy session, but you can't tell

anyone yet, especially Grayson."

"Why not?"

"Doc Jeffries says Grayson might wig out if he finds out the information before unraveling the mess inside his head. I guess something went wrong and Grayson either lost his memory because of the drug, or the C.I.A. gave him something to erase his memory. From what I gather, he escaped and ended up in the abandoned Harley shop. Either way, Doc says it's going to be some time before Grayson regains enough conscious memory to handle such a revelation."

I toss the rock into the water, not skipping it, but simply to get rid of it. "Why tell me?"

Philip guides me away from the pond. "Let's work our way to the main house. I've got a meeting in ten minutes, and I don't want to be late."

We walk along the water's edge. "You and Serenity have taken Grayson under your wing. We decided to tell you so the two of you could kind of keep an eye on him. Once he emerges from the fog, he may have some kind of emotional upheaval. Can you to take him in and have him live with you in the extra bedroom."

"Sure, Philip, but what do we look for?"

"Doc wants to talk to you. Better that it comes from him. I don't know much psychology stuff."

We round the far eastern end of the lake and start toward the main house. My leg is getting tired, and I notice myself limping, but I have one more question. "What the hell is this thing with Cowboy?"

He looks down at my limp. "Let's rest on this tree stump." He points ten yards away from the trail.

I hobble over and sit. "What about Cowboy?"

"Doc thought, and I agree, that one way to shift

Cowboy's it's-my-job-to-kill-people attitude is to have him spend time with his intended victim. You were perfect because not only are you a regular sort of guy, but now he sees you as his favorite author. The more he gets to know you, the less he's likely to want to kill you, or Serenity."

"So you want me to make him my buddy?"

"Buddies? I don't think so, but we're going to want you to spend time with him for another week or so."

"A week?"

"Until he gets what we're trying to do here."

I cross my wounded leg over my good one massaging the muscles around the soreness. "What are you trying to do anyhow?"

"I don't have time for specifics, but what's happening on the farm is the result of looking at Trillian as a gift."

"A gift? Half of earth's population was extinguished. How could you possibly see that as a gift?"

Philip takes a breath and lets it out. "I know you feel guilty for bringing this to the world, but weren't we running slightly amuck? Weren't we focusing a little too much on the individual and not so much on community? At the turn of the twenty-first century, wasn't it pretty much an every-man-for-himself philosophy?"

"Killing half the population is a gift?"

"The death of half of humanity isn't the gift part. That was a tragic situation, and if someone hadn't figured out how to team up, we all probably would have died. We learned to count on our neighbors."

"How do you see the gift?"

Philip looks at his watch and points toward the main building. "I've got that meeting in two minutes. If you're rested we can walk together. If not, I'll continue this conversation this evening after dinner."

I stand. "I'm rested enough."

We step to the path. Philip walks shoulder to shoulder with me along the wider part of the path. "The gift is, though Trillian caused so much pain and misery, it forced us to reach out to one another and to keep reaching out. Once we found this farm we simply accentuated the process. We thought if we are community animals, and I think we are, then we needed to break the individualistic conditioning."

"Is that where the narrow tables come in?"

"One of many changes we all decided to make. The key here is we all decide together. There are no leaders nor governing bodies to corrupt."

"You all get together in a big room and battle out the pros and cons of a subject until you reach a vote?"

Chapter 17

Consensus

"We tried that but it was too much like the old way, which could be easily corrupted. We tried unanimous decision making, but it took forever to come to any decision."

"What's left?"

"The Quaker's method of decision making."

I shrug.

"We sit in a circle and one at a time people throw out ideas to solve the dilemma until someone says the right thing. When everyone's head nods, the circle knows they've found the right answer."

We round the last few yards of the pond and make a diagonal trek toward the front porch.

"How can that work?"

"I don't know how it works but it does, and it's pretty painless."

"It can't work every time."

"When it doesn't, and that is seldom, either Mother Louanne steps in or we default to unanimous voting."

We reach the stairs and Philip says, "a meeting is starting right now. You want to join in?"

"Do I have to speak?"

"Decide to be a member, then you can. For right now, you'll observe." His eyes glisten and he gives me a childish grin. "It's quite exciting."

"Okay," I agree. "I need to rest my leg anyhow."

We climb the stairs, walk across the big veranda, and step in the front door. As during meals, the entire clan is present, but unlike meals, chairs are set up in a huge double circle. The inner border is a thick, pure white rope carefully positioned on the floor in a perfect circle, maybe fifteen feet in diameter. The ends are not completely connected and the rope has a small opening. Chairs and people are positioned shoulder to shoulder outside the circle. One chair and a small table with a lit candle and a large eagle feather are positioned in the center.

Philip leads me through the throng of people to a front position. He sits next to me and speaks in my ear over the din of voices. "We saved you a front row seat."

I want to respond. He already knew I was going to be here. It's too noisy so I just nod.

When the old woman hobbles into the room with her crooked wooden cane, voices quiet. She walks along the narrow aisle leading through the opening in the rope to the center of the circle. She sits on the single chair that slowly rotates on a wooden platform.

The old woman picks up the feather, and the room goes pin-drop silent. She holds it high in the air. "With this feather, I open our meeting."

She takes a small sprig of some plant and lays it over the candle. The leaf catches fire. She immediately blows it out, then raises the smoking herb. A young woman in the front row steps along the outer edges of the rope until she comes to the opening, turns into the circle and walks to the old woman, then drops to her knees. The old woman wafts some of the smoke onto her with the feather, then hands the two objects to her. The young woman stands and wafts smoke onto the old woman, then walks to the edge of the circle. After she wafts Philip, she hands the feather and smoking herb to him, and he repeats the procedure with me. He hands the objects to me and motions for me to waft smoke onto my neighbor, the young woman who asked me for a cuddle date when I first got here. I can't remember her name.

She takes the smoldering herb, smokes her neighbor, and the feather slowly works its way around the room for fifteen or twenty minutes. During the entire time not one person speaks, not even a whisper. The longer it is silent, the more energy builds in the room.

When the smoking ceremony is finished, the ancient woman blesses the entire room while remaining seated. She looks too old to stand without help.

Philip stands. "We have one single issue on the table today. Does anyone have any comments?"

A young man speaks for a moment, then an older woman, then another young man, and a girl of maybe fourteen. All along I watch the room. Each speaker takes a turn. Each person in the circle nods or shakes his or her head. When a middle-aged man speaks in a deep voice almost everyone smiles and nods. I get the feeling that it's less the fact that he was speaking and more that his view is in alignment with everyone.

Philip laughs. "We are all in agreement then? Any disagreements, raise your hand."

No one disagrees.

"Okay, then, we've successfully navigated one more issue." He stands. "I officially adjourn this meeting and suggest we prepare for dinner."

I watch a beehive of activity as the narrow tables and chairs are set up in the dinner configuration.

In twenty minutes, I take a position across from a heavyset, matronly woman with steel blue eyes. Her smile reminds me of Mom when I was a child.

"I'm Sara." She holds out her hand to shake.

I slide closer to the table, and our knees interlock. I grasp her hand. "I'm Jason."

She giggles. "I know. You're famous."

My face flushes slightly.

"I like your writing."

I let go of her hand and smile. "Thank you."

I want to change the subject. "What do you do around here?"

Her grin widens. "Bookkeeping. I'm a CPA, but the way the government is going, I don't know why I even try. Things are so screwy that if I sent them nothing, they wouldn't even know."

"Why do you?"

"I guess some day this flu will be over, and everyone will put Humpty Dumpty back together again. I figure we better have our ducks in a row when that day comes."

The first dish is set down in front of us, a chicken

dumpling affair with sliced baby carrots and peas.

Not thinking, I move closer to be able to reach her mouth with my fork feeling my knees come in a little too close. "Oh, God, I'm sorry." I slide back a few inches.

"No apologies necessary. Give a girl a thrill and she'll follow you anywhere."

She's joking, and I'm blushing. "I didn't mean. . ."

"Don't worry, Mr. Oakley. This kind of thing happen. These things aren't any big deal around here."

I cut a bite-size piece of dumpling. She takes the bite and her mouth puckers. She chews. I can almost see her tongue screaming with pleasure. Her eyes close, and she hums. She swallows the bite. "Oh, Martha outdid herself tonight."

I stab the next bite and sop up some gravy, then hold it out for her.

"Do you like our form of government?"

As she takes the bite, I say, "It's so painless."

A small amount of gravy slithers down her chin, and I snatch the napkin and wipe her.

She says. "The food is great but a little sloppy."

I smile and set the napkin back on the table. "That's why I'm here."

She snickers and takes a bite of caramelized carrots. "Oh, these are good too."

The meal continues with polite chit-chat between bites. Although we hardly say anything of importance to one another, by the time the meal is over, I feel like I know Sara intimately. Maybe it's the touching of knees, maybe feeding her, but I've made a connection.

When it's time to shift positions, I place my right hand on hers. I look into the puffy skin surrounding her eyes, and I truly love this person. "Thank you, Sara, for sharing a lovely meal with me."

She places her other hand over mine and squeezes. "The pleasure, Jason, was all mine." She slides back, stands, and rotates to another table.

A young man with a chiseled face and big brown eyes sits down. Woman to man is awkward enough, but the knee touching thing is ten times harder man to man, especially with this kid who must be six feet tall and all arms and legs.

The kid mixes knees, then slides in so much closer than Sara and I were. He does it with such an air of indifference that though he's almost touching my crotch, I'm not uncomfortable. "Hello, Mr. Oakley, I'm Billy Bob." His voice has a southern, slow-pitched twang. He puts out a wiry hand and grasps mine with a strength I wouldn't have guessed.

I want to tell him to loosen his grip, but he grabs and releases so fast I don't have time. The second plate of food is set in front of us. Billy Bob picks up the fork and cuts a dumpling, then glides it to my mouth so fast I don't have time to open. He's young and impetuous, so I give him some room to move fast. I open and take the bite, but before I have the bite half chewed, he's got another up and ready for me. "Billy, you've got to move slower for a middle-aged guy like me."

He frowns and puts his forkful on the plate. "Sorry, Mr. Oakley, I guess I'm kind of nervous, you being a famous writer and all."

"No harm, Billy."

"Bob," he says.

"What?"

"Billy Bob. The last part is important. Billy Bob."

I look up at his sharp features. "Sorry. I'll call you

Billy Bob from this point on."

"Thanks, Mr. Oakley." He raises the fork halfway, tentatively.

I nod and open my mouth. "Call me Jason."

He places a slice of delicious chicken with a small piece of dumpling in my mouth and I chew, my taste buds screaming with pleasure.

"I was wondering," the kid says, interrupting my eyes-closed taste bud experience with Martha's cooking. I open my eyes, and his face is tight like he's in pain. I raise my eyebrows while I chew the chicken.

"I was wondering, Mr. Oakley. . . well. . . just. . ." He stalls and can't finish.

I shorten my chewing and swallow. "What's up, Billy Bob?"

"I was wondering if you could. . . I mean, I have some writing, I guess."

"You want me to look at your writing?"

He blushes and picks up a scoop of food. Before I take the bite, I ask, "What are you writing?"

Once I have the food in my mouth, he smiles. "A kind of a novel, I guess."

While chewing I ask, "How far along are you?"

His eyes dance in a glistening gleam. His face relaxes. "I finished last month. I've been working on editing but I don't know the rules. I'd like you to look at it, if you don't mind." He pauses for a full three seconds, then finishes the sentence. "Mr. Oakley?"

I swallow. "Can I have a drink of water?"

"Sure thing." The kid gently helps me drink from the glass. When I'm finished, he puts the glass down and immediately scoops another bite of food.

I hold up my hand. "Wait a moment."

He puts the utensil on the plate.

"You're serious. Hell, you finished the damn thing and that is serious enough. Not many people ever start, though they mean to, and fewer finish. This is the hard part, kid. Almost none of the writers who finish want to take the trouble to make the thing readable. Where do you fit in that category?"

Without a pause, he says, "I want it to be readable."

I look at him with a serious expression. "If this is your first novel, then you must expect to have a ton of mistakes to repair on every page."

"I figure this one is my learning curve book. When I heard you were staying with us, I thought this was a perfect opportunity to learn from the master."

"I'm no master, kid. I'm just another writer. I do have twelve books under my belt, and I know more about the business than I did on my first one, but that's all."

"You wrote Baker's Corner."

"Look, Billy Bob, Baker's Corner was just another book to me. It really wasn't any better or worse than the one before it or after. It just happened to get national attention."

"Mr. Oakley, the book was good, and that's all that counts to me." He picks up the fork again. I take the bite and contemplate what he's said. With my mouth still full, I look at him with a serious expression. "Bring me the first ten pages."

He grins and unbuttons the chest of his red plaid shirt. "I hoped you'd ask, so I kinda. . ." he doesn't finish the sentence, but slides out a sheaf of papers and plops it down on the table. There must be a hundred pages.

"Is that the whole manuscript?"

"No, sir; three hundred pages. I couldn't carry it all,

so I brought the first hundred. I figured it wouldn't hurt."

I look at the first page with a bold heading. "Well Heads Relief". Under it is the kid's name, Billy Bob Granger. The type is strange and too small for me to read. I look up at him. "Do you have access to a printer?"

"Why, sure, Mr. Oakley."

"Okay then, my eyes are shot, and I can't read small type. I want you to go back and change the font to Courier twelve point, and I want you to double-space the lines so I can put in some chicken scratch notes, then print out ten pages and bring it to me."

He gets a hurt look. "You won't even have a glance at it?"

"Right now I'm eating. If I'm going to have a look, then I want to do it with no distractions. Too many people in here."

He looks around. "I guess you're right."

"How about another bite?"

He stabs some carrots. "Sorry, Mr. Oakley, I guess I got too wrapped up in the book thing. I kinda do that."

"It's okay, I know the feeling. That kind of directed energy is just what it takes to become a good writer."

I open my mouth and take the food.

"I want to become a great writer, Mr. Oakley."

While I chew the carrots, I say, "like what Hemingway said once."

"What was that?"

"'There are no great writers, only great rewriters.'"

The kid smiles. "I guess I got a lot to learn."

When dinner is finished he stands and shakes my hand. "I'll have the ten pages to you later tonight."

"I'm kinda tired. Why don't you bring them around in the morning? If I'm not up yet or I'm busy writing, just put them on the front porch."

"Okay, Mr. Oakley."

"Call me Jason."

He speaks like he's trying on a new pair of jeans. "Jason." He smiles and bolts out of the hall.

Philip steps up to my table. "You want to continue with our conversation?"

I get up from my chair and stretch my leg. "My leg hurts, so I'd like to lie down, but maybe you could walk me to my house and we could talk there."

"Sure."

I hobble to the door with him in tow.

"Maybe you need the wheelchair or a cane. We have some stored here in the office."

"I'll be okay, Philip." I push the screen door open and step out into a warm dusk. "I just need to get somewhere where I can take the pressure off. My bed would be the perfect place."

He helps me navigate the stairs and walks along the path with me. When we're out of earshot of everyone, he whispers, "I think the government has a cure for this flu, and I think they're holding out on us."

As usual with Philip, he leaves a lot of open space between sentences. Maybe he's thinking about what to say, but I believe he simply moves slowly, as he does with everything.

"What leads you to believe that?"

"I listened to Grayson's taped interview while he was under hypnotherapy. He said they gave him a shot of some yellow liquid, and he stopped getting sick. I think he was an experiment that went awry."

I stop in the dark. "What do you mean?"

"It cooked his brain. That's why he acts so simple."

"I thought he was always that way."

"Grayson was C.I.A. You don't get to be an operative with a simple mind."

We reach the top of the slight hill, and the lights of the house appear. "What do we do?"

"I think we sit down with Doc Jeffries and let him tell you the whole story."

"When?"

"Eleven tomorrow morning."

We reach the porch and he helps me up the three stairs, then into the house and to my bedroom. Once I'm settled, he goes to the door. "See you tomorrow about a quarter to eleven."

Without an answer, he closes the door behind him. The last thing I hear before the night gets silent is Philip's shoes crunching along the dirt, disappearing into the night.

Chapter 18

Writing Again

The next morning I open my computer, and for the third time in two years I write another page. It isn't much, but I'm giving myself time to get back into the groove.

Billy Bob has left his ten pages but I haven't had a chance to look at them.

I want to continue writing, but the kid's pages keep calling to me, and I go outside with my reading glasses. I sit on the porch swing and scan the first page. Setting aside the endless typos and badly constructed sentences, it's good, so I read the second page. The kid has a way of sucking the reader right in, so I read the third page. In fifteen minutes I've gone through the entire ten pages, haven't made a mark, and I want to read more. He's good.

I look out toward Philip, who is walking along my path. I wave, and he returns the gesture. He reaches the porch and leans on the rail. "It's a warm morning." His forehead is wet with perspiration.

"I guess it is. I hadn't noticed. You want something to drink?"

"That would be nice."

I gather up the ten pages, stand, and grab the screen door. Philip follows me into the sitting room and settles into one of the wicker chairs. I pour a glass of water from the refrigerator and hand it to him.

He downs the glass and hands it back. "Can I have another?"

I fill the glass.

He asks, "Are you ready to see Jeffries? He came up with something new about our Grayson."

I hand him the full glass. "Yesterday's news was big enough. What could possibly top that?"

"I should let him tell you. We have some decisions to make."

I want to pry, but in the short time I've known Philip I already know he isn't going to budge, so I don't try.

"Okay, let's go find out what new revelation Jeffries has for us."

Philip stands and together we walk out of the house. We stroll around the far side of the porch and past Grayson's garage. The door is open, and I peek in to see Grayson leaning over the Harley.

I wave and call out a good morning, but he's in one of his self-induced trances, tapping the small wrench on each separate part of the bike.

Philip motions me on, and we walk over another rise through an open field, step over an old barbed wire fence, and walk down into the bottom of the gully to a small house much like Serenity's and mine.

An ancient shingle hangs from the entrance to the porch, "Harold H. Jeffries, Ph.D." Philip knocks at the door and we hear shuffling from inside. The door opens. A wrinkled old man in his seventies looks at us. "Philip." The door swings wide. "And you must be the famous writer everyone's talking about."

"I don't know about famous, but I am a writer."

He holds out his farm-worker hand, and I shake.

"I'm Doc Jeffries."

"Jason Oakley," I say in response while he pulls me into the room. Philip and I sit on the high-backed couch. He sits in a comfortable-looking brown leather chair across from us and leans forward on his knees. "I guess we have things to talk about now, don't we?"

Philip nods. "You came up with something?"

The old man's bushy gray eyebrows rise. "Yes, a big revelation, and it may have something to do with you, Mr. Oakley."

"Call me Jason."

"Okay, Jason. Grayson was in a hypnotic trance yesterday, mind you, so nothing I say can leave this room. I'm repeating it because it directly affects you. You cannot repeat what I'm about to say to anyone, especially Grayson, because his memory has been erased, and it's going to take him awhile to reconnect all of the dots. If he gets any information before he reconnects, it may send him into overload. Not a good thing for Grayson."

"I can keep a secret, Doc."

"Good," he says, "because these last few days the young man has made some real headway."

I lean back on the couch and try to put my arm on

the back, but it's too high to reach.

"I don't like the couch for that reason too. The back is too high, but the couch is comfortable to lie on, so I keep it."

There is a moment of silence before Doc continues. "Grayson was a test case with the government, and he was cured of Trillian, but at the cost of his memory and sense of well-being. I guess they had him in some lab for awhile, but he escaped and ended up in the motorcycle shop."

"That's where I found him."

"Anyhow, the test lab is somewhere in Newcastle. That's why Grayson was in Rocklin. Those two towns can't be five miles apart."

The old man wipes his mouth like he's ready to say something so important he has to clear his palate first. "From what I've gathered, everyone in the lab contracted something nasty, and few had time to make it out of the building. Grayson was in a decontamination unit so he was unaffected."

The old man stands and walks to the roll top desk to grab a pad of yellow lined paper with scribbling. He flips the pages of notes. "Here it is. Grayson said the serum is in the lab. He gave me a detailed description of how to get to the lab, how to get in, and most important, where the serum is."

I shrug. "Why are you telling me this?"

The doc lowers into the chair, looks at the notes, then at me. "Because, according to Grayson, you were the original carrier of Trillian from the jungles of Brazil."

I feel like a trapped animal. "I never told him that."

The doc holds up one of his huge hands in a halt gesture. "Don't worry, Mr. Oakley, what is said in this room will always stay in this room. Even Grayson doesn't know this fact consciously. He told me during our third session."

I'm squirming in my seat. "I didn't bring the virus in, Sam did. I tried to get him to leave the pendant where he found it, but he wouldn't. I mean, hell, the thing must have weighed three pounds, and it was pure gold."

"The pendant?" Philip asks.

"That damn pendant. The virus must have been on the surface. We took out every town we went through getting back to the States. The pendant had some kind of curse. Sam never made it back. Last I saw of him he was chasing down some Mexican soldier."

Jeffries asks, "What happened to the pendant?"

"I got it in the mail about three months later. There was no note, no return address, nothing. Sam dropped off the face of the earth, and before he did, he sent me that cursed pendant. I heard later he died in Mexico."

"Do you have it now?"

"I gave it the researchers in Palo Alto, but I've got a strong feeling that they didn't want to test the virus. The thing brings out the worst in everyone."

"Everyone except you."

I look at the doctor. "I guess, everyone except me because I know how much pain and suffering it's caused. I had it buried for awhile until Serenity talked me into giving it to the lab."

The doctor puts one elbow on the arm of the chair and rests his head against his hand. "Grayson thinks the pendant is in the lab at Newcastle."

My voice is louder than I want it to be. "How could he possibly know?" I try to calm myself a little, then speak in a quieter tone. "Grayson had been in the motorcycle shop for a long time before we found him. From what he said it was a year, so how could he possibly know?"

"He doesn't know," Jeffries says. "His subconscious knows."

"What in the hell are you talking about?" Again my voice is loud. I go quiet and try to calm myself. "How can his subconscious know if he wasn't there? I gave the pendant to the Palo Alto people two days earlier. Grayson hadn't left the shop in a month, since Billy Black disappeared."

The doc's eyes open slightly. He poises his pencil. "Who's Billy Black?"

"Hell, Doc, I don't know. Grayson told me some guy called Billy Black had been with him for a long time, then, before we showed up, Billy left."

"Interesting." Doc absently scribbles in his note pad.

The room is quiet until he finishes. He quietly taps the eraser end of the pencil on the pad. "The fact is, Mr. Oakley, I have no clue. Grayson knows the pendant is in the Newcastle lab."

"Then it should stay there because the blasted thing is nothing but trouble."

I'm looking at my shaking hands when the doc says the next words. "We need the pendant and the serum."

I look at him, but the greedy look isn't in his eye. "You wouldn't want to bring the bad luck of the pendant to this compound. You don't know what that thing can do. I've seen it in action, and it isn't a pretty picture."

The doc looks at Philip. A nonverbal communication goes on between them, and the doc says, "okay, maybe you're right, but we need the pure form of the virus. Maybe we can take some samples then bury it with one of the properties backhoes?"

I leap to my feet and pace the room for a minute. "You want me to go into a contaminated lab and search for a pendant that is probably under some kind of government triple-redundant lock and key, and you want me to bring you the pendant?"

"Not you alone, Mr. Oakley. You'll have help."

I stop pacing and throw my arms in the air. "And having help will make everything all right?"

The two men sit quietly. I rant for who knows how long. I run out of insults and excuses. I look at both of them. "Jesus, I thought I was rid of that cursed pendant. When do you want me to go there?"

Philip stands and puts one hand on my shoulder. "When Cowboy wakes up."

"Cowboy?" I yell. "What the hell do you think I am, some kind of idiot? He wants me dead."

Philip gives me a smile. "Mother Louanne wants it that way. She says you two have some kind of destiny to work out."

"Jesus fucking H. Christ, a destiny? She sure does have a twisted sense of humor."

The old man struggles to get to his feet, then puts out his hand to shake. "Good luck, Mr. Oakley. We'll all be sending our best wishes to you because this one is not going to be easy."

I'm numb. Philip leads me out the front door and down the steps, then across the field toward my house.

Halfway to the top of the rise, he stops. "Cowboy should be waking later today. You'll be starting into your second stage in two days. I think tomorrow is a good day to do this. I'll have a team of people ready to transport you to the site. What say, oh-nine-hundred?"

He's talking like a commander in the Army, like

I'm some military grunt taking orders, do or die. In retaliation, I say, "I'll be working on my next novel until ten. If someone brings me breakfast, I'll be ready at ten-thirty."

He smiles, turns back to the hilltop and starts walking slowly. I fall into step. He says, "Ten-thirty is good."

The next morning, once I write two pages and a youthful man brings me breakfast, the young woman who first approached me for a cuddle date steps onto my porch. I'd seen her through the window so I meet her at the door.

"Hello, Mr. Oakley."

I smile because, though I have not forgotten her beauty, I have misplaced her name.

"Cowboy is waking up, and Philip wants you there."

My reaction is to cringe at the thought of welcoming that murderous bastard back to the world of the awake, but I pick a sweater from the coat rack and follow her down the steps and along the path.

She walks in front of me. "I hear you're working on another novel."

"I wouldn't say I'm writing one yet, just getting my rhythm. I'll probably end up deleting everything I've written."

She looks forward and speaks over her shoulder. "We're all happy you're working on something. You don't know how much your books mean to me."

"Thank you. I guess they mean something to me too because in the last days I've been writing, I've felt like my old self again. I'm much happier."

We reach the top of the rise. She stops and points across the small valley to the other side of the lake. "I live in that house under the pair of Digger Pines. You can visit me there sometime."

I hear the nervousness in her voice. I stop walking, and she stops with me.

"Miss?"

"Bonner. Catherine Bonner."

"Look, Miss Bonner, I'm very flattered that you're so interested in me, but Serenity is pregnant, and I'm with her these days."

She blushes and looks at me with a serious expression. "I'm not interested in you in that way, Mr. Oakley. You are much too old for romantic considerations. I want a cuddle date because you feel cuddly to me, and I'm exploring reaching out to older men because doing so brings up all of my old "Dad" feelings. After I turned twelve, my dad couldn't hold me any longer, and I felt rejected. Having a cuddle date with me sometimes is sweet, but sometimes I find myself bawling late into the night. You remind me so much of Dad that you can pretty much count on the bawling, at least for part of the night."

"I've never heard it put so succinctly."

She smiles. Her nervous teenager look is gone, replaced by a mature woman assuredness.

Now I'm feeling like a teen. "Look, Catherine, I'm not sure I would be ready for something like you propose. I have a hard enough time maintaining my own feelings when it comes to the opposite sex."

Her bright smile shifts to something unrecognizable and mysterious. "Well, then, Mr. Oakley, maybe, as old Mother Louanne suggests, something is in this for you too."

"Call me Jason."

"Jason." She speaks like she's been saying my name for years.

I ask, "Did that old woman put you up to this?"

Her face instantly turns to anger. Her eyes glare, and her cute little nose scrunches. I can see where one day, sooner than she might think, her first wrinkles will appear. "Look here, Jason, Mother Louanne is all we have around here. She is our most important asset. She never speaks casually. People hang on her every word."

"Isn't that a little dangerous?"

"No, sir, it's not dangerous. For one, Mother Louanne has the gift. So far, whenever Mother has suggested something, she's been ninety percent correct. We've learned to listen."

"I'm sorry, Catherine, I didn't mean to insult you or Mother Louanne."

Her smile returns. "Apology accepted. Now, Mr. Oakley —Jason— are you going to bite the bullet and spend the night with me or not?"

I point toward the hospital. "Maybe we should walk. Philip wants me to greet Cowboy when he awakes."

Her long, auburn hair swings behind her glistening in the sun. "Too late. He woke up twenty minutes ago. We're going to have you serve him lunch."

She takes my arm, and we walk side by side along the widening path. "I know this cuddle thing makes you nervous."

"Except for a bunch of crying, I don't know what to expect."

"Here are my rules and the rules of the rest of the community. We are dealing with emotional issues here, so any hint of sex is the first big no-no."

"What does that mean, because I don't know if I can

lie next to you and not have those feelings. I don't know if you've noticed, but you exude sex."

She says, "thanks, for the compliment, but I assure you that sex is the last thing on my mind. Not that I don't like sex once in awhile to soften the edges, but in this case what we're attempting is purely therapeutic. I need you to be there as a father."

"A father? I have no idea how to do that. I've never been a father."

"Okay, then maybe your role would be therapist."

"I've never done that, either."

She rolls her eyes. "It can't be that hard."

I stop a hundred yards from the hospital building and look at her. "This might be the hardest thing I can think of."

She gets a confused look on her face. "But why?"

"Hell, Catherine, I don't know why, it just is. The thought of lying next to you, even with our clothes on, sends me into a place I've not experienced since I was a teenager."

"Okay, then." Her eyes sparkle. Her white, straight teeth show when her full lips pull back in a wide grin. "We can both come at this like gangly teenagers. It might be the perfect approach."

I shrug. "This is the first time in my life I've had a beautiful woman trying to talk me into sleeping with her."

Her eyes narrow. "You have to agree, Jason, sleeping is all we are going to do. We have strict rules here about cuddle dates. No messing around. It's for healing.

She gives a firm nod like there will be no negotiating the issue.

She grabs my arm and walks me the last yardage

to the building, up the three steps, and into the long medicinal-smelling hall. A tray of food sits on a table just inside the door. She picks it up, hands it to me, and whispers, "Go get 'em, tiger." She disappears out the door.

I swallow and walk down the long hall. Catatonic patients lie in beds on either side of my journey.

I step up to his bed and give him a smile. "How're you doing, Cowboy?"

He looks at me. "Little dizzy, but I guess I'm back."

I set the tray on his lap.

He raises the bed to a sitting position. "What are you doing here, anyhow?"

"I was told to be here when you woke up. Guess I'm a little late."

"What, are they trying to get us to be friends or something?"

I sit on the empty bed next to his. "Friends I don't think I will ever be with you, but maybe they want us to understand each other."

Chapter 19

The Search

We stare at one another in a awkward silence for a moment before Philip opens the door at the end of the hall. In squeaky tennis shoes he walks toward us. The few people who are awake greet him when he passes. He gets close to Cowboy and me and gives us one of his puzzling grins. "How are you two doing this fine morning?"

Neither Cowboy or I respond, but I don't think it's a fine morning, especially knowing I have to dig around in a corpse-filled lab looking for the pendant.

Philip steps up, sits at the end of Cowboy's bed, and looks at him. "Have we got a job for you."

Cowboy's rigid angular face crinkles into a suspicious glare. "What do you mean?"

Philip's demeanor is so sappy even I'm suspicious. He flips an envelope at Cowboy. "Get up Boy, you've got some work to do."

Cowboy pulls at the handcuffs and makes a jangling noise on the pipe. "Can't go anywhere with these."

Philip slips his forefinger into the watch pocket of his Levis and produces a small key. "No problem, we'll have you out of those in a split second." He stands, walks to the wall and unbuckles Cowboy's right wrist, then reattaches it to himself.

Cowboy huffs with indignation.

"You almost accomplished what you came here to do. You don't think we're going to let you run wild, do you?"

Cowboy frowns. "I guess not."

Philip unsnaps the second pair of cuffs from the wall. "Let's get you cleaned up and dressed. We have a big day ahead of us."

He gathers the clean clothes sitting at the end of the bed and walks Cowboy to the shower stall.

Philip thinks for a moment then disconnects the cuffs. "We have three strapping young men outside this building. You try anything, and they will pounce on you, but this time they won't be so gentle. You going to be good?"

Cowboy smiles, nods, and closes the shower door.

When the water is on, Philip motions me to step down the hall. "You go into second stage tomorrow?"

I look at the calendar on my watch. "Yes, I guess I do. It kinda snuck up on me this time. Now that I don't have to find someone to care for me, a big part of my waking hours are left open, and I actually forgot."

"We have a team ready to go. They're going to take

you to the building. Once you find the two items, come right back. Because the lab is so close, you should be able to go there, ramble around, find what you're looking for, and get back by dinner."

"Aren't they in a safe or something?"

Philip fishes in his short-sleeve shirt pocket and pulls out a piece of paper. "This is kind of a rough layout of the building and where the safe is." He points at the five numbers chicken-scratched onto the bottom of the paper. This is the combination."

"Where did you get this?"

He gives me a sly look. "Mother Louanne."

"She gave you the map and combination?"

"Not bad, huh? She said the numbers came through, but she may not have them in the right order. You may have to dink with them a bit."

"That she was able to get the numbers at all astounds me."

Cowboy steps out of the shower completely dressed in his Levis, plaid shirt, and his ridiculous boots. I put the slip of paper in my wallet.

Philip speaks across the room. "You look a hundred percent better. Amazing what a shower will do."

Cowboy stretches his arms out and rotates like a fashion model. "I feel much better too." He walks to us. Philip pulls out the cuffs and takes one of Cowboy's arms. Cowboy grimaces. "Are those necessary?"

"They are where you're going." Philip clips the cuffs on and, in a quick motion before I have time to even speak a word of protest, he snatches my arm and snaps the other side of the cuffs on my wrist.

"Jesus, Philip, not again. Why must I be punished for what this jerk has done?"

The cuffs are securely in place. Philip looks at both of us. "If it were up to me I wouldn't give a shit, but Mother Louanne thinks this is how it's going to be today."

I blanch. "I don't want him going with me."

Philip shrugs.

Cowboy asks, "Where are we going?"

"I'll let Jason fill you in on the details. For right now, you have a job and I've got some people waiting for you." Philip leads us out of the hall and down the three steps. An older tan SUV sits parked outside the hospital. Six young men and Grayson are lounging around the SUV, and once we're outside two of the young men move into action.

Philip escorts Cowboy and me to the SUV and puts us in the back seat. Grayson gets in and the door is closed. The engine starts, and with a wave from Philip, the car moves along the long dirt road, pitching and bumping from the ruts.

The shotgun kid asks, "You're Jason Oakley?"

"It's me," I say sarcastically, still a little miffed for having to deal with Cowboy.

"You wrote Baker's Corner?"

God, I am so tired of that question. Because I'm in such a mood, my response isn't the most conducive to a long ride with two young men. "It was one book that was published."

The kid gets my snappy behavior, gives me a sour look, then looks out the windshield. He continues his conversation with the tow-headed kid driving and, oh great, I'm stuck in the back with the assassin between Grayson and I.

It's a long bumpy road, but finally we reach pavement and the ride smooths. I open a window.

Cowboy says in a matter-of-fact voice, "I'm going to have a smoke."

The kid in shotgun says, "No smoking."

Cowboy gives me a smile and puts the pack back in his top pocket.

I reach forward and tap the kid on the shoulder. He turns. "Hey, I'm sorry for snapping at you. I was just informed I was going to baby-sit dipshit here, and I wasn't too happy about it." I lift my cuffed arm.

"Hey, it's okay man, we all got jobs to do and maybe I'm not so happy about mine either."

I extend my hand over the seat. "I'm Jason."

The kid takes my hand and we shake. "Glen Baldor." He nods toward the driver. "This here's Frankie."

"Frank to you, dickhead," the driver says with a jovial voice. He adjusts the mirror. "What's it like?"

All I see are his gray eyes. "What do you mean?"

"Being famous."

His question isn't a wise-ass remark, but a genuine curiosity. Although I've heard the question posed from school children to network talk show hosts, I see the sincerity in his request.

"Sometimes it's a pain in the ass, but at times being known opens doors."

"What kind of doors?"

I snort. "It hasn't happened since Trillian, but I used to get invites to private Hollywood parties. You know, the ones with famous actors."

The kid's eyes get big. "No shit?"

"Sure, but all that ended with Trillian."

The kid's face drops like his world just ended. "Lots of stuff ended when Trillian came."

Frank looks at him. "One thing for sure, though,

we've been getting laid a lot more."

Glen laughs. "That's for sure." He holds up one palm facing the driver.

The two young men high-five and laugh.

Frank drives too fast, but still in a safety margin I can live with. We roll up the long winding hill toward town, eventually getting to the freeway and the first stoplight I've seen in a week. The light turns red, but the kid rolls through. After another five miles of freeway driving, he takes a right and drives south. In a mile, the freeway ends, and we're on a wide, fast-moving two-lane. We drive the long stretch to Auburn, through the overly developed city with its box stores and fast food restaurants, and finally onto Interstate 80. The entire time we pass only three cars on a road that used to be packed with cars day or night.

We ride the short five miles to the Newcastle turnoff, take a twisty road over the Auburn dam, then go a mile into the blond, grassy hills sprinkled with Valley Oaks and Digger Pines. We make a left into a wide driveway, and stop at a heavy-duty Cyclone gate with a sign that reads, "Government Property, No Trespassing."

Frank stops, gets out, and goes around back. Glen slides into the driver's seat. With a four-foot-long pair of bolt cutters, he steps to the fence and snaps the lock like it was butter. He pulls the gate back. Glen drives through onto the property. I'm a little nervous, being on the backside of a no-trespassing sign, but I say nothing. Frank closes the gate, gets in the car, and points to the right. "We follow the driveway behind the second building."

The SUV lurches along the bumpy road, and quickly we're hidden in the underbrush of small Cedar Trees,

Manzanita, and Deer Brush growing wild along the pavement. Frank is studying the map while Glen pulls behind a modern concrete structure the size of one of those box stores we passed in Auburn. When we reach the back of the building the driveway splits.

Frank says, "take a right. It should go around the building to an underground shipping dock. We'll enter there."

The second building is more carefully designed. The front plate glass window stands twenty feet tall to the arched roof line, with large concrete posts every thirty feet. It's the roof's only support. The illusion is that the roof is simply sitting atop the posts. A wide, concrete spiral staircase leads up to the building and another just inside the door continues the staircase effect to the tall second floor. Large, deco-designed chandeliers dot the foyer with its massive copy of Michelangelo's David sculpture in the center. "The government sure had a lot of extra money to spend at one time," Glen says, slowing to gawk at the building.

I point. "If we get a chance, I'd like to see the sculpture before we leave."

Frank nods to the left. "Go around the building."

Glen swings the SUV to the left, and in a few seconds we're pulling into a wide shipping dock and down a slope to the loading platform.

Frank, with his huge bolt cutters, leaps out of the car and moves across the loading dock with the speed of a cat.

Glen shuts the engine off. "We're supposed to wait here until Frank finds his way into the building."

Cowboy, who hasn't said much during the entire trip, jangles his cuffs. "How about we take these things off so I can have better motion?"

"I would if I could, but Philip has the key."

Frank returns with the bolt cutters hanging from one hand. He opens the back door of the SUV. "All of the locks are on the inside. I'll have to take another approach." He stows the cutters, pulls out a portable welding torch with a cutting tip. He carries it to the main door, where he fires the thing and cuts a hole in the steel. He returns and stows the torch in the back. "Okay, let's get going. I don't know how much time we have here. Maybe the silent alarms are still active, maybe not."

I get out. Cowboy is forced to follow. Grayson gets out on the far side. He walks to us, and looks at the building. "I never came in this way, but maybe once we're inside I'll recognize it."

Glen leans on the fender. "I'll hang around out here and keep an eye on things. He hands Frank a walkie-talkie, then beeps it. "I'll keep you posted."

We follow Frank through the seared hole in the door. "God, it smells in here." He takes a white salve and rubs some under his nose, then hands the tin to me. "This'll keep you from puking."

I take a finger full and pass the container to Cowboy. I put the salve under my nose. It stinks to high heaven, but it'll cover the stench of death inside the building.

Grayson rubs the salve under his nose and we all put on surgical masks. He looks around. "This way to the lab."

He walks across the concrete slab of the warehouse toward a small steel door to the left. We reach the door. He opens it and passes into a long, dark hall. He finds and turns on the light. When the lights come on, we're faced with the reality of the situation. Three half-decomposed bodies lie atop one another on the floor. Two lie farther along the hall. Although I can't smell the grizzly scene, I almost puke from looking at half-exposed skulls, ragged shop clothes, skeletal fingers with rings still attached.

After swallowing my gorge three times, I'm able to speak. "Looks like they closed this place up and never came back."

Frank tracks around the pile of decomposed human flesh. "We've run into this scene more than you think, especially in government buildings. I know something is still going on back in Washington, but we're looking at a bare bones operation these days."

Cowboy and I maneuver our way around the corpses with Grayson tailing us. Farther down the hall two bodies are spread out and easy to step over.

Grayson says, "at the end of the hall make a right. We'll have another hall, then the lab will be at the end."

We step over four more dead people by the time we get to the end of the hall, then come to a small waiting room with plush couches and high-backed chairs.

"There." Grayson points at a glassed wall and moves out ahead of us. He opens one of five doors and looks in. "They kept me here for almost a year. Looks like he wasn't as lucky."

Cowboy and I look in the door as Frank gets out his map. A corpse lies wasted across the bed. I look at Grayson. "How did you escape?"

"Maybe some kind of accident. The lock was always jamming, and they had to mess with it a lot. One night the guard wasn't at his best, and he simply forgot to set the lock. Getting out wasn't easy, with all of the armed guards, but I managed."

Grayson's face is flushed. His eyes are glassy. "I didn't

remember any of this until we got here."

Frank looks at the map. "The office is around the bend. Mother Louanne thinks the safe is in the office."

He steps left and disappears around the corner.

Grayson is about to either have a breakdown or an epiphany, and I'm not leaving him alone. "You okay, Grayson?"

In a whiny voice, he blubbers, "They robbed me of a year, damn them, and they left me with a wasted memory."

I put my right hand on his big shoulder. "You are getting your memory back. That's something"

"I guess, but why'd they do it?"

"Who knows the why of governments? It's all so unnecessary."

Cowboy speaks for the first time since we left the community. "Our job was to never ask why."

Grayson says, "don't you think it's just a little bit weird, never asking why of a government that is so random and self-serving?"

"It's our job." Cowboy says.

"Why did your government want Jason and Serenity killed?"

Cowboy shrugs. "I don't have a clue. I simply did as I was told."

"Because I ran my car into some symbol of wealth, the Senator sent you to kill me. Because I wrecked his precious little fountain?"

Cowboy says, "I'm sorry, Jason, I didn't know."

"You didn't know because you never asked. Do you see how dangerous that is? Your senator is completely disconnected from spirit. If he's going to send someone like you out to do such a despicable errand, then the guy has no redeamable humanity."

I look at Grayson. "They did give you a gift, though."

"What's that?"

"They cured you of Trillian, and that is a gift you can share with all of us, once we find the safe and get the pendant and serum."

Grayson gives me an incredulous glare. "Is that why we are here, to find the pendant?"

"And the serum they used on you."

"I had a dream about the pendant last night. It's a big gold disk with some deep embossed inscriptions and gold beads for the necklace."

"That was in your dream?"

"Yup, and if that's the necklace, the pendant was never here. It's still in Palo Alto."

Cowboy's face drops, but I feel lighter. "The pendant is nothing but bad luck. From the second I saw it, the thing gave Sam and me nothing but trouble."

Frank steps up. "We got to look anyhow, right?"

"Hell," I say. "I could just as easily go home."

Cowboy lifts his arm, pulling mine with him, then remembers and lifts his other arm to rub his face in a gesture of clearing his thoughts. He says, "We gotta look anyhow. What if Grayson is wrong?"

"I dropped it in Palo Alto a little over a week ago. Who in his right mind would venture into this building and store it here?"

He smiles. "The government."

Grayson continues to stare into his old cell. "In my dream we look for the safe, but trouble comes."

"What kind of trouble?"

"I don't know, but it's going to be a problem."

"It's just a dream," Cowboy says.

The walkie-talkie cracks and Glen's voice breaks the silence. "Frank? You there Frank?"

"I'm here, Glen. What's up?"

"We've got company."

Frank turns to us. "I say we get out of here."

We all go toward the exit. Cowboy pulls at my cuffs. "Wait, we got to look."

I say, "what the fuck for? You heard Grayson; we've got to get out of here."

"What if he's is wrong? Maybe the pendant is here?"

"Then it should stay here," I say. "The thing is nothing but bad news."

I yank at the handcuffs and pull Cowboy along, though he is still resistant. I look back at him and his eyes are bugged, his face is contorted, but I don't have time to stop. I've seen the look of greed before.

Frank and Grayson are pulling away from Cowboy and me. I wish I had the keys to the cuffs, I would definitely unhook Cowboy and leave him to his greed and his precious pendant.

"Come on, Cowboy, we've got to get out of here."

He continues to drag on my handcuff. He refuses to leave.

"Frank," I yell when he rounds the corner of the long hall, some twenty yards ahead of us. In a second, he pokes his head around and looks at me dragging Cowboy.

"I need some help."

He yells at Grayson, and the two of them sprint back to me. I'm surprised when Frank produces the key. "Mother Louanne said to leave him here if he puts up a fight." He unhooks the cuff from Cowboy's side.

Cowboy reaches out. "Give me the combination."

I shake my head and dig out the slip of paper from

my watch pocket. I hand it to him. "Keep the fucking pendant if you find it, but bring us the serum."

He nods and runs into the bowels of the building.

"Frank?" Glen's voice cracks in the silent halls.

We sprint into the big warehouse. Frank answers with a quick voice. "What's up?"

"Two cars are driving up the driveway. I hear them around back."

"Get out of the car and hide in the bushes."

The radio is silent for a moment. We reach the torched opening in the big bay doors. Frank peeks around the opening. The radio squawks. He turns the sound down as Glen says, "two military, each with three people."

The radio goes silent, then squawks again. "Shit, they have guns."

Frank looks around behind us and points at an office built high on the back wall overlooking the warehouse. He whispers, "get in the office."

He runs up the stairs with Grayson and me a few steps behind. He opens the door to a grisly scene. One security guard lies across the desk and another is slumped against the far wall. Even the stinky nose balm doesn't help in close quarters. I hold my breath.

Frank goes through a back door. "In here." He signals for Grayson and me to follow.

We enter a little bathroom, with its one small window overlooking steel storage racks. I hear movement on the concrete below and whispered voices.

Frank quietly closes the door of the bathroom. I peek out the window.

Five heavily armed soldiers fan out and search the open floor below us.

In a few minutes they're going to come up the stairs and find us. Frank picks up the gun laying on the table and points at the door. His face is pale.

I whisper, "Put down the gun, Frank."

After a moment of considering, he quietly sets the gun back on the desk, then stands next to Grayson and me. He leans against the wall when a soldier takes the first step up the wooden staircase making the entire office vibrate with every step. I can count each step he takes —ten, eleven, twelve— and the office door opens.

My memory goes back to the last time I saw Sam.

Chapter 20

Mexico

Sam and I talked about it, and the idiot was willing to take the risk. I told him I was getting on the plane. I found my seat and looked through the window. I saw him being escorted to a military Jeep. His hands weren't cuffed, but a soldier got in next to him with a sidearm drawn.

I was on my way home. I'd be in Los Angeles in a few hours. I had some time before the flu came back, and I hoped to be safe in my house before I got sick again.

The plane taxied along the runway, made a wide U-turn onto the active runway and rocketed into the air. We climbed at a sharp angle and banked left. I saw the ground maybe a thousand feet below. Three Jeeps were traveling along the single highway leading toward town. I knew Sam was in one of the Jeeps. He wasn't coming home for awhile. I felt guilty for leaving him behind, but I had given him too many opportunities to ditch the pendant. Hell, he could have sold it anywhere along the way, but he got greedy.

Sam was on his way to a Mexican military compound and I was going home, which I should have never left in the first place. I planned to stay home for a long time.

The plane leveled out at who-knows-how-many miles above the earth and a young, dark-haired stewardess filled a cart with drinks. I was sitting in the fifth row looking over the Sea of Cortez, wanting to be home.

Two long hours with a newborn fussing behind me, a small boy's constant questions to his mother, magazine reading, and looking at the passing landscape, the plane descended into a cloudless pea soup of a yellow muck they called Los Angeles airspace. The atmosphere was so dense we could see only a few miles beyond our air bubble. When the wheels touched down, I felt a little seasick. By the time the plane pulled up to the terminal, I had a slight fever. As I left the plane, I had the shakes, and sweat was pouring from my forehead. I was halfway along the passageway. I saw people waiting for their loved ones. A man in a business suit held a white sign with blue letters that read, "Mr. Phelps."

I turned toward the carpeted wall and that terrible lunch, the eggs and sausage I'd eaten for breakfast in Mexico and the wine I'd bought on the plane, all came spewing out. I collapsed. A woman in a business suit called for help. I was put on a gurney and taken to some hospital room. My condition worsened.

The most frightening part was being alone. I finally

woke up what felt like a week later. Other than a minute headache and soreness from days of being in bed, I felt great.

The hospital was empty; not completely empty, but almost no one was staffing the patients.

I got out of bed and found my clothes. I dressed, walked along the hall to the elevator, and went down five stories to the ground floor. I passed five people who looked like they needed to be in bed.

No one was at the desk, so I walked out the door without signing out and looked for a taxi. Eventually, I was forced to call a cab, but got only an answering machine. The machine was full so I couldn't leave a message.

I walked to a bus stop, but no buses came. In time, I walked one long block after another with so little traffic I couldn't believe I was in Los Angeles.

When I came to a newspaper rack, I dropped my fifty cents in the slot and pulled a paper, then sat on the bench in the shade of a Pepper Tree.

The headline read in big letters across the top of the page, "Killer Flu Hits L.A."

"A new strain of flu swept the Los Angeles area forcing ninety-five percent of the population to their beds," the first line of a quarter-page article read.

When I noticed the date, I was astounded that I'd been in a Los Angeles hospital for ten days. Where was I? What had happened to me?

Then the entire scenario hit me. Sam and that damn pendant of his put me in my condition. I was the one who brought the virus into the States. The entire Los Angeles Basin was infected because of me.

I sat at the bus stop in shock for a good portion of

the morning. I was trying to think about what to do. I just wanted to get home without infecting anyone else.

Behind me was a used car dealership. I went onto the lot expecting to be assailed by a salesman. I walked the entire lot and saw no one. I went to the office and pushed the door open. A large, football-player-type hunched over his desk, his head in a puddle of vomit.

I shook him, but all I got was a moan. I picked up his head and slid the paper between him and the puke.

"I'm going to buy one of your cars, if you don't mind," I said and searched his drawers for a piece of paper to write a note to him. If he had what I had, he'd eventually wake up. He could contact me.

I found the keys and drove away in a silver midsize convertible. I wondered if I'd get into big trouble doing such a thing, but it was an emergency.

I stopped at a gas station for directions but it was closed. At the third gas station, I finally found one young girl sitting pasty-faced at the cash register. She looked like she wasn't going to hold out for long. She directed me to the right on-ramp, and in five minutes I was driving an almost empty freeways heading north.

In an hour, I was over the Grapevine and down onto the long boring drive of the Imperial Valley, up Interstate five, through nothing but open fields with an occasional orchard or cattle ranch.

When the gas got low, I pulled into one of the few exits with gas stations but nothing was open. No one was around. A sign on one of the station windows said, "Out sick. Back in a few days."

In the last station of the group of five, I drove to the front door. The glass was shattered. I pulled to the pump and slid my credit card through the self-serve slot, hoping the pumps were active. The machine accepted my card and the pump activated. I filled my tank and got out of that ghost town of a rest stop before something happened.

While driving through Stockton, then Sacramento, I passed a handful of cars, then gassed up again at a station where I regularly stop. The station was shattered. Every window was missing, with each gas pump violated in some way.

I looked around the station at the various businesses and they also had broken windows. A furniture store had pieces of leather furniture lying askew on the front lawn. The local grocery had boxes of food and drinks strewn in the parking lot. A liquor store where I often stopped was still smoldering, burned to the ground. Nothing was left but a few embers.

The car dealership across the street had a few cars scattered across the lot.

I always knew that part of Sacramento was a powder keg, but the place looked like a war zone.

The headline showing through the window of the newspaper rack read, "Flu Hits Sacramento."

One car drove along the street toward Manzanita Boulevard while I tried each pump until I found one that was functional. I swiped my card, pumped the gas, then got the hell out of that part of town before whoever destroyed that corner, returned.

On the road, I looked more carefully at businesses facing the freeway and noticed endless lines of broken windows .

Once out of the frightening part of Sacramento and into the suburbs, things returned to normal, or maybe the chaos was not as apparent. Either way, I relaxed into my journey, and for the first time I turned the radio on. Every station I tried —and the radio had one of those search options— I found nothing but static.

What had happened? Did I cause all of that, or did some other kind of catastrophe happen?

I got off the freeway in Auburn and headed north, driving past a five-mile string of auto parts stores, restaurants, movie houses, gas stations, car dealers, and big box stores, all empty. Most were vandalized with merchandise strewn in the parking lots. I didn't see a single moving car and few people.

I got through that small city and began the long drive, moving ever uphill through open country of grassy fields peppered with Valley Oak and Live Oaks, with an occasional austere quality of the Digger Pine.

By the time I'd traveled the thirty miles to my town and the road opened into three miles of freeway, my fear meter had dropped back into an acceptable range. The Brunswick Basin was pretty much closed, but none of the stores were ransacked. Other than few people being around, the place looked normal.

Knowing I had no food at the house, I pulled off the freeway and went to my favorite grocery store.

It was open, thank the gods, but only one employee was at the register. The shelves were almost empty. I managed to find some apples, a six-pack of warm beer, and some canned goods, but anything fresh was gone.

When the kid rang up my purchases he did so with listless movements. I tried to engage him, but he didn't say much. His face was pale, and he could hardly push the keys of the register. When he scanned, he was barely able to hold up the beer.

I paid with cash I'd gotten from an ATM in Los

Angeles, and he handed me a fistful of change.

"They're getting close," Frank whispers, which brings me out of my reverie and back to the problem.

I say, "it sounds like two people."

Each of the wooden steps outside the office creaks, as the weight of the men transfers onto a higher step. The sound reaches the top platform and a loud crash of breaking glass comes from deep inside the building. The sound of careful footsteps stops, then, without a word, the two soldiers rush down the steps. The footfalls of boots across concrete fade toward the crash and the big warehouse is silent again.

Frank looks at us. "Let's get out of here."

I grab his shirtsleeve. "They could have left someone behind."

Frank leads the way out of the dinky bathroom and across the office, then peeks through the closed blinds and studies the layout. "I'm going down first in case someone's waiting. If I don't get stopped, I'll wave you down."

Grayson puts his hand on Frank's shoulder. "I've still got C.I.A. status. If anyone should go, it's me."

Frank nods.

Grayson grabs a big envelope off of the desk, opens the door like he owns the place, and stomps down the stairs like he was too busy in the office to notice that anyone was in the building.

When he reaches the concrete floor, a single word echoes across the room. "Halt."

I peek through the blinds. Grayson says, "what the hell is going on out here?"

A young soldier paces across the hall. His rifle is

pointed directly at Grayson. "Don't move."

Both of Grayson's hands are high in the air. He has a casual attitude.

I whisper, "Grayson amazes me."

"The guy does have some balls," Frank says.

The young soldier marches at Grayson's chest, gun pointed, and gets distracted trying to get his radio to work. Grayson makes a lightning-fast pirouette. He snaps the gun out of the kid's hands. In a wild kung-fu display rivaling a ninja movie, he chops the kid at the base of the skull. The kid drops like a sack of potatoes and Grayson helps him to the floor. With his finger, Grayson motions for us to join him. We rush for the door, then run down the steps. We hit the concrete, following Grayson to the hole in the metal door. He looks out. "Someone is out there too."

He rushes back for the rifle and picks it up. I whisper, "No Grayson. No one gets hurt."

He smiles and puts his finger to his lips in a silencing gesture, then returns holding up the rifle. "To disable their truck so they can't follow. The real soldiers are inside where the action is. They left the kids to do the grunt work. I'll distract the guard long enough for you to get in the car. "Who here has used a rifle?"

Both Frank and I look at him with stupid stares, then we look at each other.

"Okay, it's real simple. Here's the trigger. Aim and pull the trigger. You've seen it in the movies, right?"

Frank takes the rifle.

"Make sure no one is anywhere close to where you point and you'll be all right. Start the car, then blast the radiator of their Jeep. You've got fifteen or twenty rounds. Empty them into the car and get out of here."

"Where are you going?" I ask.

"If I can't disable the kid, I still have C.I.A. status. I can get out of something like this without much trouble. They might question me for awhile, but they'll have to let me go eventually. I'll find my way back to the farm when I think it's safe and I'm not being followed."

He stands and walks through the opening in the steel door, then yells to get the guard's attention.

The guard meets him halfway across the driveway. This guard is more careful and makes Grayson stop fifteen feet away. His gun is trained on Grayson. The exchange of words is covered as two bursts of automatic gunfire ring out from deep inside the building. I want to see where the sound is coming from, but I continue to watch the guard and Grayson.

Grayson bends with his hands still high in the air. In yet another one of his lightning-quick, ballsy moves, Grayson leaps across the fifteen feet to the guard, slides in low, and scissors his legs around the guard. The kid goes down on his back as a single shot from the gun rings out. The rifle spins in the air and lands against a concrete wall thirty feet away. Grayson chops the kid and leaps to his feet. He motions for us to come out.

I race across the yard.

Frank calls on the radio. "Glen, get your butt out of the brush, and let's get out of here."

I reach the SUV.

Grayson picks up the gun.

Glen leaps into the driver's seat. I find my position in the back and close the door. "Swing around and get Grayson."

The engine comes to life and Glen slams the shifter into gear. He makes a wide arc to Grayson. I open the back door. Glen slams on the brakes and Grayson leaps in.

"Give me a clear shot of the jeep," Grayson yells, and Glen, in a wide swing toward the front gate, gives Grayson a view of the parked Jeep. The rifle report is deafening this close. Eighteen or twenty rounds pierce the military-green grill. The headlights shatter. Both front tires turn into shreds.

We get to the top of the hill. Gunshots roar out and the back window of our SUV explodes. A hole the size of my thumb opens in the roof lining, and sunlight streams onto my lap. Bullets zing by but no others make contact. In another second we're over the hill and out of range.

The gunfire stops. I look back. "Holy shit, someone could have gotten hurt."

Frank has a flushed grin. "Wasn't that a rush?"

Grayson focuses forward through the windshield and points. "It isn't over yet."

A green military truck blocks the gate. Two soldiers stand with rifles poised.

"Shit." Glen slows to a stop, but Grayson yells, "They're just kids. Go around them." He aims the rifle out the window at the grill and lets go of three rounds. The two guards scatter when Glen slams the closed gate, tossing it into the air toward the truck. Our SUV careens past the truck and along the driveway. Shots ring out behind us, but nothing comes close.

We slide around the turn, pull out onto the main roadway, and race for the dam.

"We have to dump this car," Grayson says.

Five minutes later we're slowly cruising a residential side street looking at the never-ending rows of dusty cars. Grayson points at an older Chevy parked in a driveway. The layer of dust is so thick the car looks like it has a plastic cover. "Pull around the corner, and I'll see what I can do."

"Why the old wreck?" Frank asks.

Grayson says, "because the older cars don't have steering wheel locks and they're easier to hot wire. Computerized cars are impossible."

"Good point," I note. "I say we drive the wreck."

Glen parks behind a hedge, and we wait two minutes before Grayson pulls around the corner. The engine is sputtering as he parks and motions for us to get in. We abandon the SUV and pile into the Chevy. Grayson shifts into first and we drive away. The engine misfires often while we slowly gain speed. I'm riding shotgun. "Are we going to make it? This car sounds like it's on its last leg."

Grayson makes an abrupt stop in front of a house two blocks from where we dropped the SUV. "The engine hasn't been started in two years. It's going to need a little time to get all the moving parts lubricated again; then it'll run fine." He leaves the car running, jumps out, and grabs a garden hose. He turns on the water and squirts the dusty surface of the car. "Get out and help get this dust off."

We pile out of the car and, with bare hands, scrub the faded yellow paint and windows. In a minute the car looks acceptable. Grayson gives it one last rinse, turns off the hose, and we drive away.

The motor sounds better by the time Grayson shifts into second gear and we leave the neighborhood.

"The engine isn't running well enough to get on the freeway yet, so we'll need to take the back roads for a while. Does anyone know this area?"

Glen says, "Make a right here, then a quick left, and

we can follow the frontage road."

Grayson makes the turns and we poke along, the engine misfiring enough that he can't shift into third gear.

By the time we've funneled onto the freeway, the car has smoothed out enough to get to forty. Traffic on the freeway is almost nonexistent. The ride to Auburn at this poky speed is no problem.

When Grayson gets off the freeway, we've reached fifty miles an hour and the engine has smoothed out.

We're headed home.

Chapter 21

Home

"We didn't get the pendant," I say to Philip as he steps onto the porch where I'm resting on the swing seat. "We failed completely."

"We didn't expect you'd succeed."

"What?"

"The pendant's not there."

My temper rises. "Then why did you send us?"

"I didn't send you, Mother Louanne sent you to help Grayson remember. Another month and the vaccine will be ready. We didn't need the pendant."

My hackles and my face relax. "In that case, our mission is accomplished. Grayson became his old self once he saw the room they'd kept him in. I don't know, something clicked and he was normal again."

"Just in time, from what I gather from Frank."

I smile. "Single-handedly, Grayson got us out of that mess, and no one got hurt. A few vehicles need some help, but I was proud of him."

Philip sits next to me. "Mother Louanne wasn't sure if Grayson's memories would be jogged when he saw the room, but it was worth a try."

Serenity opens the screen door and steps onto the porch. "You boys want some lemonade?"

Philip nods, and I say, "Two, please."

She disappears into the house.

"What about Cowboy?" I ask. "We left him to deal with the military."

"I wouldn't worry about Cowboy. He knows how to take care of himself."

"I guess you're right."

"Mother Louanne told Frank to release him once Grayson remembered the room. She knew Cowboy would distract the soldiers away from you."

"No kidding?"

"She has the power of sight, She's saved the day more times than you can know."

"I certainly believe that."

Serenity brings out drinks and sits across from us on a wicker chair. We relax in silence while looking out over the meadow, listening to the meadowlarks, starlings, and a distant cow mooing. I hear the sound of bees, and a feeling of contentment overcomes me. It's the first feeling like this I've had since I left for Brazil with Sam.

I take a long drink of Serenity's lemonade. When I'm finished, I set the glass on the little table next to the porch swing. "What about the pendant? I thought you needed to study the Trillian virus."

"We have the next best thing."

Serenity, still holding her glass, looks at Philip. "What's the next best thing?"

He says, "we have Jason here, who contracted the virus first. Our research team thinks what's inside you is pretty close to the original virus."

Philip looks at me. "When are you going to have that cuddle date with Catherine?"

I look at Serenity, then to Philip. "Probably never."

Serenity puts her hand on mine. "Philip helped me with the cuddle date concept and I believe it's worth looking into."

I get a deer-in-the-headlights look. "Well, I don't like it one bit." I put my hand up and count off my fingers. "First, she's young and beautiful and how am I supposed to not feel sexual toward her? Second, what am I going to do with a sobbing woman? Third, I'm with you. Finally fourth, why the hell would I want to submit myself to that kind of emotional overload for an entire night anyhow?"

Philip smiles. "Because it's not just for her that this little experiment is performed. I've had cuddle dates with several women in our compound and what I came away with far exceeded the balance of what I gave. There's something about being with a woman as a sister that helps me live more fully in my emotions. And, I don't know if you agree, but us men could use a little more emotion."

Serenity smiles. "Jason, I want you to do it. Catherine has asked for your help."

Philip says, "This is the first time Catherine has asked for a cuddle date from anyone. This is no small thing."

I take a deep breath and let it out. "I'll think about it."

He lifts his arm and, with a thumb, points over his shoulder to Grayson who is walking along the path toward us. "We have Grayson, too. He's probably going to be our best subject because he beat the virus, and we're looking at his immune system to see how he counteracts it."

We all look at Grayson who is still fifty yards away. Serenity asks the obvious. "He's better, but still a little lost. Will he ever be normal again?"

Philip leans forward and puts his hand on her shoulder. "Mother Louanne sent him on the trip to Newcastle to jog his memory. She believes if anything is going to happen, it'll be by going back to the original event, but I'm not sure."

I say, "I don't get it, he changes when there's trouble, then reverts to his simple self after the danger is over."

Philip smiles when Grayson gets within twenty feet of us. "Automatic response," is all he can say before Grayson gets within earshot.

I open my arms and speak before Philip can finish his sentence. "Grayson, buddy. What the heck is going on?"

He takes his final steps to the three of us and stops, facing Serenity. "Something happened while we were in Newcastle."

Serenity rises and steps forward to take Grayson's hands. "I know, Jason was telling us. Sounds like you barely got out of there in time."

"No, I mean something happened to me."

"What?"

He rubs both his temples. "My head has cleared, not completely, but some. I can remember who I was and what I was doing before I went into the research lab."

Serenity gives him a grin. "Grayson, that's great."

His face creases into a mass of worry. "The problem is I don't like who I was. I wasn't a nice person, and I don't remember ever knowing nice people like you."

Philip speaks with an air of authority. "It's not who you were that counts, Grayson, it's who you are now."

Grayson says, "that's the problem, Philip. Now that I remember, maybe my niceness will go away, and I might revert to who I was."

Philip speaks. "You're among friends now, son. We'll take good care of you and help to keep you from falling back into your old life."

Although no tears spill down his cheeks, Grayson's eyes brim with tears. "I killed people."

I'm shocked, but I try not to show it. "It's not what you did, Grayson, but what you plan to do with the rest of your life."

His lip quivers and his voice is shaky. "I don't want to ever do anything like that again, but I don't know if I can keep such a promise. It's ingrained in me." Grayson lets go of Serenity's hand and lifts his hand to his face. His sobs are quiet at first, then get stronger. From between his hands he speaks words of finality. "I'm a horrible person."

Once the words are out, he breaks into deep sobs.

Philip motions us to come in closer. He wraps one arm around Grayson and the other around my shoulder, then pulls me in.

Serenity puts one arm around Grayson and the other around me, and we all pull Grayson in tight to us. His sobs slowly increase to full blown cries.

We stand in our tight circle, holding one another,

supporting Grayson while he blubbers soft, unintelligible sentences. There is a sweetness about the moment.

Five minutes later, Grayson's emotional upheaval lessens. In another minute, he pulls away slightly and looks each of us in the eyes one at a time. When he's finished, though his voice still quavers, he speaks. "I want to be a good person again. I really do."

He goes into another crying bout and we pull him in close. Philip speaks softly. "Maybe you could get the motorcycle up and running."

Grayson gives him a guilty look. "Tell the truth, I know nothing about motorcycles."

"Jack Blanko can help you. He's a mechanic."

Grayson perks up. "Who is he?"

"He lives here on the farm. I'll introduce you at dinner tonight. The two of you together might just get that thing running."

Grayson gets a faraway look. "That would be nice, but I don't know how to ride a motorcycle either."

"That'll be the fun part," I say. "Maybe we could all learn."

The End

Nik's Favorite Story

"... a very interesting metaphysical science fiction novel structured around the soft science of psychology, sociology and futurism. The plot is fast paced and shoots off in unexpected directions." Bob Spears Grit Lit

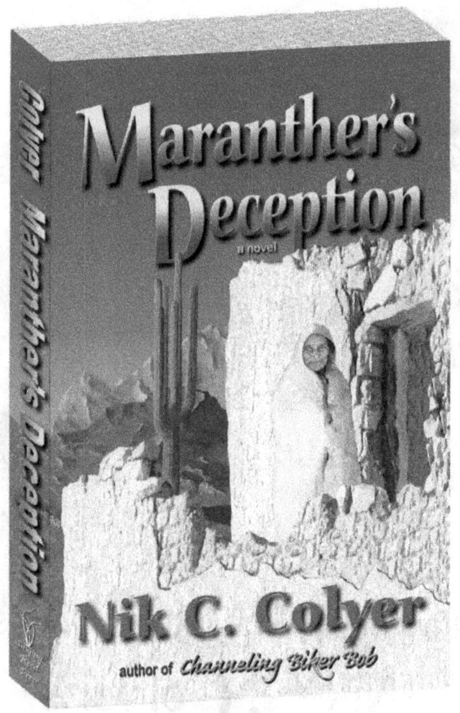

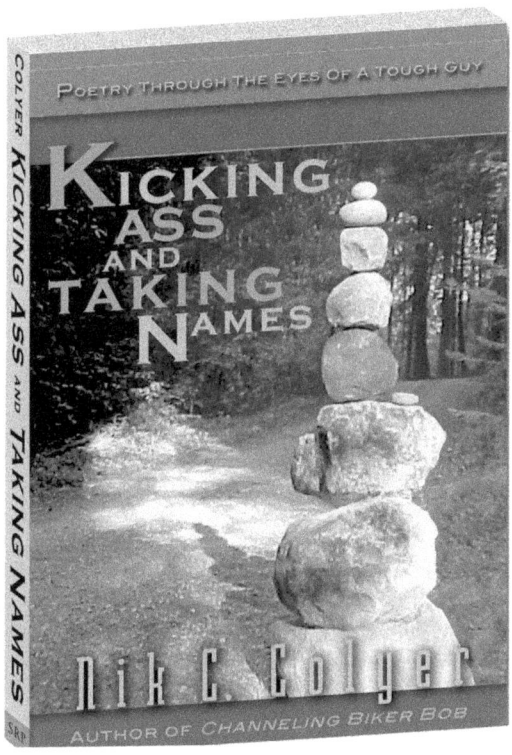

Books to come by

Nik C. Colyer

Trillian Rising Discussion Guide

1. Why hadn't Jason written anything in years?
2. Who did Jason go to the Amazon with?
3. What was the problem returning to the USA?
4. Which way was the virus fatal?
5. What were the three phases?
6. When did Jason know the medallion was cursed?
7. What was the meaning of their forehead tattoo?
8. Why did he pick Serenity?
9. What was so important about getting pregnant?
10. What roll did Baker's Corner play?
11. Why did they get stranded in San Francisco?
12. Who was Cowboy working for?
13. Why did everyone want the medallion?
14. What curse came with possessing the medallion?
15. What condition was Grayson suffering from?
16. Why did he want to work on motorcycles?
17. Why was Mother Louanne so important?
18. How many people lived on the farm?
19. Why did Philip put Cowboy and Jason together?
20. Was Grayson happy with his new home?
21. Why were the eating tables cut so narrow?
22. What was a cuddle date?
23. What real reason did Mother Louanne have for sending the men to the lab in Newcastle?
24. Why did she send Cowboy?
25. How did they get back to the farm?

www.ingramcontent.com/pod-product-compliance
Lightning Source LLC
Chambersburg PA
CBHW050126170426
43197CB00011B/1734

* 9 7 8 0 9 7 0 8 1 6 3 8 2 *